WTF?

WTF?

Robert Peston

HODDER &
STOUGHTON

First published in Great Britain in 2017 by Hodder & Stoughton
An Hachette UK company

1

Copyright © Robert Peston 2017

A CIP catalogue record for this title is available from the British Library

ISBN 9781473661295
eBook ISBN 9781473661325
Tradeback ISBN 9781473661301

Typeset in Plantin Light by Hewer Text UK Ltd, Edinburgh
Printed and bound in Great Britain by Clays Ltd, St Ives plc

Hodder & Stoughton policy is to use papers that are natural, renewable
and recyclable products and made from wood grown in sustainable
forests. The logging and manufacturing processes are expected to
conform to the environmental regulations of the country of origin.

Hodder & Stoughton Ltd
Carmelite House
50 Victoria Embankment
London EC4Y 0DZ

www.hodder.co.uk

For Mum, who is equally to blame

CONTENTS

CHAPTER 1
DEAR DAD

Dear Dad,

Before you died in April of last year, you and I acknowledged that the popularity of Donald Trump in the Republican state primaries, which choose the candidate to be the GOP's nominee for the next US president, was troubling. It showed how 'bonkers' – a word I inherited from you – politics had become in the rich West. But you were too respectful of America and Americans to think that they would ever actually elect an impulsive, superficial, narcissistic, sexist, borderline racist as their president.

Nor did you or I anticipate that the British people would vote to leave the EU; it was obvious that choosing to do so would be a choice to make all of us poorer, and to make Europe less stable and secure; and for all Britain's permanent crisis of European identity, the country would surely never choose self-harm. We might not love the bureaucracy and remoteness of the EU, but what defined us as a nation was moaning about it, not actually tearing up our membership card.

As for the 2017 general election, you would have seen that as comedy and tragedy. This was a battle led by a Tory with a Nelsonian eye to the crisis in public services, who was claiming to want to fight injustice and inequality wherever it lurks, and yet offered policies that were too much about sacrifice and not enough about hope. Her unlikely near-nemesis? He was a Labour leader with a charming if naive conviction that the state can solve literally everything, largely by spending other people's money.

When I learned the outcome of this battle, at 9.20 p.m. on 8 June with the top-secret release of the exit poll to broadcasters, my brain briefly short-circuited with the surge of new information about what the British people want – or perhaps do not want. Labour and Tories further apart in ideas and ideology than at any time since 1983, but only a comedy fart apart in percentage of votes cast. The nation seemed to be as torn as I had become. Collectively, we had in practice opted for 'none of the above'. So what do we really want?

As if the world had not become weird enough, then along came Emmanuel Macron, another outsider, but the anti-Trump. Proudly internationalist, this Europhile, young former banker trounced both the usual French political suspects of left and right, and the extreme illiberalism of Marine Le Pen, to become French president. He is a quintessential French contradiction: a member of the corps of France's elite technocrats, who have run all its big institutions for decades, but a repudiator of the party that first gave him harbour, the Parti Socialiste, and all the established parties. You would have been wary of the resonances with Blair, a leader you never desperately admired. Whether Macron is the salvation of liberal values or their desperate last gasp – all stylish, narrow-leg Paris pantaloons and global-banker soundbites – is unclear.

For any one of Trump, Brexit, Corbyn, Macron or May to define the Western world would have been unlikely at any point over the past thirty years. They are all newcomers in their different ways, a break from the men who typically run things and the traditional way things have been run. For all five to coalesce blows up most of what you and I would have seen as not just the normal order of things, but the reasonable order of things. *WTF?* as they say, although you never would.

Among the WTF-est of nights was 8–9 November. It was 4 a.m. at the harsh concrete modernist American Embassy in London's Mayfair, which has since been abandoned to the developers, to be reborn under the ownership of the Qataris as a luxury hotel for sheikhs and oligarchs. I had expected the loud-mouth, billionaire reality-TV star Trump to be victorious. All night, I cruelly teased young members of the State Department with my prediction. But when prediction became reality, I was probably less emotionally prepared than anyone. It was devastating. The Democrat ambassador Matthew Barzun, a close friend of and fund-raiser for Obama, kept a stiff upper lip. But the professional officials, who aren't supposed to take sides, were nonetheless flattened, like *Looney Tunes* characters run over by a steamroller. It was the Titanic for the despised liberal metropolitan elite, those Theresa May had chided as 'citizens of nowhere'.

The motives and mores of a globalisation that had lifted hundreds of millions out of poverty, though not in America, Britain or the rest of the EU, were drowning. The world felt a scarier place than at any time I could remember. All I could think was that I wanted to hug my two boys. Instead I hugged an *FT* columnist, a fellow bruised, battered and besieged liberal-minded metrosexual, and therefore the nearest I could find to family. Goodbye to all that.

Even if Trump is not forever, he is doing a spectacular job of widening divisions at home and abroad, of bringing resentment and conflict where once there was grudging tolerance. And Brexit will be forever, as a redefinition of who we are as a people more profound than anything I have lived through and probably ever will. Theresa May insisted new Britain would be 'Global Britain', while simultaneously saying it would be much harder for brains, money and people to come here. To much of the rest of the world, new Britain is horrid Little England. They are right.

We fucked up, didn't we, Dad – all of us who prospered in a borderless world for capital and labour? We ignored the complaints of those whose way of life was being dismantled.

So belatedly, I think the revolt against how a liberal plutocracy has run everything since around 1980 was long overdue. I didn't vote for Brexit, and I would never have voted for Trump. But – and please don't throw me out of the family – I now fear that those who did were on the right side of an important argument and the right side of history. Which is not to say that Brexit and Trump are benign events. They are not. They are poisonous. But they are probably the last chance to reform global capitalism and make the distribution of its fruits fairer – before there is a powerful movement to raze everything to the ground.

I am a hopeless optimist that governments will understand what happened and will rise to the challenge. Well actually, not governments, because it is not easy to have supreme confidence in the pack of leaders currently in power or knocking on the door all over the West. But I have faith that out of the current swamp, a new generation of politicians with credible new ideas will emerge primped and pristine on the shoreline of our ageing democracies.

I am writing this book, partly so that I can better understand the nature of that challenge, to come up with a few ideas about how we could fix things, and partly as therapy, exculpation for my many years of blindness to the growing sense of hopelessness and helplessness felt by so many. There was so much I got wrong for years about the lives and convictions of half my British compatriots, or at least the half and a bit who voted for Brexit.

Dad, given that our family's story is one of self-improvement without the help of inherited wealth or purchased education – we are inverted snobs about schools, comps rule! – I discounted how trapped millions of people could justifiably feel. And it never occurred to me that the EU could look like a threat to many, a challenge to the comfortable order, rather than simply part of our identity.

Why was I so blinkered for so long? Perhaps, Dad, because of nature and nurture, being descended from Ashkenazi East European Jews and being taken by you and Mum aged eleven or so to the promenade at Dieppe, to get childishly drunk on the excitement of abroad and delicious Normandy cider. So much beauty stemmed from across the Channel, not least its football. For all my irrational and constantly disappointed hope that one day the England football team would consistently outplay Germany, France or Italy, I swooned at the elegance and sophistication of the Dutch team in the 1970s and the French in the late 1990s. Who wouldn't want to identify with Cruyff and Zidane. Surely we all did?

And then there was school, a comprehensive in North London in the 1970s, which would feel familiar to millions in its school-uniformed rowdiness. History, taught by the twinkling Ruby Galili – who had a misshapen hand, never went to university and was a more serious and enthusiastic historian than most academics – rooted this island's story in that of the Continent, giving appropriate weight in rumbustious lessons to Francis II and Henry IV of France, the Revolt of the Low Countries, the Thirty Years War, the rise and fall of the Holy

Roman Empire and the English Revolution. This was not sinister, pro-European brainwashing. It was understanding who we are.

Being a Jew, even if an unbelieving one, made a difference, too. When I was growing up in the 1960s and 1970s, Adolf Hitler was still a bogeyman, scarier than the Daleks. A book-ish, voluble, neurotic boy – nothing much has changed – I was terrified by all those myths that he had somehow escaped the bunker. And from the back of our white Hillman estate car, as we drove past bombsites and trolley buses, the war seemed near. Hitler had been beaten only fifteen years before the year of my birth, 1960, closer than 9/11 is to someone born in 2017. And that is one reason why I was so shocked that the vast majority of people of my generation and older wanted Brexit, given that if the EU and its predecessor insti-tutions have achieved anything – and they have achieved a great deal – they have brought a longer period of peace and sustained prosperity to this continent of Europe than at any time in its volatile history.

The point of the EU – founded in 1951 as the European Coal and Steel Community and succeeded by the Common Market – was to bind the economies of European countries so intimately as to make war between them unthinkable. And here's the rub for us in the UK: arguably, it was a great British idea, and Churchill's for that matter, in that he argued in his famous 1946 speech in Zurich that Europeans could soon be as free and happy as the Swiss, if only they were to 'build a kind of United States of Europe'.

But obviously for many British people, it was a peace project for them, not us. How else to explain that a decisive majority of those over fifty-five, many of whom were alive during the war, voted to leave? Well over sixty per cent of them voted for Brexit, say YouGov,[1] a bit fewer according to the British Election Study. It is appalling that the trope of plucky Britain standing alone in Europe's darkest hour trumped the reality of the security and prosperity that can be achieved when European nations bind themselves together to make money, not war.

EU membership has made us richer, by providing our businesses with cheaper access to an enormous market on our doorstep. In the UK of my early teenage years in the 1970s, we struggled to keep the lights on, doing homework by candlelight when the power was routinely switched off. Ours was a country beset by strikes and whose economic performance lagged by a margin those of our historic enemies, Germany and France. Back then – and this was a reason we voted for Common Market membership in the first plebiscite in 1975 – being more like them seemed a good thing, in an economic sense.

Today, economists are divided about the net impact of EU membership on our economy, partly because the counterfactual of how we would have invested and traded on the outside is fraught with uncertainties. What is incontrovertible is that the UK's biggest economic defects – the wealth and income gaps between north and south, old and young, for example – cannot be laid at the EU's door.

Taking sides is also about identifying with those in the vanguard of the competing arguments. In 1975, it was a choice between pro-Common Market Roy Jenkins – the intellectual, bon-viveur son of a miner – and Tony Benn, the hard-left aristocrat who saw membership as an attack on the working class. In the early 1980s, it was between the then pro-European Margaret Thatcher and shambling Labour leader Michael

---

1 Peter Moore, 'How Britain Voted', YouGov, June 2016.

Foot. In the 1990s, it was a choice between a young and hopeful Tony Blair and a very angry John Redwood. So, for most of the last fifty years, history and optimism seemed to be on the side of those who wanted us more intimately integrated into the great European project. Those who preferred us out were – let's not be coy about it – nutters.

Here is what fills me with dread and despair, Dad: *we* are the nutters now. Any talk of keeping us in the EU, against the revealed wishes of the British people, is obviously the talk of a fundamentalist obsessive.

Sir Bill Cash, who devoted his entire life to campaigning to get us out of the EU as a latter-day Savonarola, is the calm and measured select-committee chairman who understands Britain and Britons better than you and me – as, obviously, does David Davis, an anti-European ideologue who is the minister in charge of getting us out of the EU in one piece.

OK, I am exaggerating slightly for effect. But only slightly. A couple of years ago, I would have casually described both of them as Eurosceptic obsessives incapable of seeing the wood for the trees, and no one in my circle would have batted an eyelid. Today I feel as alienated, perhaps more, from pro-European ultras like Blair, George Osborne, Chuka Umunna, Peter Mandelson and Nick Clegg when they vow to die in a ditch to avoid a so-called bad Brexit, or to give British people the chance to vote again. Who are the fanatics now?

It is not that it is an affront to democracy in any sense to argue that the vote was wrong, as some on the Eurosceptic right argue – with supreme hypocrisy given that they never accepted the result of the 1975 referendum, and would not sleep until it was overturned. Nor was the totemic 52 to 48 victory margin so great as to settle decisively the question of our national identity forever: if admitting kinship with the UK

Independence Party is a proxy for being a diehard anti-European, only around two-thirds of those who voted for Brexit are probably immovable forever in their commitment to it.[2]

But we ignore at our supreme peril the fact it was the government and almost the entire establishment, including the seemingly reluctant leadership of the Labour Party, that lost the argument. It was the official position of the British state to remain in the EU, and the people said no. That cannot be brushed aside as just one of those things. The Leave side may have conducted itself in a tricksy and mendacious way, but it is to patronise our countrymen in a disgusting way to say they did not know what they were voting for.

To deny the result would be legitimising violent protest, because we would be saying there is no point trying to settle disputes with the ballot box. Which does not mean there are no conceivable circumstances in which it would make sense to have another vote. But for a government or parliament to go back to the country on this without betraying our democracy would require the British people to make it clear, in an unambiguous and decisive way, that they had made a terrible mistake. Right now, there is no sign of that.

The distinction here is that pro-European politicians must follow public opinion, not lead it. There is no staying in the EU unless the costs of not doing so prove decisively greater than most Brexit supporters expected. Those costs cannot be pre-empted by well-meaning, pro-EU campaigners. They have to be lived. In fact, the more that voters hear from the Blairs and Cleggs that they were idiotic and wrong, the more entrenched they will become that Brexit must be forever.

---

2 Jonathan Mellon & Geoffrey Evans, 'Are Leave Voters Mainly UKIP?', British Election Study, July 2016.

We are all just prisoners, of course, of our own device. These days when I make factual statements about the complexity of leaving the EU – putting in place new arrangements for European aeroplanes to land here, for new medicines to be licensed, for goods to be exported and imported without excessive delays or cost, for banks to offer services all over Europe – I am accused of being unduly negative. I think that is wrong, but I cannot be wholly certain that I am controlling the voice and instincts of the disappointed pro-European in me. But at least I was not like Tim Farron in the 2017 general election, talking about the imperative of holding another EU referendum to a British people sick to the back teeth of voting.

Even with the supposed safety valve of the Brexit vote – or possibly because of it – there has been a hideously rising incidence of hate. The frenzied, near-fatal attack by a mob in Croydon on a seventeen-year-old Iranian Kurdish refugee, Reker Ahmed, seemed a manifestation in the real world of the disgusting assaults that are the daily discourse of social media. Many of my non-white and non-indigenous friends say that since the vote they no longer feel welcome here. This is not paranoia. They have faced racist abuse for the first time. Some are making plans to leave Britain, or trying to acquire citizenships of other countries as an insurance policy. I even know two Jewish families, whose antecedents escaped extermination in the concentration camps, who have applied for German citizenship. Which makes me weep.

The question is whether these racial, ethnic and other tensions would be eased or worsened if MPs suddenly decided the Brexit vote had all been a terrible mistake. I fear they would encourage and license the most poisonous extremism. Which is only one reason why it makes sense for most of us to attempt to make Brexit a success, in good faith, unless and until it can be proved beyond any reasonable doubt that there is no good Brexit.

A good Brexit? I cannot pretend believing in it will be easy, partly because of the power of groupthink. The thing is that I know thousands of people, because of the day job, and most of them wanted us to remain in the EU; more starkly, in my closest circle of perhaps a hundred family members and friends, no one voted to leave the EU. It turns out I have not really been living in the United Kingdom, but in a privileged metropolitan bubble or ghetto. That makes me sick, because if I am passionate about anything, it is that in a community – that can be as large as a nation, or larger still – we have a minimal duty to know and understand each other.

Now here is a good joke at my expense: for most of my myopic life, I took for granted that because I went to a state school with an uncanny resemblance to Grange Hill, I would instinctively be in tune with the great, state-school-educated majority of this nation. FFS.

Dad, I don't regret for an instant yours and Mum's ideological commitment to comprehensive education. I am glad that unlike most of your Labour peers, you were not a hypocrite who decided that what was good enough for the country was not good enough for your kids; there was never a thought of sending us to fee-paying schools. And I had the time of my life at Highgate Wood School in Crouch End.

The only serious tension in the school was between the Greek and Turkish Cypriots, or Bowie fans versus Bolan's. My teachers were working-class autodidacts, who did teacher training after national service without the benefit of a university education. The most important things they taught me were self-reliance, the ability to find out things by myself and the love of learning as a good in itself.

But what shocks me today is that an educational experiment that was all about encouraging social mobility and the
sense that we're all in it together has left me more out of touch
with most of the country than would probably have been true
of my family when I started school in 1971. I was certainly
upwardly mobile, but just at the time when social mobility
was ossifying. Forty years on, I spend almost all my time with
people like me – many of whom went to those posh public
schools you and I rejected, Dad – and people like us don't
appear to be living in the same Britain as much of the rest of
the country.

I got a sense of my difference and distance from much of
Britain when reporting during the EU referendum campaign.
In Leicester, I assumed it was a collective wind-up when
almost every Asian I met said to me that they would be voting
for Brexit, in part because of their concerns about what they
perceived to be excessive immigration (although nationally
two-thirds of non-whites voted to remain).[3]

On the eastern seaboard, and in Kent and Essex, I met
white families who said that the political establishment, the
leadership of the Tories and Labour, ignored them and didn't
understand that the country they love was going to the dogs.
Nigel (Farage) would sort it out for them, they said – which is
not a phrase heard often up North London.

Many of the English Brexiteers were the usual suspects, the
traditional hardcore of anti-metropolitan, anti-immigration,
anti-Europeans – white, male, retired homeowners, living in the
country. But the more important new noise was coming from
those on lower incomes, also predominantly white, whose living

---

3 Gideon Skinner & Glenn Gottfried, 'How Britain voted in the 2016 EU
referendum', Ipsos Mori, September 2016.

standards had been flat or declining for years. Here is the Brexit coalition of the older haves and the younger (but not young) have-nots: there were clear majorities for leaving the EU among those retired, the unemployed and those not working but looking after the home; and Brexit was backed both by those who own their homes outright, with no mortgage, and those in council homes and other social housing.[4]

Victorious Leave was a coalition of those who feared they had lost control of their country and those who feared they had lost control of their livelihoods. They wanted an end to the humiliation of kowtowing to foreigners and an easing of the never-ending struggle to make ends meet. Boris, Gove and the leaders of Vote Leave promised all that. Whereas from the other side, the Stronger In camp, it was all dire warnings from David Cameron and George Osborne that things would only get shittier if we left the EU. It was hope versus fear. And for millions who didn't think their lives could get much worse – and who quite liked the idea of giving a bloody nose to the posh boys, Cameron and Osborne – hope inevitably won.

Osborne and Cameron believed that economics, the robust claim that Brexit would make us poorer, would always beat arguments that leaving would give us more control over our lives and laws, and – especially – over immigration. They didn't realise that national self-determination would be such a powerful message to voters. And more importantly, after their years of austerity that were taking a heavy toll on vital public services, Cameron and Osborne had no credible response to the Leave campaign's claim that Brexit could save the NHS by giving us control of the £350 million a week we send to Brussels – even though that claim was spurious, at best.

---

4 ibid.

Robert Peston

And, of course, the people were right and Osborne and Cameron were wrong, in that they grossly exaggerated the immediate damage to our living standards of Brexit, if not the likely long-term costs; the increase in uncertainties, costs and frictions for our companies in their trade with the rest of the EU, the most important external market for our goods and services, is making Britain poorer but slowly and cancerously, not with a bang.

I suspect, Dad, that you, like me, would have said in the imme-diate aftermath of the vote that poorer people who voted for Brexit were cutting off their noses to spite their faces, that the lower growth in national income that would flow from Brexit would hurt them, the poorest and most vulnerable, the most: it would lead to fewer job opportunities for them, a further squeeze in their already depressed incomes, and an extension of austerity in public spending that would see their benefit payments cut further and a worsening in the vital services provided by schools and hospitals. And although Theresa May delayed by five years the moment when the budget was supposed to be balanced, austerity was not abandoned, so public services and benefits will remain under pressure for years.

But poor people who voted for Brexit were not wrong, in that it was probably the best opportunity they would ever have to give the establishment a proper kicking, for ignoring them, for forgetting they exist. During most of the previous thirty-odd years, Britain and most of the rich West had been run on a deceitful prospectus. Labour and Tories had argued, and even for the most part believed, that they were governing for the whole nation. But that was tosh. They were governing for themselves and for those who work in the City and the service sector in London and the South-East. They were governing for property owners. They were governing for a highly skilled, internationally mobile elite of corporate executives, bankers and entrepreneurs. This is not revolutionary rhetoric, it is observable fact, which cannot be ignored by left or right.

For a while, though, a system of stewardship that favoured the richest seemed to benefit everyone. Between 1992 and 2008, the British economy grew faster and more consistently than at any time since the nineteenth century. We could have our cake and binge on it. The rich became unconscionably wealthier. And the tax revenues spewing from an acceleration in growth allowed more money to be spent on schools, hospitals and tax-credit subsidies for jobs.

However, this seeming golden economic age was a dangerous illusion. Much of the growth was generated by dangerous risks taken by banks and other financial institutions in the City, which it was convenient for the government of Blair and Gordon Brown to ignore. They wilfully ignored the unbalanced and unsustainable structure of our economy – too reliant on the City and household spending, too little on investment and manufacturing, too much on debt shipped in from abroad to finance our lifestyles.

But even in these seemingly boom years, millions of poorer people saw only modest improvements in their living standards and their life chances, while the owners of capital were taking more and more of the overall pie, leaving workers with less and less. And even before the Crash of 2008, output per worker, or productivity – the underpinning of living standards – was not converging fast enough with the much higher levels of our major competitors, such as America, Germany and France.

Another lie was that public-spending cuts and the economic recovery plan devised by the coalition government of Tories and Lib Dems after 2010 would distribute the pain equally between the rich and the poor. The crisis we are seeing now in social care for the elderly and in hospitals, the severe funding squeeze for schools, the cuts in benefit payments and tax credits, these are the direct consequence of decisions taken by Osborne, Cameron and Clegg. And their initial cuts in investment spending permanently harmed the UK's growth potential, and therefore tax revenues available to fund schools and hospitals.

Meanwhile, with the 2010, 2015 and 2017 governments all putting the onus on balancing the books, rather than helping the poorest, it was left to the Bank of England to restore and retain economic momentum. But the tools it employed to stimulate the economy, the slashing of interest rates and the creation of £435 billion of new money, disproportionately helped the rich: as a deliberate aim of policy, cutting the price of money inflates the price of assets, such as houses, property, shares and government bonds. To state the bleedin' obvious, poor people don't own houses or significant assets. So the very measures taken to save us from the worst effects of the banking crisis actually widened the wealth gap between rich and poor.

This does not make the Bank of England the avowed enemy of the people. But by sticking to the tramlines of its *modus operandi* – creating cheap money to push up the price of assets, thereby increasing the confidence of owners and encouraging them to spend and invest more to foster growth – the Bank worsened endemic inequality.

So, what were poor families in the North-East and North-West, who were just about succeeding in keeping their heads above water, to think when they saw the government apparently shaping economic policy largely to help their friends in the South? Even George Osborne's Northern Powerhouse of transport and infrastructure investment plans seemed tilted particularly towards his then constituency base by Manchester, rather than more depressed Sunderland and Middlesborough.

Of course, the under-employed and economically insecure of Sunderland, Braintree and Margate had no compunction in whacking the Camerons and the Osbornes. Every time David Cameron insisted that the referendum campaign should not be seen as a test of his popularity or competence, voters thought the precise opposite, that this was an opportunity to give him a bloody good hiding. And the refusal of Jeremy Corbyn to share a platform with him, even once, reinforced the idea that this was all about Cameron, and not about the EU.

What matters now is the response to the Brexit vote of government, central banks, those who run our big companies, religious leaders and anyone with the power to influence how our income is made and distributed. For a brief moment in the summer of 2016, it looked as though Theresa May got it. Her very first pledge on the street in front of 10 Downing Street, on 13 July, was that her number one priority would be to help those on modest incomes, the people she styled those 'just about managing'. Maybe it was all going to be OK after all, because this introverted child of a country vicar seemed to have captured the mood of the nation:

> If you're from an ordinary working-class family, life is much harder than many people in Westminster realise. You have a job, but you don't always have job security. You have your own home, but you worry about paying a mortgage. You can just about manage, but you worry about the cost of living and getting your kids into a good school.

If you're one of those families, if you're just managing, I want to address you directly. I know you're working around the clock, I know you're doing your best, and I know that sometimes life can be a struggle. The government I lead will be driven not by the interests of the privileged few, but by yours. We will do everything we can to give you more control over your lives. When we take the big calls, we'll think not of the powerful, but you. When we pass new laws, we'll listen not to the mighty but to you. When it comes to taxes, we'll prioritise not the wealthy, but you. When it comes to opportunity, we won't entrench the advantages of the fortunate few. We will do everything we can to help anybody, whatever your background, to go as far as your talents will take you.

She clearly saw that the establishment had been put on warning, that its grip on power had become much more conditional, that the distribution of the fruits of our toils has to become fairer. But then there followed, well, not very much – a lot of words about, for example, increasing the power of workers relative to bosses, and too few deeds. Perhaps the cause of her inaction on an agenda that could have established her as a great reforming Tory premier was a quite extraordinary act of self and national harm she committed in the autumn of 2016, perhaps the most wilful act of vandalism by a serving prime minister. That was her declaration at the Tories' annual conference on 2 October 2016 that she would trigger the EU's Article 50 process for beginning Brexit negotiations with the rest of the EU by the end of March 2017.

The announcement was a conference gimmick to warm the cockles of the arch Brexiteers in her party and reassure them that she would respect the result of the referendum, and the UK really would be leaving the EU. But it imposed an arbitrary and hard deadline of the end of March 2019 for the moment we would be out of the EU – and therefore gave away almost all of her negotiating power, not only to the twenty-seven EU countries on the other side of the talks, but also to any critic in the UK parliament or outside parliament with the power to slow up or frustrate the process. At that fateful juncture, she capitulated to France and Germany on perhaps the single most important Brexit issue, that negotiating timetable, in that it is not remotely practical or possible to agree all the important terms of Brexit within Article 50's two years.

Of course, the official EU position was that the two-year timetable was not up for negotiation. But that is to ignore real-politik. For the brief few months when May refused to name a date for triggering Article 50, the rest of the EU was in agony. They hated our presence at EU decision-making councils as a hostile member. And it was fantastically frustrating for them not knowing when we would be properly gone, for good. So May should have exploited their discomfort by saying she would not agree to trigger Article 50 unless and until in (probably secret) informal discussions they settled some of the big issues of the UK's future relationship with the EU, such as the outline of a trade deal, for example.

If that proved impossible, she could have refused to trigger Article 50 till the other EU 27 agreed to vote that there would be whatever extensions to the talks beyond two years might prove to be necessary. And again, if that ran into the sand, she could have insisted that as and when the talks began, the terms of Brexit should be negotiated simultaneously with our future relationship with the EU. The fundamental point is that literally the single card she held of any significance was that only she could initiate the beginning of the Brexit talks, and once she had played that card, the UK was at the abject mercy of the rest of the EU. Having now done so without obtaining anything from the rest of the EU, she has guaranteed that the Brexit talks will yield a sub-optimal outcome for the UK – and could well be a total disaster.

This was such an abdication of the UK's national interest, I am staggered the Cabinet Secretary Sir Jeremy Heywood did not try to prevent May. I am sure that her announcement of the triggering date was consistent with the legal advice he and she would have been getting that there could be no negotiation before Article 50 was triggered. But all EU negotiations are in practice always about politics, not law. The notion that she could not have called the rest of the EU's bluff on this is craven – and tragic for Britain. When I think about it, I weep. And it is not irrelevant that during the referendum, when the campaign director Dominic Cummings was asked whether a commitment should be given to triggering Article 50 without securing concessions from the rest of the EU, he said to do so would be the equivalent of putting a loaded gun in one's own mouth.

The point is that when May subsequently said, in her famous speech in ornate Lancaster House in January 2017, that 'no deal is better than a bad deal', she was talking something quite close to piffle, cock and balderdash. If the UK was to tumble out of the EU on 1 April 2019 without a formal deal, quite a few very bad things might well happen. Because we would be outside of the EU's customs union, there would have to be new border checks on the more than forty per cent of our two-way trade that is with the EU. Unless new warehouses are built now, more border guards recruited, roads widened, new IT systems put in place, the delays in everything from food to cars coming into Britain and going to the EU could be hideous.

There could be queues of lorries at Dover going back tens of miles. Certain foods could become scarce in supermarkets. Brexit for a while would be ugly. And that would be to ignore the very real risk that aeroplanes from the rest of the EU could not land here. That security co-operation with police and security services in the rest of the EU would be made more cumbersome and fractious. Or that EU citizens living here and Britons living in the rest of the EU would be in agonies of uncertainty about their residency rights. Oh, and the rest of the EU would probably sue us for the €50 billion to €100 billion they think we owe them in relation to promises we made to fund the EU budget before voting to leave.

As soon as she established the end of March 2019 as the moment we would again be an independent state, it became almost impossible for her to have any agenda at all other than the political, legal and technical preparations for Brexit, because that was life and death, and everything else could wait.

But even so, at the moment Article 50 was triggered, Mrs May and her Brexit secretary David Davis were woefully under-prepared. That was partly because she made another extraordinary misjudgement, which was to challenge the case brought in the autumn of 2016 by Gina Miller and others that the process to leave the EU required parliamentary approval. If the vote for Brexit meant anything at all, it was to reassert the sovereignty of the British parliament. So for May to wish to argue in the courts that parliament should not debate and approve the most important constitutional decision of our time – and for her to claim that her office, the executive, was all powerful – was nothing short of a scandal. And because the

Supreme Court did not rule for Miller until January, the historic parliamentary debates that ultimately gave her the authority to trigger Article 50 took place much closer to her self-imposed deadline than was necessary, and were therefore yet another distraction from the far more important job of working out what we want from Brexit.

Then came the third misjudgement and act of self-harm. Having left the parliamentary debate so close to the wire, when the shock of the referendum result had worn off and MPs and Lords had regained their mojo, May spotted that they were very unlikely to give her a blank cheque for the Brexit talks. She realised she could not be confident, with her slim majority in the Commons, that parliament would in the forthcoming months back her in all the necessary Brexit-related votes. So in April she made a fateful decision to call a snap general election, in the confident hope that it would deliver her a huge parliamentary majority and personal mandate to deliver whatever version of Brexit ultimately suited her.

The result could hardly have been further from what she hoped and wanted. In one of the most turbulent campaigns in history, disrupted by two terrible terrorist atrocities, the unprecedented leak of Labour's manifesto and the equally unprecedented U-turn by May on a flagship manifesto policy (about funding social care for the elderly), British voters turned their backs on the small parties, and especially UKIP, and coalesced around the Tories and Labour as they had not done for decades.

Labour's share of the vote increased by almost ten percentage points to forty per cent, its greatest gain since the era-defining 1945 election that saw Labour's Clement Attlee replace Winston Churchill. May did win more votes than Blair ever did, but she lost her majority in the Commons. Although Brexit was rarely at the forefront of rhetoric in the two-month battle, in the end the outcome was a re-run by proxy of the referendum – with those wanting a more abrupt exit from the EU voting for the Conservatives and those wanting a more emollient approach and a closer long-term relationship with the EU opting for Labour.

May was told in no uncertain terms that she cannot be confident of popular backing for whatever version of Brexit she scrabbles together. And she is now the hostage of ten DUP MPs from Northern Ireland, who sold her a so-called Confidence and Supply agreement – that guarantees her DUP support in the votes she needs to win to sustain herself in power, although not all votes – for £1.5 billion of investment in the province. Her authority is seriously weakened, and there is no prospect of her leading the Tories into the next general election. And for what it is worth, my view is that she sealed her fate, as a disappointed and disappointing PM, when she put party interest before national interest by citing March as the date for commencing those Brexit discussions.

Maybe she can claw back credit for herself and party, if she can turn that Downing Street promise to govern for everybody into reality. The imperative of doing so was only made more conspicuous after the incineration of Grenfell Tower, and the deaths of around eighty of its inhabitants, which showed this rich country letting down the poorest and most vulnerable to an extent I never expected. But with her grip on power so fragile, and her party bitterly divided on what it really is and what it stands for – the Tories are yet again fighting over whether the economic liberalism of Thatcher and her determination to shrink the state were aberrations or their true essence – the prospects of May healing our wounds as a nation are slight.

This second-ever woman prime minister for Britain initially seemed the counterpoint to Thatcher, restoring to the Tories their belief in intervening and fixing markets and capitalism when they deliver unjust outcomes. The Tory party may well return to what it used to call One Nation values, but it will happen because that is where her MPs eventually take it, and not because she will lead them there.

Our democracy gave us what I think we want and need, which is a national debate about who we are, while the prime minister is held prisoner by a divided party, parliament and country. Better that than what America's democracy gave Americans as their president – a showman, liar and hypocrite. Trump was elected thanks in part to his appeal to those on low – but not the lowest – incomes, and especially to the white middle classes outside of the great metropolises (families who in Britain would be described as 'working class'), but he has created a top government team out of billionaires and the super-rich. And although some of his promises, such as big infrastructure spending, may create jobs and incomes, the Wall Street he denigrated as being in the 'swamp' is salivating at an expected loosening in the important Dodd-Frank restrictions on how they make money. Worse still, he wanted to strip health and welfare benefits from the poor while cutting tax for the rich; it is a blessing he is being blocked.

Here again, Dad, I have to distinguish between my own horror at Trump's divisive, hate-generating rhetoric and narrow nationalism on the one hand, and the motives of those who backed him. The point is that the crisis for white Americans in its declining industrial heartlands is even more acute than in England's, manifested in epidemics of opioid and alcohol abuse, worsening suicide rates, a reversal of decades of people living longer. And Trump appeared to listen to them in a way that Hillary Clinton did not. He spoke their language.

He seemed to understand their despair that their incomes had not risen for years, even if his policies stand little chance of seriously helping. He respected their Christian and family values, when Clinton and the Democrats in Washington seemed to be embarrassed by them – and to value them less than they did Latino and black people. Like the choice of Brexit, a vote for Trump was a vote for hope, even if it was a naive hope, against a status quo that left many feeling like second-class citizens. The measure of the failure of the Democrats and Clinton was that a majority of white women on low-to-middle incomes voted for him and not Hillary after all his 'pussy-grabbing' and eye-bleeding hate language.

The votes for Trump and Brexit were not the ignorant mistakes of the misguided. They were declarations by millions of families that they will no longer tolerate the countries they love being run against their values and economic interests by a self-renewing elite. The surge in the vote for Corbyn also has to be seen in that framework. Corbyn supporters were, of course, largely those who opposed Brexit. But Corbynmania captured the other side of divided Britain and points to what is most worrying about this place today, in that it is fissured and fragmenting to an extent we have perhaps not experienced since it was created in its current form by the Acts of Union more than three hundred years ago.

So, what I will now explore is:

- Why the economy has been skewing rewards so much more to the richest.
- How and whether it can be reconfigured to fulfil its fundamental purpose of lifting up everyone, and especially those with least.
- Why trust in so many of the institutions and people who have run things for years is at an all-time low among the general public, though not among the elite.
- And whether it may be possible to persuade those most alienated from mainstream politics that they have a voice that matters.

What I will assess is whether finance can be fairer, whether robots can create meaningful satisfying employment rather than stealing our jobs, whether workers can unite to demand improved living standards in a way that does not undermine growth, whether the denigration of experts that is so pernicious for our faith in organisations vital to our prosperity is actually reasonable, and whether digital technologies offer hope of a more open and democratic approach to decision making, or the threat of tyranny.

In a way, this book could be seen as the fourth in a series: by accident the quartet I have written can be seen as the story of how the optimism of the Blair–Brown early years has led directly – and causally – to the cynicism and disappointments of today.

My first book, *Brown's Britain*, a biography of Gordon Brown as a creator of New Labour and as the longest serving chancellor since the nineteenth century, explored the origins of the cult of austerity, the extraordinary and arguably excessive power of the Treasury and the birth of the politics of 'triangulation', which saw Labour abandon its core principles and embrace many of those of the Tories. The greatest tragedy of these years was perhaps the way the all-powerful Treasury deified services and the City, ordained that manufacturing did not matter, and more or less killed any serious attempt at an industrial strategy that might have reinvigorated the ailing former industrial heartlands of the Midlands and the North.

Then came *Who Runs Britain?*, which was a lament about the widening gap between rich and poor, the collapse of social mobility and the rise and rise of a plutocracy. Latterly, *How Do We Fix This Mess?* was about how Western governments effectively subsidised banks to take insane risks in the cause of generating giant profits and vast bonuses.

These three themes, the long-term neglect of depressed places and people, worsening inequality and the perceived unfairness of financial globalisation, have brought us directly to where we are today. We are a divided country – in fact in the West, we are divided countries – at a crossroads, where hate and mistrust are more prevalent and more mainstream than at any time that I can recall, and with respective populations uncertain whether they can still rally and unite around a single flag and a set of basic, civilised values.

Dad, we would not be in such a mess if your voice, and others like yours, warning that you can't allow millions of people to be left behind and then expect them to feel grateful, had been heeded. I wish you were here to help me solve the puzzle of what needs to be done to restore the march of progress, rather than fatalistically accepting fracture and managing endemic failure.

You died in a great NHS hospital that was operating at dangerously close to full capacity, from multiple infections you picked up while in the hospital. It was the worst, the most tragic luck. Your doctors were magnificent – so diligent, so expert, so hard-working. Shortly before you died, you made characteristic light of your perilous condition, when you told the consultant physician that as an economist, you could see the marginal utility of trying to keep you alive was probably now less than the marginal cost. You broke my heart with that display of selflessness, humour and rationality – the qualities that defined you. They are also great British virtues. Which is why neither you nor I would ever give up on this country we love.

Dad, you would be shocked, appalled, by how fragile it all feels. So, tell me please, what the fuck do we do now?

CHAPTER 2
THE DEATH OF PROGRESS

Britain, Europe and America have become much more ossified. Fewer people are escaping a disadvantaged start in life, especially compared with the immediate post-war years, which is when my dad really got going on his journey from Bayston Road in London's immigrant East End to the House of Lords. There is less social mobility. And something else malign has happened that affects all of us more conspicuously, a global economic cooling that has put a stop to a longstanding rising tide that lifted all boats. In much of the rich West, economic growth has slowed very significantly, and the fruits of what growth there is have gone disproportionately to the richest. We have been experiencing the harmful combination of worsening inequality and possible secular stagnation (to use Larry Summer's resonant phrase).

Most of my dad's generation, known as the silent generation, enjoyed huge improvements in the quality of their lives – and they rightly expected the same for my baby-boom generation. That optimism has dissipated. One of the most important social phenomena of our age is the collapse in confidence that our children will be better off than us. It is no longer rational for someone born today to hope that their lives will improve as much as someone born eighty years ago, if at all. And if hope for a better life is progress, this is the death of progress.

My dad's story tells us something about how the West is not the hopeful place it was. Maurice (named after Chevalier) Harry Peston was born in 1931 and brought up in London's Jewish Stoke Newington. He was the eldest son of Abraham, always and mysteriously known as Bob, who jointly owned a small skirt-pleating business, Sun Ray, and who in family mythology lost a small fortune gambling on the greyhounds. His father was Solomon Pastein, a cabinet maker from Warsaw, and his mother was Golda Goldman.

Abraham-known-as-Bob's wife Yetta (née Malt – described as a typist in the census) died when my dad was fifteen, which is a jarring rhyme of life, since my beloved wife Siân died when our son Maximilian was fifteen. Dad's sister Myra left school at thirteen to cook and clean for the family and bring up their baby sister and brother, Barbara and David. The day after Yetta died, Dad returned to school and my granddad went back to working sixteen-hour days.

Dad, who was six foot tall at thirteen, was the acknowledged genius of the family, the star pupil at the Grocers' Company School, which became Hackney Downs. He was the first in his family to go to university and the only one of his four siblings to do so, when he went to the London School of Economics. There he was a protégé of Lionel Robbins, one of the founders of modern British economics and a much more right-wing and free-market economist than Dad was to become.

From there, Maurice Harry Peston won a scholarship to Princeton, whence he wrote home of a university then boasting John Nash, Oskar Morgenstern and John von Neumann on its staff (and Einstein as a resident), where in the common room the conversation was:

> . . . of an extraordinarily low level . . . much more like that of old men than the flower of a nation's youth . . . From what I have seen of it, this society is most noteworthy for its mediocrity, which does not mean there are no exceptions or that time will not persuade me to change my mind.

Time changed Dad's mind. As a fellow at Princeton, he became a member of Oskar Morgenstern's research group, and therefore one of the first British people to understand and practise game theory. After three years, he came home to do his national service, but – unknown to him – Morgenstern wrote to the Chicf of the Imperial General Staff, saying that under no circumstances should my dad be allowed to do normal national service. Dad got a call from the War Office asking him instead to help them understand how game theory could have military applications, and he therefore joined the Army Operational Research Group: he used to boast to me that by his mid-twenties, he had the rank of colonel.

By the time I was two years old, he was a successful academic at the London School of Economics, with a substantial semi-detached house and garden, backing on to ancient oak woodlands – Queen's Wood – in North London. There was a parquet wooden floor in the hall, a boudoir grand piano and books everywhere. Economists, journalists, writers and actors came to my parents' many parties. Social mobility was something you could see, feel, touch, eat (we were the first in our road to eat avocados – or so we claimed) and buy (we were definitely the first to have a colour telly – it felt like being given the gift of sight). It was also how we talked. Mum, born

Helen Cohen – the only daughter of a Jewish tailor, Joe, and his wife Rose, who managed a ladies' dress shop in Waterloo's The Cut – banned the word 'toilet', because that was not something people like us said.

We were not alone in moving up. This was the 1960s and 70s, when all of Britain seemed to be switching from black and white to colour, from Spam to prawn cocktails, when extraordinary numbers of people were enjoying standards of living that their parents would have regarded as an impossible dream. By contrast, what I have done in life and where I have ended up is not especially surprising, given where I started – although the greatest gifts my parents gave me were an over-developed work ethic and a fear that I could lose everything if I relax.

Of course, not everyone born eighty years ago had the optimism and confidence of my dad. As children in the hard years of austerity after 1945, they would have been rational to fear the worst. But in practice, their lives and those of their offspring would be transformed for the better, by state education, the health service, council housing, the welfare state – whereas those born in the last thirty-odd years are typically experiencing chronic work insecurity, inability to buy a home or even rent a decent one at an affordable price, and inadequate opportunities to save for a decent retirement.

The tide started to go out before the Crash of 2007–8, but it was made much worse by the collapse of banks and the temporary breakdown of their essential function, that of financing growth. And a paradox in the weft of this book is that our digital industrial revolution is compounding the breakdown of the primary function of the economy, to reward all of us, by directing its rewards to a decreasingly small number of people.

These are the important inter-connecting currents: less

dynamism in our social structures and less movement of people from one social class or income group to another; the apparent end of economic growth that rewards all; widening wealth and income gaps between rich and poor.

Social mobility really matters, because of an intrinsic sense of what we think is fair. One way of seeing this is that if we had to design a society with ignorance of what our own place in that society was likely to be, and all we knew was that total equality ran counter to what was practically or theoretically possible, we would probably demand that at the very least we all had a decent chance of bettering ourselves, in whatever circumstances we were born (this is a bastardised version of John Rawls's veil of ignorance). This would seem to be the very minimum of what a decent society would deliver. The same point is expressed differently by Alan Milburn's Social Mobility Commission:

> Low levels of social mobility infringe our nation's social contract: that those who work hard will have a fair chance to succeed. That is why social mobility is not just about the prospects of those at the very bottom of society. Nor is it just about opening up the top levels of society . . . it is about whether your background holds you back, whatever your social position. Too often seen as being about only a minority in our country, social mobility is an issue for the majority.[5]

But that is where the important political arguments begin, because there are so many different ways of defining 'a fair

---

5 'State of the Nation 2016: Social Mobility in Great Britain', Social Mobility Commission, November 2016, p. 1.

chance to succeed', especially the extent to which the state can and should intervene to help the poor better themselves and also to prevent the rich pulling up the ladder to keep those lower down trapped in their places. Deciding where we draw the line between help from the state that facilitates self-development and self-improvement, and help that encourages dependency, is still, after all these years, the big dispute between left and right, and in this country between Labour and Tory.

There is no doubt, however, that the line has been drawn in the wrong place for years, because a weakening of social mobility is nothing new. A 2007 study[6] showed a significant decline of upward travel between the Baby-Boom and Generation X eras. Those born in 1958 whose parents were among the poorest 25%, or quartile, in Britain had a relatively low 30% chance of staying in that bottom quartile. But that had risen to just under 40% for those born poor in 1970.

What is more, almost 20% of those in the poorest fifth, or quintile in 1958 succeeded in climbing into the richest quintile – whereas only 11% achieved this ascent among the 1970 cohort. Or to put it another way, between the 1950s and 1970s, it became significantly harder for the poor to break free from the shackles of where they were born.

As for what has happened more recently, the Social Mobility Commission looked at data for those in work aged between twenty-nine and thirty-six in 2015. It showed no significant improvement in intergenerational income changes: any man born into the richest fifth was three times more likely to be there as an adult than someone born in the poorest fifth;

---

6 Jo Blanden & Stephen Machin, 'Recent changes in intergenerational mobility in Britain', Sutton Trust, December 2007.

strikingly the advantage of being born rich for a woman was a little bit less, but still significant.

What has gone wrong? Well, the first thing to point out is that the significant social progress of the post-war years, the rapid expansion of the middle class, was always going to lead to a slowdown in social mobility, almost by definition. The 1944 Butler Education Act's step-change improvement in state education was bound to give a relatively rapid and dramatic boost to the economic prospects of the poorest, that would etiolate as extremes of wealth and income were reduced, as they were until the 1980s.

And one problem with the bloomin' middle classes – the problem with me – is we want the best for our children, and we do what we can to deploy our resources to reinforce their prospects of having the most comfortable possible life. Collectively, when we make sure our kids go to the best schools, or have all the books they need, or we hire tutors, we capture most of the available university places for our children – keeping out children from poorer backgrounds.

The statistics bear out the idea that a swelling middle class tends to keep a diminished working class in a ghetto. Among those born in the 1958 group, 5% of those from the poorest quintile eventually got a degree, compared with 20% for the most prosperous fifth. Now it may look like progress that 7% of the bottom fifth from 1970 babies graduated in the late 1990s, but some 37% of the richest got a degree. And the point is that social mobility is conditioned by relative educational attainment, not absolute. Among the later Generation X, the richest were pulling away from the poorest; degree attainment between rich and poor widened from fifteen percentage points for Baby Boomers to thirty percentage points for Gen X.

Within the picture of declining general social mobility there are connected stories about gender and ethnic mobility, which show trends that are positive, but may also be storing up problems for later. A recent survey by the Sutton Trust showed girls saying they are more likely than boys to go to university, by a margin of seven percentage points, while black, Asian and minority ethnic (BAME) school students had greater expectations of a university education than whites by an eleven-percentage-point margin. If that were to translate over time into better jobs and earnings for women and ethnic minorities, it would also translate into a fairer country. But if it reflects, which it may, a collapse of ambition and hope by poor, white working-class boys, that would be a long-term source of division and resentment.

In respect of the gender pay gap, we are a million miles from the problem being inadequate pay for men. Nationally the gap is still 18% between men and women. And at the top, the difference is even more yawning. The BBC was recently savaged by the media for the huge pay disparity in favour of its male stars, such as Gary Lineker, Graham Norton and Jeremy Vine, and the fact that only a third of its highest paid stars were women, while almost none were non-whites. But there was some disingenuousness here in the attacks on the corporation: such yawning gaps to the benefit of men are rife all over industry, the media and – especially – in the City.

The difference is that the BBC, funded by all of us, has a greater responsibility to reflect national mores – and it is in the vulnerable position that it succumbed to government pressure to be more transparent about pay than any private-sector business. The BBC claims that its pay gap across the board is just 10%, which is significantly better than most employers. That said, it does not reflect well on the BBC that

45% of its top-paid people were privately educated, almost seven times the proportion of British people who went to fee-paying schools. The BBC is not a utopian microcosm of the kind of socially mobile country we would all love to inhabit. But then, nor are any of our most powerful public or private institutions.

To digress, self-indulgently, for a moment, the BBC's admission that its prizes disproportionately go to old white men should perhaps have given pause for thought to the right-wingers and libertarians, such as Breitbart, who had laid into me on social media and in columns for the policy at ITV of recruiting an intern for my show *Peston on Sunday* via Creative Access – which meant that only members of ethnic minorities could apply. This attempt to build a team that better reflects our nation was apparently 'racist'. But the inescapable fact that my company, like most others, is largely run by white men is not a problem worth addressing, apparently.

The gender imbalance is as much about power as money. Take the most powerful economic institution in the UK, the Bank of England, where none of the five governors (the name for the governor and four deputy governors) is a woman (although a fifth governor was a woman till recently), where the Bank's court (its fancy name for the board) contains nine men and just two women, and all of them are white, and where its interest-rate-setting monetary policy committee contains one woman out of eight (and again all are white).

Does this mean that the Bank of England and BBC discriminate in an identical way in favour of men? Not quite, according to a former senior official: 'The BoE has a slightly different dynamic from the BBC: few women get into top positions, but there's pay parity. So, if you get there, you're paid the same, but it's harder to get there. Interestingly, the

Bank has been impervious to change despite the presence of Mark Carney [the Bank's reforming Canadian governor].'

As for equality at HM Treasury, the most important of the government's departments, that is a slightly hilarious example of work in progress. The top two, the permanent secretary and second permanent secretary, are both men, there is one woman among the five directors general, but at the third tier of directors – of which there are five – every single one is a woman.

Then there are the stories I routinely come across of jobs being given by one mob of privileged white men to their friends, at the institutions that dominate our culture – and of women being turfed out or excluded. It is extraordinary that Theresa May in effect ousted Rona Fairhead from the role of chairman of the BBC Board, by forcing her to re-apply, and then appointed a genial, bright, posh, white former banker, in the form of Sir David Clementi. This looked like active discrimination in favour of an ex-public schoolboy by a prime minister who claimed to be cracking down on privilege.

Even worse, perhaps, was the vetoing by Karen Bradley, the culture secretary, of the black, former deputy chief executive Althea Efunshile from appointment to the Channel 4 board, not to mention the resignation honours dished out by David Cameron – peerages, knighthoods and assorted gongs – to pretty much all his Downing Street team and allies, although they had all had the time of their lives working for him and none needed their social status reinforcing.

What bliss it is to be born rich and powerful in Britain. But the system is massively tilted against you, if you are born poor. And the same story, of class and income rigidities between generations, is true in other rich countries. The American

Dream, that anyone can achieve anything with determination in the land of opportunity across the Atlantic, has been more myth than way of life for decades.

Perceptions that America is more of a can-do place than Europe are incredibly resilient, however. According to World Values Survey data, just 29% of Americans think that the poor are trapped in poverty and 30% that income is determined by luck rather than education and application. Europeans are much more fatalistic, because 60% are convinced that where you are born is where you end, and 54% see chance as the only way out. Which explains why 60% of Americans think the poor are 'lazy and lack willpower' compared with just 26% for Europeans.[7]

But although it is probably good for the US that Americans believe anything is possible, it is a socially useful lie. In the Victorian era, social mobility in the US did significantly outstrip that of the UK – largely because the movement off farms into factories and white-collar jobs happened much earlier in Britain. But that social-mobility gap had disappeared by the latter half of the twentieth century.[8] To be clear, it is not (as you know) that social mobility has increased in Britain, but that it fell very sharply in the US.

The circumstances of birth, even in America, are the most significant determinant of life prospects. Around 40% of those born to parents in the poorest 20% will never get themselves off that bottom rung. And although 60% will rise,

---

7 Roland Benabou & Jean Tirole, 'Belief in a just world and redistributive politics', *The Quarterly Journal of Economics*, Vol. 121, Issue 2, May 2006, pp. 699–746.

8 Jason Long & Joseph Ferrie, 'Intergenerational Occupational Mobility in Great Britain and the United States since 1850', *American Economic Review*, Vol. 103, No. 4, June 2013, pp. 1109–37.

most of them will not get more than one or two rungs high-er.[9] And like the UK, this absence of serious mobility is less new than you might think: a 'millennial' child, born in the bottom fifth in 1986, had just a 9% chance of getting to the top fifth, which was exactly the same probability as for a Generation X baby born in 1971.[10] Individual social mobility showed no improvement between the decades 1986–96 and 1996–2005.[11] Meanwhile, those lucky enough to be born into the top 5% have a 22% probability of staying there as adults. As for the impact of ethnicity, well, white workers are a staggering ten times more likely to make it into the top earnings quartile than African Americans.

It is the impact of the widening gap between rich and poor that makes declining social mobility especially damaging. With income and wealth inequality increasing considerably from the mid-1990s on, it is arguably much more worrying that we lack the institutions to help the poorest break free of their income and class shackles. The burden of being born poor increases as the rich become richer, because those with the most money can throw even more resources at their own offspring's educations and life prospects, compared with what is possible for the rest. And this eats away at the bonds between us, increasing resentments between poor and rich, reinforcing the idea that the way things are run, the institutions of the

9 Julia B. Isaacs, Isabel V. Sawhill & Ron Haskins, 'Getting Ahead or Losing Ground', Economic Mobility Project of Pew Charitable Trust and the Brookings Institution, February 2008.

10 Raj Chetty, Nathaniel Hendren, Patrick Kline, Emmanuel Saez & Nicholas Turner, 'Is the United States Still a Land of Opportunity? Recent Trends in Intergenerational Mobility', National Bureau of Economic Research, Working Paper No. 19844, January 2014.

11 'Poorer than their parents? Flat and falling incomes in advanced economies', McKinsey Global Institute, July 2016.

state, are there only to serve the rich and privileged, and to keep the rest in their place.

If, as I do, you believe that the votes for Trump, Brexit and Corbyn were to some extent protests against the unfairness of how society is organised and run, then there is a connection between these votes and the combination of declining social mobility and worsening inequality. But it cannot be the whole story, since the combination of the widening gap between rich and poor and less social mobility has been evident for decades, at least since the advent of Margaret Thatcher and Ronald Reagan in the early 1980s. What made these regressive trends more toxic was the collapse of economic growth after 2008, because it is easier to put up with seeing others get relatively bigger pieces of cake, so long as everyone receives at least a little bit more cake.

Those at the bottom of the income scale are likely to be less fractious if economic growth is making them less poor in absolute terms, if not in relative terms. And for around a decade, that has not been happening. According to McKinsey, a staggering two-thirds of households in advanced economies – or up to 580 million people – saw their incomes before benefits and other forms of state top-up fall or stagnate between 2005 and 2014. Just to give you an idea of the magnitude of this massive income squeeze, the comparable number of people undergoing flatlining or falling incomes between 1993 and 2005 was less than 10 million.

This represents a catastrophic breakdown of the economic system throughout the rich West. If it does not exist to make most of us richer, what is its point?

Liberal-market capitalism stopped working.

Meanwhile there has been partial redemption for the role of the state. Handouts from government cushioned the income fall for many: after public-sector transfers and tax, there was no improvement or a worsening in disposable income for 210 million people; so the intervention of governments cut by more than half the numbers whose incomes were reduced. And what is amazing is that it was in America, where the safety net has always been less comprehensive and generous than in Europe, that this state help offset the worst of the squeeze. In the US, disposable incomes for those on middle incomes actually rose 1% in the decade to 2014, a tiny bit better than nothing, though down from a 15% increment between 1993 and 2005.

The paradox, of course, is that state intervention worked, and was simultaneously declared unaffordable by the politicians in office. The very large sums disbursed by governments for in-work or out-of-work benefits – to those on low incomes or unemployed – were made during the recession when tax revenues were collapsing, and governments' debts rose at unsustainably fast rates, though not (yet) to unsustainably high levels. So just as the safety nets have been proved to work, they are being scaled down and even withdrawn in some countries, including Britain.

As McKinsey says:

In the future, governments may find it difficult to sustain this level of spending without substantial revenue increases; government debt as a share of GDP increased over the past seven years in five of the six countries we studied. For example, central government debt is close to 100% of GDP or higher in Italy, the United Kingdom, and the United States. In the United States, it rose from 56% of GDP in 2005 to 97% of GDP in 2016.[12]

---

12 ibid., p. 14.

The case for rapid reductions in government deficits is often exaggerated. But we would be doomed to endure static or falling living standards, unless we can revive the growth of incomes in the market economy, or unless we can become less dependent on state handouts. McKinsey warns of a plausible low-growth scenario that would lead even more of us – up to 80% of Western households – to suffer falling or stagnating incomes in the decade to 2025. This is not our inescapable fate. But we need to understand what underlies the plausibility of the idea that the squeeze on our living standards could be the new natural order of things.

There are several reasons for the ratcheting down of what we have been earning and may henceforth be capable of earning in our jobs. First are what McKinsey styles 'aggregate demand factors', which in the current instance is a euphemism for the global financial crisis. A decade on from its onset, the negative impact on growth is still being felt. The banking boom that turned to bust, caused by bankers' greed and regulators' negligence, left us permanently and seriously poorer, because of the costs that fell on taxpayers of the bailout and the way it undermined the banking system's capacity to fund sensible and productive economic activity. Even now there is plenty of evidence, before our eyes, that banks continue to finance asset and property bubbles, rather than the new wealth and job-creating enterprises that the world needs.

Then there are the important changes in the structure of populations, or demographic factors. In the rich West, we are ageing societies, whose households are shrinking. This reduction in the intrinsic size of the workforce, relative to non-productive older people who need support from the state, is a brake on growth. It is a brake lessened in places such as the UK and US by the immigration that has taken place, but which in both countries has become controversial and hated by many.

Then there is the decline in what we earn on savings and investments, dividends from shares and businesses and interest on cash deposits. This income has been falling, in part because central banks slashed interest rates to revive the economy after the crash.

Finally, there are what McKinsey calls 'labour-market factors', which include one of the most important of all economic trends of the past forty years or so, the declining share of national income that has been distributed to workers in the form of salaries and wages, or what is known as the labour share of income. This fall in the proportion of our economic output that goes to people to reward them for their toil and effort is another way of seeing the widening gap between rich and poor, because its corollary is an increasing share of the cake taken by the owners of capital, or those with stakes in businesses and property. The cause of this important rise in returns for capital and diminution in earnings for workers has in some measure been the exceptional returns or profits made by new technologies, especially in the digital age – which is not necessarily bad, because it is associated with an improvement in the quality of our lives as we enjoy new things and services (smartphones, Uber, Google and so on).

Workers' earnings in the West have also been squeezed by globalisation, competition from the low-wage economies of China and Asia. But the fall in the wages of low-skilled Westerners as a result of factories shifting to China has not been all bad for us. Our living standards have been improved by deflation imported from China: when we can buy a Chinese laptop or mobile phone for half what it cost a few years ago, we are relatively richer.

There is an argument that the trend to bigger and bigger companies, especially through mergers, reduced competition and channelled rewards to owners rather than workers. But perhaps the most important reason why the labour share of national income has been declining – because it represents a political choice, rather than a hard-to-resist global economic trend – is that trade unions have been crushed, especially in the UK and especially by Thatcher.

So, what are the important numbers? McKinsey calculates that from 1970 to 2014, with the exception of a short-lived spike during the 1973–4 oil crisis, the average wage-share collectively fell by 5% on an indexed basis in six countries it studied, the US, UK, France, Italy, Sweden and the Netherlands. But the UK's drop was much bigger than that average. It was 13% over these forty-four years, which would represent a huge distribution of income from workers to the owners of capital. Now the most plausible explanation for the exceptionalism of the UK is Margaret Thatcher, or rather the way that she tried to and largely succeeded in ending the ability of British trade unions to boss businesses and government.

Until she took office, trade unions expected – especially when Labour was in power – to determine wage rates in private and public sectors. Before her, trade unions could bring entire industries, indeed the nation, to its knees, by supporting each other on picket lines and in strikes. She massively circumscribed their rights, to work together and indeed to strike at all. And that fall in their disruptive power was a fall in their economic clout. This humbling of union leaders and bigging-up of the board room was sustained by Tony Blair and New Labour, after his 1997 landslide. It was a matter of principle for him to keep the trade unions shackled in their new place, because he felt Labour would be more popular if it seemed to be on the side of the capitalists, but also he did not want to be held to ransom by trade union leaders in the way that so many of his predecessors had been.

The statistics underpin the notion that it was Thatcher who undermined workers' incomes, because – as the IMF has pointed out[13] – after the early 1990s, workers' or labour's share of national income in Britain stopped deteriorating and actually rose very slightly. That said, it is not all about Thatcher. Research by the Bank of England[14] showed labour's share of income fell a significant five percentage points after 2009, which could be the mirror of a recession that reduced the relative value of work, but also raises questions about how new forms of working, on the shortest possible contracts and for new digital companies, are weakening the power of workers.

The other side of squeezed pay for employees was soaring company profits and sky-rocketing executive rewards. Because with unions castrated, there was a void when it came to holding boardrooms to account. Of course, that void should have been filled by the owners of businesses. But these owners, largely institutional shareholders – pension funds, hedge funds, insurance companies and other collective investment schemes – did not take their responsibilities seriously: they had and still have a culture of selling the shares of companies that are performing badly, rather than instructing the respective managers of their companies to shape up.

Big shareholders, often and paradoxically the de facto

13 'World Economic Outlook: Gaining Momentum?', International Monetary Fund, April 2017, pp. 126–7.
14 Andrew G. Haldane, 'Labour's Share', speech at the Trades Union Congress, London, November 2015.

representatives of the workers as managers of their pension savings, were absentee landlords, unwilling or unable to rein in chief executives who were lining their own pockets out of all proportion to their talents, or the wealth they were generating for their owners or the economy. In 1989, after Margaret Thatcher had done her best to liberate company directors, the typical chief executive of a big company earned twenty times workers' average pay. Today that ratio is around 130:1.[15] So have executives become 110 times more talented, special and valuable than their workers over the past thirty-odd years, which is what would justify that huge increase in pay differentials? Or have they simply become 110 times more powerful? I think everyone – including the lucky bosses – knows the answer.

The bosses, predictably, would say that they are in a global market, and that they could earn even more elsewhere, especially in the US (where the ratio of top pay to workers' is more than 300). And even in Germany the gap is at least as great as in the UK, on one measure. But our response should probably be (1) go and work in America, Dubai or Switzerland then, and let us see if we miss you more than you miss us; and (2) the whole investment universe exaggerates the contribution of all but a handful of genuine management geniuses.

That said, it would be wrong to suggest that underlying corporate performance has not improved. It has, very significantly. In the words of McKinsey, 'profits for North American and Western European corporations in the past three decades have been exceptional, with after-tax operating profits rising to 9.8% of global GDP in 2013, from 7.6% in 1980, an increase

---

15 'Executive Pay: a review of FTSE 100 executive pay packages', CIPD in conjunction with High Pay Centre, August 2017, p. 4: mean ratio between FTSE 100 CEO and full-time UK worker is 132:1.

of nearly 30%. Between 2010 and 2014, after-tax profits of US firms measured as a share of national income even exceeded the 10.1% level last reached in 1929.'[16] Again this heightened profitability is a corollary of shrinking workers' rewards.

Which might be tolerable if these profits were reinvested in these businesses or others to generate additional employment, or more remunerative activities for their workers. Or if they were devoted to creating exciting new products – life-saving drugs, for example – from which we all benefit. But too many companies, especially the biggest multinationals, deploy their cash to buy their own shares to drive up the share price, which triggers huge paydays for bosses under their bonus and incentive schemes. Or they simply hoard the cash, often offshore, to minimise the tax they pay in the countries that give them the shelter and services they need to prosper. When companies behave like enemies of the people in this way, they turn profit into a dirty word, which it should never be, because in the absence of profit, there is no life-improving investment.

None of which is to argue that trade union reforms were all bad, but only that they may have gone too far in weakening and humiliating the unions. Thatcher's transfer of power from union bosses to corporate executives – barons to fat cats – was good for Britain for many years: it underpinned our golden age of sustained, well-above-average, employment-creating economic growth, from 1992 to 2007. Also the flexibility of Britain's labour market – or the confidence of companies that they can hire and fire almost at will, and can manage employee costs to match demand for their goods and services – is one reason why unemployment in the UK did not soar in the way

---

16 'Poorer than their parents?', McKinsey Global Institute, op. cit., p. 10.

it did in most of the EU after the 2007–8 Crash. Unemployment has since fallen to levels we haven't seen since the mid-1970s.

For me, however, it is the lesson of Sweden that we must heed. Because the Swedish experience suggests the UK may have gone too far in empowering capital over labour. Of the six countries studied by McKinsey, Sweden was the only one where the majority of people did not endure a flatlining or a significant fall in earnings from 2005 to 2014 – and this was true of their market-based income and their disposable income after state transfers. McKinsey says:

> At one extreme is Italy, which experienced a severe economic contraction in the recession after the 2008 financial crisis and has had a very weak recovery since. There, real market incomes were flat or falling for virtually the entire population. At the other extreme is Sweden, where only 20 percent of the population had flat or falling market incomes. In each of the four other focus countries – France, the Netherlands, the United Kingdom, and the United States – the proportion of segments whose market incomes did not advance was in the 60 to 80 percent range.[17]

What has Sweden got that the others lack? The answer is relatively successful trade unions: almost 70% of workers are union members (on the basis of the latest available data) compared with just 25% in the UK. In Sweden the typical working family has increased its share of national income, and from 2005–14 enjoyed faster rises in living standards than non-unionised workers at the very top and the very bottom of

---

17 ibid., p. 3.

the income scales. In the long term, Swedish workers are
protected by contracts that guarantee wage rates and hours
worked. And in a crisis, such as the 2008 global banking and
economic crisis, the unions were prepared to work with the
Swedish government to reduce working hours temporarily, to
help keep companies afloat and preserve jobs.

And for the avoidance of doubt, and to challenge the
consensus in Britain and America that there is a correlation
between union power and economic under-performance,
Sweden is a rich, successful country. It is richer per head than
the UK, and depending on how you measure it, more or less
as rich as the US.

What should give us in the UK most pause for thought,
perhaps, is that despite the Swedish government topping up
the income of the poorest with benefit payments during the
recession on a more generous scale than most countries did,
and despite entering the recession ten years ago with government debts roughly equivalent to those of the UK, Swedish
state debts today are less than half ours (and half those of the
US).

Sweden is a story about how collaboration between labour
and capital can generate prosperity and growth from which
everyone benefits. Apart from anything else, if you accept the
proposition that when productivity or output per worker rises
it is only fair that wages rise, then Sweden is one of the few
countries on the planet operating in a fair way – because
unions have the power to rein in the natural propensity of the
owners of capital to scoop disproportionate gains.

Britain and America lack the cultural cohesion of Sweden
that underpins this closer alignment of capital and labour.
And when the power of collective labour increases, companies have a strong incentive to substitute capital for workers.

So rises in living standards can be associated with socially damaging rises in joblessness. But it is also striking that despite its much higher unemployment rate, France has so far turned its back on the populist Marine Le Pen, who had been arguing for her country to leave the eurozone and even the EU. The pervasive sense of hopelessness in many depressed parts of France is no worse than the hopelessness in parts of the UK, where employment is higher, but job security and wages are much lower.

We need to learn from Sweden's success. The sense that the dice are loaded against us would be lessened if we built new models of social solidarity, of organised, co-operating labour. I will explore some new possible models of how workers united can win a fairer share of income. But for now, it also needs to be said that workers can have all the power in the world, but they (we) will not become sustainably richer if each of us fails to produce more on average, if our productivity cannot be revived.

So when we organise ourselves as a counterweight to employers, to bosses, the aim must be to work with them to increase revenues, rather than against them to eliminate profits. That kind of shared purpose would provide hope that progress, with all its beautiful plumage, is not the very dead parrot it seems.

CHAPTER 3
THE AGE OF EMOTION

There has never been a more exciting time to be a journalist – and the corollary probably also holds for audiences and readers. The sheer number of ways of delivering a story and of receiving information, on social and digital media, together with television, radio and the press, is thrilling. But it is also confusing and troubling, because the parameters of what I do are much more complicated than they used to be.

From when I started as a cub reporter in 1984 till comparatively recently, the essence of what I did changed little: I would try to find out important stuff happening in the world, on good days I would get that information before my rivals, and then I would try to present what I had found out as accurately and impartially as possible. The measure of my success was whether that story was the splash in my newspaper or the lead item on TV and radio news. My judge and jury were my newspaper and television editors and bosses, who decided if my story was any good. And if they liked it, they would give it the prominence that automatically delivered a huge audience.

That model of journalism still exists. And indeed, I am still playing that game. But I also spend a huge amount of time trying to deliver 'content' (horrible word) on social media. I started when it was great fun, because I love industrial change, and there was something compelling about its conversational nature and immediacy. These days it is an essential part of my working life, because that is where the massive audiences are to be found. I started on Twitter in 2009, and was re-energised by the way readers would challenge what I tweeted and proffered their own views and news. Since the start of 2016, I have invested considerable time and effort producing short videos and written commentary for transmission on Facebook. I am currently trying to get to grips with Instagram, in a bumbling way.

These new media have been adopted by me with enthusiasm. But that does not mean I lack concerns and anxieties about the way they are changing journalism and politics. What generates a huge audience on them – so-called reach and views – is not the kind of hard news journalism I have been doing all my life. When I put out a scoop on Twitter or Facebook, it will be welcomed politely by my followers and seen by a few thousand or ten thousands of people. But when I publish something angry or emotional, which may contain nothing new of a factual nature but is just me expressing raw sentiment, the audience swells to hundreds of thousands and even millions.

A furious post I put out on Facebook about Trump at 6 a.m. on 9 November 2016, after it was clear he was being elected, and another outraged one on the betrayal of the residents of Grenfell Tower, had an impact incomparably greater than detailed forensic investigations into the people and institutions that run the country and world. Emotion generates excitement on social media, in the way that cold hard facts – however important – rarely do. And for the journalist (me), that is seductive, almost corrupting. I won't pretend I was not flattered when drivers stopped their cars to congratulate me on what I had said about Grenfell.

But social media as the empire of emotions and feelings is dangerous for journalism, and for democracy. I have spent my entire working life striving never to be a propagandist, to try to shine a bright light on power and let people make up their own minds about it. But if nobody cares unless I inject my own pain into my reporting of what is going on – well, that is a big problem, because if I faithfully followed the diktats of the new social media market, my journalism would necessarily become much more skewed and tendentious.

I would look only for stories that make me cry or laugh, which would mean ignoring huge acres of the important news landscape. And my presentation of those stories would be at least as slanted and biased as my everyday conversation, possibly more so. I would abandon all my training to see both sides of a story and present the fairest picture. I would become more pamphleteer than journalist, but with the ability to insinuate myself into every home. This is not a notional risk. The ecosystem of digital media is driving journalism in this pernicious direction – because that is where the clicks and views are to be found, and the money can be made.

Of course, we have been fed tendentious news 'with attitude' for decades. Arguably the *Mail* and the *Sun* were avant-garde – 'post-truth' – before the internet had been invented and that too-slick concept was employed to define the symbiosis between a modern genus of populist politician and new media. Some would say that the importance of George Osborne CH, a former Tory chancellor, becoming editor of London's *Evening Standard* is confirmation that all 'mainstream media' is the vehicle of politically motivated plutocrats – although that was an allegation arguably more plausible about the Fleet Street of the 1930s to the 1950s, when Lord Beaverbrook could make or break any government or politician as owner of the *Express*, in the Black Lubianka building, or about Rupert Murdoch in any recent decade.

But we are now in a madhouse where lies on social media are obviously true, because we have a personal relationship with social media that validates everything we watch and read there, and everything that is in newspapers is obviously a lie, even the truth, because they are owned and controlled either by evil commercial interests, or are the sinister tools of the left-leaning metropolitan elite. Oh, and for some it is all a Jewish conspiracy (again).

I am exaggerating. But only a bit. What is harder to assess is whether we end up with chaos, in which the distinctions between fact and fiction are appallingly blurred. Or whether we are drifting towards the tyranny of the deep-pocketed technocrats, whose ability to use algorithms to invade our digital lives, and find out all about our hopes and fears, will give them power not only to target messages at us to get us to buy stuff we did not know we wanted, but also to vote for parties and people we had not thought we supported. That is what this and the next chapter will explore. When China's government is already using algorithms to screen a billion accounts of the message service WeChat for anti-government messages and sentiments, it is probably rational to fear the worst.

Today, as social media bosses everything, and Donald Trump is apparently running the free world through his Twitter account, perhaps I sound like a flat-earther. Are journalists like me, and organisations like the *FT*, ITV and BBC, who seek what we think of as truth, self-deluding and naive? Perhaps our truth is merely another self-interested version of reality – and ours is worse because we deny that and pretend superiority. If so, those who accuse me on Twitter and

Facebook of simply inventing any story that jars with their reality (I am by turns accused of being a Tory, a leftie, an EU lover, an EU hater, an opponent of Scots independence, a proponent of Scottish independence, a Blairite, a centrist, a member of the establishment, a hater of enterprise, a modern-day Freemason, part of the international Jewish conspiracy, *inter alia*) are the sane ones.

They are not, though. A world in which all news is perceived as convenient fiction is one susceptible to take-over by tyrants. It is the world in which a Putin is most comfortable, because in it he cannot be held to account. To use the Silicon Valley jargon, he was an early adopter of technology and processes to exploit social media and the internet to subvert the truth and condition public opinion – with notorious troll factories, in which Russians are paid to write disinformation about foreign elections in posts or blogs, and insert pro-Putin propaganda into otherwise anodyne articles, and automated social media 'bots' that parrot propaganda.

It is hideously apt that Russia should have intervened in a US presidential election on behalf of a candidate who is a genius at making wholly contradictory statements and never conceding the contradictions. A world where no news story can be believed, or *per contra* every news story is equally right, is a world in which emotion and brute force, not reason, rules. It is a world in which we are too vulnerable to being seduced by a new Mussolini, or even a Hitler.

It really matters that reason is not buried, either in the media or politics. So we need to understand why it is now so much under threat. Here are the important and connected trends:

- *political disintermediation,* or the ability of a demagogue like Donald Trump to go around the established media and communicate directly with the public via social media, and in his case through Twitter.
- *fake news,* or the proliferation in the digital sphere of fictional news pretending to be fact – either to distort political debate for malign ends or to attract clicks, readers and advertising revenue.
- *data mining by self-learning algorithms,* which monitor our behaviour on social media and the web, and learn about our habits, preferences, hopes and fears – so that news and messages can be sent to us that are guaranteed to make an emotional connection with us.
- *echo chambers,* or our imprisonment in social media newsfeeds that give us only the news and views that correspond with our revealed prejudices and biases – and never challenge our respective views of the world.
- *the shock-jock hegemony,* or the growing tendency, even in conventional news media, to merge news and comment, to disguise campaigns and propaganda as objective reporting, much as shock jocks have done on radio for years.
- *the defenestration of experts,* or the collapse of confidence and trust in any kind of traditional authority, but especially institutions and individuals with claims to expertise, and including the traditional media.

Donald J. Trump is a seventy-one-year-old, who apparently understands better than most politicians half his age the value of going round the back of the established media to talk directly with voters. As he told the *FT,* 'without the tweets, I wouldn't be here...I have over 100 million followers between Facebook, Twitter [and] Instagram. Over 100 million. I don't have to go to the fake media.'[18] And he made mistrust of the established institutions in Washington, the mainstream media and Wall Street recurring themes in his election rhetoric, (but although he continues to pillory the press and television, this attack on the rest of the establishment is a less important pillar of his actual government – in practice his policies are very likely to enrich banks, private equity firms and hedge funds, because of the way he wants to lighten regulations for them).

His campaign was conducted to a revolutionary unprecedented extent in 140-character slogans, claims, pledges, attacks and rebuttals on Twitter. A reality TV star, he intuitively understood the power of communicating in shocking, sensational headlines – 'Hillary Clinton should have been prosecuted', 'With Mexico being one of the highest crime nations in the world, we must have THE WALL', 'MAKE AMERICA GREAT AGAIN', and so on.

It reinforced his 'authenticity', which would have been put at risk if he had allowed himself to be mediated – packaged and interpreted – by traditional television and newspapers. And he has spectacularly deflected popular attention from serious charges against him and his family, such as the alleged improper contact between his colleagues and family and the misinformation machine of the Russian state, by making outrageous claims against his opponents. But if the rewards for him are boundless, the costs to America are huge, because he reinforces an image of the world's most powerful and important nation as being in permanent crisis. It is as though the chaos and interpersonal conflict that daily reigns on

---

18 *Financial Times*, 2 April 2017.

Twitter, Facebook, Instagram and the other social media services has taken up residence in the White House.

The competing realities of the President of the United States on the one hand and the conventional media he attacks daily for allegedly making things up have become the status quo, a given, frighteningly fast. When we are forced to accept that we can either have confidence in the president, or in the press, but not in both, we are dangerously close to the collapse of democracy. But that is where we are. Trump's denigration of anything that challenges his views or authority as 'fake' is destroying the fabric of the state; and he is breaching the great trust and responsibility conferred on him when he was elected. The cancer is made more malignant because one of the tensions between press and president is over the role played by Putin and Russia in subverting fair news coverage of his contest for the White House with Hillary Clinton.

Proper and important questions about whether he was helped to power by selective leaking of Russian hacks of Democratic National Committee emails become for him evidence of a liberal conspiracy to do him in. His defence is to lash out, typically by alleging worse against Clinton and Obama. Other instances of political misdirection have been his attacks on public officials, like James Comey – the director of the FBI he fired – and extraordinary public disputes between members of his own staff.

In Western political annals, there has never been anything quite like Anthony Scaramucci – Trump's communications director for a little longer than the blink of an eye – telling the *New Yorker* that unlike Trump's chief strategist, Steve Bannon, 'I'm not trying to suck my own cock.' When all of government is turned into a very public soap opera of backstabbing, or in the case of Scaramucci his preferred 'frontstabbing', all complaints against the presidency, serious and minor, become trivialised. How do you find a reason to impeach or get rid of Trump, when everything is a reason?

A collapse in public confidence in powerful organisations – or what the public relations firm Edelman calls 'trust in institutions' – is linked to the votes for Brexit and Trump. On its annual survey,[19] what it categorises as the 'mass' of people mistrusted government, business, media and non-governmental organisations in both Britain and America. But probably more important is the widening gap between the trust of the 'informed public', the elite, and that of the great 'mass' of people – which was nineteen and twenty-one percentage points respectively for Britain and America, the widest trust gap of all twenty-eight countries in the survey (in the UK, for example, 56% of the supposedly informed public trust the four big categories of social and economic institutions, whereas just 37% of the whole population do).

Broadly, the people who run the world trust themselves, and the rest of the population mistrust them. That augurs ill, for the stability and cohesiveness of our countries. Strikingly, the country where this trust gap between the informed public and the mass population is next largest, at eighteen percentage points, is France – which goes a long way to explain both the popularity of the extreme right-wing French nationalist Marine Le Pen, and why the French population was prepared to take the risk of electing the relatively unknown and untested Emmanuel Macron as president.

As for trust in the media, that has fallen to all-time lows in twenty-three out of the twenty-eight countries surveyed

19 '2017 Edelman Trust Barometer: Global Report', Edelman, January 2017.

– with just 32% trusting it in Britain and 33% in France. A much higher 47% trust it in the US, though – and some may think this is a bad joke – only in India, Indonesia and China is significant positive trust recorded. Call me too unimaginative, but I am not sure China offers an attractive model for how to rebuild confidence in the media.

What we have been witnessing are two self-reinforcing trends. First, national institutions, whose function was to unite us or at least serve all of us, and that we used to trust, have been exposed as flawed and perhaps too human for our tastes. This does not just include the Treasury, Bank of England and International Monetary Fund, but parliament, monarchy and church – parliament, because of the scandal of MPs claiming excessive and inappropriate expenses; the monarchy, after years of tawdry revelations about Prince Charles' unstable marriage to Diana; and the church as a result of shocking disclosures that child abuse by vicars and priests was ignored and covered up for years.

What is routinely now denigrated as 'mainstream' media – the big newspapers and broadcasters, like the ones that have employed me for thirty-five years – are savagely mistrusted, too. Having blown the whistle on what's wrong with the powerful and mighty, they have been infected by the consequential collapse in confidence in any institution that pretends to know what is best for us – and in their case, also by a booze-and-testosterone-fuelled arrogance that led them to hack voicemails and use illegal methods to obtain information beyond what could be justified in the public interest (fewer British people trust the media than government, according to Edelman, and while the reputation of government has improved a bit since 2012, that is not true of press, TV and radio).

Many of us have decided we only trust people we know, or

can name. 'Where once trust was anonymised, institutionalised and centralised, today it is increasingly personalised, socialised and distributed,' said Andy Haldane, in a speech about what the Bank of England may need to do to regain the confidence of all of us.[20] What this means is that we increasingly trust services that rely more on visible recommendations from identified customers than the views of the institution itself. So digital platforms such as Uber, Airbnb, Spotify, Google, Amazon, Deliveroo and Facebook are partly successful because of their convenience and the fact they have driven down the price of goods and services we want and need, from transport, to communication, information, accommodation, entertainment and every conceivable bit of stuff. But what also matters about all of them is that we rate and leave reviews about Uber's drivers, or apartments listed on Airbnb, or things sold by Amazon and the suppliers in its marketplace.

Confidence in them is earned by the quality of how they perform, and how they are rated by us, rather than being taken for granted. And second, they give us the sense, which is sometimes an illusion, that we are in charge and in the driving seat. Facebook and Twitter are in the same mould: we can 'like' and 'follow' any number of voices on those social media platforms, to keep us informed about the stuff we have decided matters, rather than being told by the *Daily Mail*, *The Times* and BBC what they think we need to know,

There is the all-important rub. Because when it comes to news and important information, social media empowers us to find out more about what is going on, but also traps us in

---

20 Andrew G. Haldane, 'A little more conversation, a little less action', speech at Federal Reserve Bank of San Francisco Macroeconomics and Monetary Policy Conference, March 2017.

opinion strands that make us feel better about ourselves, rather than challenging us, and also makes us much more susceptible to being misled by the wilfully and accidentally mendacious. Facebook's and Google's algorithms, the formulae that put items in our respective newsfeeds, select for us news and views that they assess scientifically as likely to resonate with us, based on our previous reading and viewing habits. So they put us in a bubble away from competing narratives, which reinforces our prejudices, rather than healthily challenging them.

When applied to news, the rating or 'liking' system, which works well if we are hiring a plumber, buying an espresso machine or planning to watch a movie – though serious questions have to be asked about the power of an Amazon or Google to make the rules of these new huge markets – can be cancerous to the proper functioning of democracy: false news and lying propaganda that happens to strike a chord can be liked, shared and retweeted with the self-reinforcing momentum of the hysterical mob, and is then read, watched and taken as truth by gazillions of people.

Of course, a newspaper with a strong personality, like the *Daily Mail*, gives a skewed view of the world, too, but could never screen out all information that conflicts with our prejudices and way of seeing, in the way that an algorithm can do. The *Daily Mail* is necessarily broad in sweep by dint of having to be bought by millions of people: the cost of creating a personalised paper *Daily Mail* for each of us would be prohibitive. And when newspapers print stories that are wrong, they face sanctions that simply do not exist at the fringes of the digital wild west – although there are many who lack confidence in the Independent Press Standards Organisation or IPSO, the newspapers' watchdog.

More and more of us get our news online: in 2016, 50% of Americans under twenty-nine, 49% of those thirty to forty-nine, according to Pew Research.[21] And it is very hard to overstate the consequences of what is, in effect, a revolution in the way we hold power to account. It is not all bad. Social media has given more of us the opportunity to shout loudly. There is the potential for almost anyone to write a blog and attract millions of readers, completely independently of the newspaper and television brands that have for decades had almost total control over the voices we hear.

For believers in competition, especially the competition of ideas, that is a great thing. But professionals in the mainstream media played two very useful functions that are in danger of disappearing in the social media babel: they carried out extensive fact checking and verification (not always successfully, but better than nothing); and they identified stories that they regarded as interesting or important, that we would never find if left to our own devices, even in a digital world. They delivered to us largely accurate news and serendipitous tales that enriched our lives. And in the shift from analogue to digital, from institutional media to social media, the danger is not simply that we end up being vulnerable to lies and manipulation in that digital space. There is also a negative feedback to the traditional media, which has become more shrill and extreme in order to compete with social media and seemingly stay relevant. So social media has in that sense weakened and undermined the most basic virtues of traditional media.

---

21 Amy Mitchell, Jeffrey Gottfried, Michael Barthel & Elisa Shearer, 'The Modern News Consumer: news attitudes and practices in the digital era', Pew Research Center, July 2016.

The fragmentation of media caused by the digital explosion is the big reason why the 2017 general election was the first in living memory whose outcome was not determined or won by the *Mail* and the *Sun*. They were as vicious about Corbyn as it was possible to be, and hopelessly and helplessly enamoured of May, increasingly against the sentiments and instinct even of their own readers. To put this into context, their attacks were more devastating about Corbyn than their character assassinations of Neil Kinnock in 1992 and Ed Miliband in 2015. Yet when it came to election day, Kinnock and Miliband were kept from 10 Downing Street by support for the Labour party that turned out to be weaker than widely expected, while Corbyn's Labour polled massively better than even he had anticipated.

And in case you have forgotten that the *Daily Mail* saw Theresa May as an earthly angel, here is a reminder – from a rare interview she gave to their star writer, Jan Moir:

Near neighbours are George and Amal Clooney, although the couples' paths have yet to cross. 'No, I have not seen him,' she [May] says. 'In fact, I think I am the only person in the village who hasn't met him.' Perhaps she should put him on the guest list for one of her spicy lamb suppers? 'I don't think I was intending to invite him, so no,' she says. Well, that is Very Theresa, if I may say so, very much a plank of Mayism . . . She just wants to get on with doing her best for everyone in Britain – and finding time to experiment with outre pudding recipes. Underneath her re-purposed jackets and smart slacks, behind her armour-plated prudence and persistence, she is a truly remarkable woman, the genuine article in a world of careerist phoneys. Amen to that, as she might say herself.[22]

The painful irony for the *Mail*, of course, is that it was Corbyn – not May – who was widely seen as 'the genuine article in a world of careerist phoneys'. Although everything that Moir wrote was doubtless true about her, it was negated by the internal contradiction in her campaign, which is that it was all about her, in presidential style, and yet she refused to have a public television debate with him, Corbyn. It just didn't smell right, to millions of British people.

It is not that most of those who voted Labour were ardent Corbyn followers; most were bemused by the hysterical worship of him by a mob of panting young fans. But their innate sense of fair play was offended by the *Mail*'s and *Sun*'s front pages on 7 June, the day before the polls opened, which were nasty and vindictive. The *Mail* showed pictures of Corbyn, his shadow chancellor John McDonnell and the shadow home secretary Diane Abbott, and called them 'Apologists for Terror', in huge sombre type – adding 'the *Mail* accuses this troika of befriending Britain's enemies and scorning the institutions that keep us safe'.

Meanwhile the *Sun*, under the screaming headline 'Jezza's Jihadi Comrades', instructed its readers to 'make sure they vote for the Tories' because Corbyn – it claimed – had been 'at rally with Islamic hate mob'. At a time when the whole nation was feeling raw and anxious after the Manchester and London terrorist atrocities, this was a character assassination too far, because although it was perfectly legitimate to point out that as a lefty activist he had routinely kept rum company over

---

22 *Daily Mail*, 12 May 2017.

many years, and to raise questions about his judgement, it was altogether another level of innuendo to imply we would all be more at risk of being slaughtered by terrorists if ever he became prime minister.

It was the kind of slur that made the newspapers – and by extension the Tories and May, too – seem desperate. That it failed to stem his surge in the polls has damaged the authority of all three, and for the newspapers the damage could be very long lasting. On the day after the election, Rupert Murdoch was seen in the men's room of his newspapers' London office with his head in his hands. It seems apt.

Which is not to say that newspapers are an irrelevance. In the spring of 2017, George Osborne chose to edit London's *Evening Standard* newspaper, in preference to remaining a backbench MP, and not out of nostalgia for a lost world of inky national influence. He calculated that the *Standard*'s estimated readership of two million in a capital city of global clout would give him a voice to challenge the direction of the government that he would never have as a backbench MP. What Osborne's appointment represents is a greater blurring of the lines between politics and all media.

There has never been an unimpeachable *cordon sanitaire* between press and politicos. Richard Crossman, for example, was a cabinet minister in Wilson's 1960s administration, and then editor of the *New Statesman* in 1970. For much of Boris Johnson's tenure as editor of the *Spectator*, from 1999 to 2005, he was also a Tory MP. But the *Statesman* is conspicuously and proudly Labour and the *Spectator* avowedly Tory, whereas a paper like the *Standard* has not been party-political in the same explicit way. Also, the modern Tory party seems to have attracted a disproportionate number of bright young men who never seem quite sure whether they are writing government policy or a news-paper column.

Look at how Michael Gove flitted between membership of the Cabinet and being a *Times* columnist and back again to Cabinet. That included an interview in January 2017 with President Trump for *The Times*, when Rupert Murdoch was an observer in the room, though hardly a neutral one. Which of Gove's many hats was he wearing at the time? Was he there as a story-seeking *Times* journalist? Or as a former leader of the Brexit campaign with a vested interest in Trump saying something positive (as he did) about a future trade deal with Britain? Or as an MP keen to be reappointed to Theresa May's government and therefore highly unlikely to ask questions of Trump that could embarrass her? Or as the well-paid employee and friend of Rupert Murdoch, whose huge American media businesses would presumably not wish to be seen by the president as an enemy? With so many hats delicately balanced on his noggin, Gove elicited the devastating insight from Trump that 'Brexit will be a great thing.' Which was not really a surprise.

The other senior minister with whom the line between Westminster and media seems particularly fuzzy is Boris Johnson, the foreign secretary and – coincidentally – former figurehead, with Gove, of the Leave campaign. Johnson was seemingly offered the *Standard* job before Osborne, or at least *The Sunday Times* quoted 'friends of Johnson' as saying that the foreign secretary had been the first choice of the *Standard*'s proprietor, Evgeny Lebedev, son of the former KGB agent and Russian oligarch Alexander Lebedev. Those 'friends' of his presumably knew what they were talking about, because the author of the news story, Tim Shipman, had been hanging out with Johnson that week for an interview with him, which appeared in the same 26 March 2017 edition.

Certainly Johnson and Lebedev seem close: for five years, every October from 2011 to 2016, Johnson spent a weekend at Lebedev's lavish Palazzo Terranova, in Umbria (described by *Condé Naste Traveller* as a beautiful former palace in an idyllic location and with sublime views) – usually accompanied by his wife Marina, and even on occasion being flown there and back by Lebedev in a private jet. Some would argue it is unsettling that Johnson as the mayor of London and then foreign secretary thought it appropriate to take hospitality from a Russian-born media mogul, whose oligarch father's relationship with President Putin and the Kremlin is much debated, and is certainly opaque. But the trips were disclosed under public-sector 'transparency' rules.

As for Osborne, he is using the *Standard*'s front page and editorials to put pressure on the Tory Party to move its centre of gravity nearer to the values and policies he favours – that the government should not abandon his version of austerity, and if we are to leave the EU, we must not also leave its single market. The paper's criticism of Theresa May has been waspish. The *Standard* did ultimately endorse her towards the end of her general election campaign, but only as the least toxic of a rum choice of candidates. And when she failed to win the majority she sought, he labelled her a 'dead woman walking' (on the BBC's *The Andrew Marr Show*), after first recalling ruefully that when she sacked him as chancellor in July 2016, she advised him to 'get to know my party better'.

At a time when media power is shifting so much to social media, one slightly odd phenomenon is that traditional media and government have rarely been so intimately linked, with a series of both civil-service and political jobs in Downing Street, the Treasury and other departments going to editorial executives and journalists from the BBC and *Daily Mail* in particular (and the most senior post in Jeremy Corbyn's private office went to a senior writer from the *Guardian*). There have always been career journeys from press to Westminster and Whitehall, but there seems to be more such travel than ever.

Whether the creation of these networks of hacks – using both senses of the term – has impaired the capacity of the press to scrutinise government with neither fear nor favour, or at least worse than in the past, cannot be judged scientifically. But it does mean that ministers and senior civil servants probably receive rather too much expert advice on a part of the media whose authority and influence is in decline, and not enough about new media. And it may also distort political judgements, such that ministers may be encouraged more than ever to think about what will appease newspapers and TV, rather than what is in the national interest.

During the election, in some parts of the press there was an almost total abandonment of any balance in reporting. And that had a deeply unhelpful consequence for all of the traditional media, which is that it lent spurious legitimacy to the widespread view that none of what has come to be denigrated as 'mainstream media' is to be trusted. That includes the BBC, all newspapers, ITV and me (of course). The ferocious attacks on Corbyn in the tabloids also make it harder for those of us with an old-fashioned attachment to the ideals of objectivity and accuracy in reporting (albeit only ever half-attained, and always through well-meaning approximation and compromise) to denigrate the ferocious and biased promotion of

Corbyn's Labour on new left-wing websites such as Skwawkbox, Evolve Politics, Another Angry Voice and the Canary.

I hate propaganda in any form, but I can almost see the case for what has come to be known as the 'Alt Left' – the nomenclature is a nod to the extreme populist Alt Right sites, like Breitbart, that helped usher Trump to power – when such loud voices as the *Sun* and the *Mail* are explicit cheerleaders for the Tories. And by the way, this is not because I am anti-Tory, but simply because democracies thrive on plurality in the media.

Here is an irate Thomas G. Clark, author of the blog 'Another Angry Voice', who has 320,000 Facebook followers, expressing at the end of July 2017 much of what drives and excites the Alt Left:

> One of the obvious reasons the Tories have got away with this sustained ideological assault on ordinary working people is the fact that the complicit mainstream media barely ever covers the issue. The facts that British workers have suffered the worst wage collapse since records began should be the narrative that underpins pretty much every newspaper article about politics or the economy, but some-how the ideologically driven Tory war on wages is a story that only ever pops up intermittently, with much greater prominence given to absolute drivel like Diane Abbott's bouts of innumeracy, fake stories about Jeremy Corbyn breaking a student debt promise he never made, and endless hate-mongering attacks against any public figure who dares argue for anything but the most extreme-right anti-emocratic interpretation of Brexit. Not only have the mainstream media been complicit with the Tory war on

wages by omission, they've also desperately failed to ridi-
cule the ridiculous Orwellian propaganda narrative from
the Tories that they're the party for hardworking people.[23]

Sites like his write stories and comments that go ferociously
viral on social media – and probably, on a shoestring, had as
much impact on the election outcome as the Tory-supporting
traditional press with its vast (if shrinking) resources. Jim
Waterson of Buzzfeed – another new media player, though
one that tries to be objective – identified the importance of the
Alt Left sites long before most, but even he failed to see how
influential they would be, because at the start of the general
election campaign, his big question was how they would cope
after Theresa May delivered the inevitable knockout blow to
Corbyn. Instead they and Corbyn are more secure and influential than ever.

What shows perhaps how little firm ground there is in the
media landscape today is that the *Mail* and the Alt Left do
have one common enemy: both work themselves into a lather
about what they see as the disgraceful bias of the BBC, the Alt
Left because of what it sees as the BBC's corrupt refusal to be
fair to Corbyn, the *Mail* because of its conviction that the
BBC is corruptly hostile to Brexit.

Another concern about the Alt Left sites is how they may
have helped to create giant ghettos of political intolerance.
The point is that the Canary and the *Daily Mail* are both in
their distinctive ways echo chambers for the views of very
different groups of British people, who feel validated to read
what are often their own prejudices given respectability by

---

23 Thomas G. Clark, 'How the Tories used "divide and conquer" tactics
to trash all of our wages', Another Angry Voice, 26 July 2017.

them. But the Canary, unlike the *Daily Mail,* is a huge social media phenomenon. As such it is an important part of a social media community that is largely shown only those news and other items that reinforce its members' emotional reaction to events, thanks to the algorithms that screen out serendipity and randomness from what we see in our timelines and newsfeeds. In the case of the *Daily Mail* in paper form, the equivalent of the algorithm is Paul Dacre, the editor. And because he is a flawed human being, not a computer program, there is more of a chance that a typical edition will contain a few stories that do not reinforce a particular dogma.

Now you will have noticed that I have not said all that much about the fashionable subject of 'fake news' – either the real fake news (if that's not an oxymoron), such as mendacious stories invented in Eastern Europe to harvest ad revenues from Facebook, which tended to favour Trump during the 2016 presidential elections; or, for that matter, Trump's routine slur as president that any story critical of him must be fake news. That's because fake news is a symptom of the bigger problem that information dropping in our newsfeeds is routinely misleading, even if not explicitly false.

It is welcome that Facebook is belatedly taking small steps to help users identify the most lying stories, through working with fact checkers like snopes.com and then putting a tag on the story notifying that it has been 'disputed by snopes, etc.'. But the wider problem goes to the heart of the business model of digital services, which is that the automatic computer programs of Facebook and Google, their algorithms, curate content to generate maximum activity on their services, rather than to assess the accuracy of the content. And what generates excitement and sharing by Facebook users is an idea that makes us laugh or cry or shout with anger, because it resonates with us in some way, it triggers emotions. To state the bleedin' obvious, a story does not have to be true to trigger those emotions – we only have to think it may be true.

Now on the plus side, curation of how we get our news by a machine intelligence rather than a human intelligence should protect us from the deliberate distortion of the news we read by a Joseph Goebbels – that is until a twenty-first-century Goebbels somehow manages to hack the social media algorithms to reinforce the control of a modern-day Hitler. But curation of our news by artificial intelligence lays us wide open to believing that half-truths and innuendo, that happen to be causing mass hysteria in online communities, are true or more important than is actually the case.

During the election campaign, for example, the Tories said they would abolish the provision of free school meals for all infants, which had been introduced just a few years earlier by the coalition government. But on Facebook and Twitter this was translated in shorthand by many angry people as a Tory plan to abolish all free school meals, including for children from disadvantaged backgrounds, which had been part of the spine of the state education system for decades. A form of online Chinese whispers turned one controversial policy into a truly shocking one. In more cynical cases, there have been deliberate and damaging personal slurs posted about MPs, which have then triggered hideous abuse of those MPs by credulous people. And sometimes satirical stories or even ads have been misunderstood as works of fact.

There is a life-or-death question for democracy here – about whether a small number of elite technocrats, with both superior skills in scraping relevant information from the net about our preferences and vulnerabilities and a genius for constructing propaganda to send to our social media timelines, will end up controlling the outcome of elections. I will return to this in the next chapter, when looking more explicitly at the digital battles for Brexit and in the last general election.

In many ways Facebook, Twitter and the rest have enriched our lives, but we are at a juncture where they may be fracturing nations. Trump used social media to win over the white working class of America, those who in America are called middle class, by sending them tailored messages over social media that preyed on their insecurities, their outrage that those they saw as foreigners were taking their jobs and their country. They then voted for him as a baying mob, especially in the rust belt, in the old industrial states, and carried him on their shoulders into the White House – thanks to an eccentric electoral college system that rewards popular victories in individual states, rather than overall share of the national vote.

Trump beat Clinton, even though she received almost three million more votes across America than him, out of 137 million votes cast. Maybe American democracy will survive one such massive transfer of power from left to right, from socially liberal to illiberal, against the revealed preference of the majority of American citizens. But no institutional structure can survive for long when it delivers a result contrary to the will of a majority of the people.

The role of Facebook was especially toxic, because of the way that it facilitated the spread like wildfire of false and damaging stories about Clinton – 'Hillary's ISIS email just leaked and it's worse than anyone could have imagined' – and absurdly positive fictional stories about Trump – 'Pope Francis shocks world, endorses Donald Trump for President'. Much of the fake or false news was invented for commercial rather than political reasons, to encourage online activity of hits that in turn generated ad revenues (the cottage industry of a hundred US political websites run from Macedonia was about the money, not the influence). But that does not make it less harmful.

Facebook and Google were created in effect by libertarians who, although their founders are now multi-billionaires, are desperate not to become 'the man' – the traditional publisher who vets and quality controls what goes on their platforms. They started as ways to empower you and me, by giving us the freedom to reach out to vast amounts of information and vast numbers of people. But that libertarian model is now unsustainable. They have gradually and belatedly recognised that hate videos, paedophile pornography, recruiting rooms for paedophiles and terrorists and films of executions, *inter alia*, cannot be allowed to proliferate on their platforms. And they are trying to prevent creators of fake news from profiting from that fake news. But they are still tolerating content on their platforms beyond what most of us would deem to be acceptable.

In the end, they will do themselves in if they do not take greater steps to expel the hateful, the harmful and the lies. The danger for them is that mainstream politicians – thankfully not yet all seduced by the power they can gain from astute use of social media – will unite across borders to rein them in. That could turn Facebook and the rest into the kind of regulated publishing houses that they would feel was a living death. Better surely to deploy some of their billions of dollars of idle cash to reform themselves.

Whatever Google and Facebook do, however, we cannot be certain democracy will be secure. Sooner rather than later, fake news will be created in video form using computer generated images that cannot be distinguished from reality.

Someone influential, a celebrity or politician probably, will appear in a clip saying things that may shock or move us. And it will be fiction almost impossible to distinguish from fact, a film manufactured from real images and recordings of that person, so perfectly put together that the joins will be impossible to see.

According to a recent report by the Belfer Center at Harvard University's Kennedy School, photo-realistic HD video, audio and document forgeries will shortly be possible 'even for amateurs' to generate, and these forgeries will be good enough to fool even 'some types of forensic analysis'.[24] They will be near perfect lies. Just imagine the impact when that video lie, accompanied by a vicious fake news story, goes viral on social media and the internet. Think of the potential chaos. The technology to do this is almost with us. As and when fake news looks as good and convincing as real news, it could be cynically exploited by a rogue trader's desire to move markets for a profit. It could be deployed in cyber warfare against the West by China or Russia. Or it could become the tool of a modern Goebbels. The credulousness that almost all of us are prone to when online will be ruthlessly exploited.

The marriage of money and technology, which has always created the risk of the will of the people being subverted, is perhaps more dangerous today than it has ever been.

---

24 Greg Allen & Taniel Chan, 'Artificial Intelligence and National Security', Harvard Kennedy School, Belfer Center for Science and International Affairs, July 2017.

CHAPTER 4
ALGORITHMS WIN ELECTIONS

At about 10 p.m. on 11 May 2016, an unexpected press release issued by Vote Leave was forwarded to me by a journalist friend. It had been sent to most political reporters and editors, but not to me. It quoted a 'Vote Leave source' as saying:

> The Establishment has tried everything from spending taxpayers money on pro-EU propaganda to funding the IN campaign via Goldman Sachs. The polls have stayed fifty-fifty. They're now fixing the debates to shut out the official campaign. ITV is led by people like Robert Peston who campaigned for Britain to join the euro. ITV has lied to us in private while secretly stitching up a deal with Cameron to stop Boris Johnson or Michael Gove debating the issues properly. ITV has effectively joined the official IN campaign and there will be consequences for its future – the people in No. 10 won't be there for long.

Was this a mad lashing-out by Vote Leave and its campaign director Dominic Cummings, or insidious and genius reinforcement of a powerful and resonant idea, that Vote Leave was the plucky small platoon versus Remain's bludgeoning corporate state? Gawd only knows. The notion that Johnson (Eton, Balliol, President of the Oxford Union) and Gove (Robert Gordon's College, Lady Margaret Hall, President of the Oxford Union) represent the anti-Establishment, the people, the anti-toffs, may be laughable – but for the few weeks of the EU referendum battle, it became a conceit that captured the diversity of the interests supporting exit from the EU. Remain did look like the voice of big multinational companies, big banks, senior Whitehall civil servants and the London plutocracy, because that look was reality.

Please forgive me for pointing out that the Vote Leave statement contains a couple of pretty substantial fibs. I never campaigned to support joining the euro, because my role as a journalist seeking to communicate in an objective way trumps whatever my personal leanings may be. Apart from anything else, I would have been sacked had I rallied to the euro cause, because at the relevant time – in the late 1990s – I was political editor of the *Financial Times*, a newspaper that obliged me to be neutral. And in my role as political editor and presenter at ITV, I had no involvement in determining which representative of the Leave side of the argument would debate on our channel with David Cameron – and I still feel a slight conflict of interest in even asking my bosses about it.

I imagine that ITV went with Nigel Farage as the countervoice to Cameron for the legitimate reason that he had been the living embodiment of the argument for withdrawal from the EU for years longer than Gove and Johnson. But I understand Cummings' pain. He was trying to build a coalition of political and social interests to vote for Brexit, and he was acutely aware that very large numbers of middle-class voters who think of themselves as liberal recoil at the idea of backing anything associated with Farage. As and when Johnson or

Gove becomes PM (don't laugh please – anything is possible these days), I simply don't know whether they will follow through on Vote Leave's threat and wreak their revenge on ITV and me.

The important point, as the young Tory MP Kemi Badenoch, elected in 2017, bemoans, is that in politics 'the age of reason is dead and the age of sentiment has begun',[25] which is analogous to my complaint that in journalism the age of fact is dead and the age of emotion has arrived. One toxic aspect of this has been the threatening and intimidation of parliamentary candidates, by their ideological opponents, and especially on social media. It is literally everywhere in political discourse. As everyone's social media stream will attest, the standard response today to a fact that challenges our view of the world is not to change our minds, but to aver that the fact is invented or in some way distorted by vested interests.

If political leaders are belatedly trying to reintroduce a degree of civility into debate, they are culpable for its debasement and the extreme mistrust of the state and anger at its representatives that is felt by many. They have wilfully weakened the foundation of the state by making promises they have not honoured, and by making reckless warnings of consequences if their chosen path is not followed, and this was especially true during the referendum campaign.

The most notorious example of a 'fact' or claim that was astonishingly influential, but has left a terrible legacy of mistrust of politicians, was the assertion made by the official Brexit campaign, Vote Leave, that when we left the EU we would have an additional £350 million every week to spend

---

25 Kemi Badenoch, 'The Tories must put an end to divisive identity politics', *Daily Telegraph*, 11 August 2017.

on the NHS. It was widely believed, but Theresa May's government has shown no interest in honouring it. That she was not on the Leave side of the campaign at the time does not matter. If the promises of the officially appointed campaign organisation, Vote Leave, carry no weight at all, what on earth is the point of referendums and democracy?

Of course, it was a charlatan claim in the first place, because:

1. It was a gross figure for our contribution to the EU's budget and took no account of the rebate we get from the EU.

2. It skated over the fact that much of the contribution we make to the EU budget comes back to us in the form of support for agriculture, rural communities and university research, and that farmers, universities and others would each face painful cuts if all our Brexit savings were to go to the NHS.

3. It ignored the possible imperative of continuing to make some payments to the EU to secure free-trade access to the EU's markets for our businesses.

But had it been total fiction, it would not have worked. The huge slogan painted on the side of Vote Leave's battle bus, which said, 'We send the EU £350 million a week, let's fund our NHS instead', was referring (roughly) to our gross contribution to the EU. But its implication that £350m could easily and practically be channelled to hospitals at the moment of Brexit was – as we now painfully see – an exaggeration. And even if Vote Leave had put the actual number that might be available, £150m a week, on its bus, that would have been a distortion in a sense, too. Because the campaign was trying to suggest that leaving the EU would take the NHS from its parlous financial state to the sunny uplands of ample resources, which was impossible, in that £150m would add just 6% to the NHS's funding, a useful but not transformative sum.

But whether or not in practice the cash would rescue the NHS, there is considerable evidence that it was the bus slogan that won it for Vote Leave. Its campaign director Cummings says the £350m claim was:

> the most effective argument not only with the crucial swing fifth [of voters] but with *almost every demographic*. Even with UKIP voters it was level-pegging with immigration. Would we have won without immigration? No. *Would we have won without £350m/NHS? All our research and the close result strongly suggests No* ... The IN campaign realised the effectiveness of this, as [Andrew] Cooper, [Ryan] Coetze and others said after 23 June, e.g., 'The power of their £350 million a week can't be overstated.' [Andrew Cooper, director of strategy for the IN campaign][26]

When I toured the country asking random people, on and off camera, why they were voting, those who were planning to vote for leaving the EU almost all mentioned the attraction of directing that lovely £350m from Brussels to our beloved NHS. One reason why it resonated so powerfully is that the NHS has all the qualities we value in an institution, and is so different in that sense from the EU: the NHS helps us in practical ways we can touch and feel, where the EU feels remote and amorphous; we created the NHS, whereas the EU is a club created by others; we own the NHS.

---

26 Dominic Cummings, 'How the Brexit referendum was won', *Spectator*, 9 January 2017.

Even today, on *Peston on Sunday*, whenever we ask viewers for questions to put to ministers, by a country mile the most popular is, 'Where is the £350 million?' With May's decision to reject the slogan as not hers, it has become a cancer eating away at our trust in mainstream politicians: it reinforces the widespread idea that 'they're all crooks'.

That said, the other side – the campaign to keep us in the EU – was almost as misleading in its arguments. And in one way what it did was worse, because its distortions went under the name not only of ministers but of HM Treasury, the most important Whitehall department, which is always supposed to be neutral and objective.

In May 2016, the Treasury gave its name to an official paper called 'The Immediate Economic Impact of Leaving the EU', whose central thesis was: 'a vote to leave would cause an immediate and profound economic shock creating instability and uncertainty . . . The central conclusion of the analysis is that the effect of the profound shock would be to push the UK into recession and lead to a sharp rise in unemployment.' The Treasury expected unemployment to rise in every part of the country by around 500,000 over two years and for the size of the economy to be 3.6% smaller than would otherwise have been the case. In fact, the slowdown in growth has been more gentle than that, and unemployment has so far continued to fall, to a rate we haven't seen since 1975!

None of which is to argue that over time there will not be sizeable economic costs to Brexit. In fact, the pain could end up being worse over the long term than the Treasury apparently feared. But it is damaging to the constitutional tradition that the Treasury and the whole civil service should be politically impartial that it lent its name to forecasts that were highly speculative; the Treasury seemed to be the politically malleable tool of a chancellor desperate to keep the UK in the EU. And, perhaps worse still, when the forecasts turned out to be so wrong, the Treasury looked incompetent. I cannot imagine why the then permanent secretary, Sir Nick (now Baron) Macpherson gambled the Treasury's authority in that way.

Which takes us to that moment in the referendum battle that captured the new madness of fiction-based political argument. On 6 June 2016, Michael Gove said on Sky News that 'the people of this country have had enough of experts'. He was ridiculed, because he was interpreted as denigrating all experts – from cancer specialists, to aeroplane mechanics to even the office of Lord Chancellor, which was Gove's at the time. How could the man in charge of a legal system that underpins our very way of life be so dangerously disrespectful?

And, of course, this comedy version of what he was thought to have said did little harm to anyone but himself, because it was seen as so bonkers. However, the truth (yes, that tricky concept) was that he was traduced, because a vital few words in what he said were ignored. The full quote was: 'The people of this country have had enough of experts from organisations with acronyms, saying that they know what is best, and getting it consistently wrong.'

Here Gove was on to something – although he was unfair to single out acronymic institutions, since it is not only them who have let us down. It is a legitimate concern when the Treasury makes tendentious claims that go seriously awry. And many other important government and official institutions that underpin our way of life – charged, for example, with maintaining stability in the economy and financial system – have in recent years been defined by the spectacular unreliability of their stewardship and forecasts.

Some have Gove's acronyms, like the OECD, IMF and FSA;

some, like the Bank of England and HM Treasury, do not. Most notoriously, they collectively failed to warn of the Great Crash of 2007–8, even when the evidence of banks' recklessness was in front of their noses, and they collectively erred in the other direction in respect of Brexit, by saying it would be an almost instant economic disaster, for us and the world.

None of this inspires faith in a certain kind of expert, as Gove averred. And it has had a number of highly damaging effects. Right now, the humiliation of the doomsaying 'experts' has lured the UK into a fool's paradise, where the real long-term risks and costs of leaving the EU are dismissed as the rantings of pro-EU nutters, rather than the real and present dangers we would be wise to debate and seek to mitigate or navigate around.

It has also created the impression that the man in the street knows more about the workings of the economy than a Chancellor of the Exchequer. And on this occasion, the people were right and their elected representative wrong. The man and woman in the street knew that they were not going to stop spending after the referendum, although the chancellor forecast differently. And so when shoppers kept on shopping, against expectations in the Treasury, the economy kept growing. But that doesn't prove all economists are always wrong and have nothing to say. But it does explain why, according to a YouGov poll in February 2017, civil servants and economists are among the two least-trusted professions in the UK – much less trusted than historians, scientists and, naturally, doctors. Only 'your local MP', which of course would include Michael Gove, was less trusted, along with politicians in general.

Now it is all very well coming up with a brilliant tendentious claim, like £350m for the NHS. But if it cannot be communicated effectively, then it has no force at all. What the

EU referendum demonstrated above all was the remarkable power of the astute use of social media to promote a simple positive statement. And it begs the question whether the remarkable disparity in knowledge of how to use social media in politics creates the risk that elections and referendums will be, and are being, decided less by rational decision-making by the electorate, and more by the sophistication of how emotionally loaded messages are targeted at susceptible voters.

There is no doubt, for example, that Vote Leave understood far better than Britain Stronger In (the official campaign to keep the UK in the EU) the opportunity presented by new technologies for gathering information about potential voters and then communicating with them. Looking back on the contest, Vote Leave was deploying a *Star Wars* battle cruiser against Wild West gunslingers on the other side. In some ways, it is miraculous that the margin of victory for Leave was not greater.

The best way of seeing this is through the competing accounts of what happened offered by Sir Craig Oliver, Cameron's director of politics and communications, who effectively ran the Remain campaign, and by Dominic Cummings, the campaign director of Vote Leave. The story told by Oliver in his book *Unleashing Demons* is mostly about rows with the BBC and conventional media over how the arguments were being presented, and bickering between the leading players on his side (Craig is particularly testy about the difficulty of persuading Theresa May to argue the case in public).

Cummings, by contrast, in a series of online blogs rather than a book, while also bemoaning what he saw as the vanity and negative contribution of Nigel Farage and many Eurosceptic MPs, focuses on the sophistication of Vote Leave's use of Facebook and the powerful software it developed to analyse gathered data about voters and their possible intentions.

In the months prior to the historic vote, Cummings astutely devoted his energies to what most politicians detest, namely process and management, as opposed to ideas. He aimed to deliver a small number of simple messages – mainly that dubious though effective message about Brexit liberating £350m a week for the NHS – to the most persuadable people as cheaply as possible, largely via social media, and also by banging on doors.

The focus of Stronger In and Oliver was much more traditional, and was seemingly all about TV coverage, leafleting every home and trying to minimise the benefit for Leave of its many supporters in the press. Their approach would not have seemed alien in the first EU referendum in June 1975. Against all expectations, the fact that Stronger In was a coalition of all the main party leaders, and could deploy all the resources of the state till the last weeks of the battle proper, made it a much more unwieldy and amorphous effort. The In campaign's treasurer, Roland Rudd, is withering about what was wrong with his side's polling, approach to social media and fundamental message: 'Craig Oliver ran the campaign on the slogan "Don't Risk it",' he says. 'What we failed to understand was there were too many voters with absolutely nothing to risk.'

The executive team around Cummings appears to have been much more cohesive, and smart. Cummings himself loves physics and physicists, because he believes – like his hero Charlie Munger (right-hand man of the world's greatest investor, Warren Buffett) – they ask the questions that help to prevent those with a social science background (like me), or perhaps history (like him), being fooled by crap. So, Vote Leave appears to have been set up rather like a hedge fund, staffed by rocket scientists rewarded to find new systems to beat the market by just a few basis points – or in this case, to find systems to make the limited amount of money allowed by the rules for wooing voters, £7 million, to be used a bit more effectively.

The star performer for Vote Leave, according to Cummings, was its operations director, Victoria Woodcock, who now works for the business software company Sage. According to Cummings, Woodcock was the 'the most indispensable person in the campaign; if she'd gone under a bus, Remain would have won . . . Some people are fifty times more effective than others. She is one of them.'[27]

What she did that was so valuable, for Cummings, was manage the creation of new 'canvassing software', which was appropriately named after her, as VICS or Voter Intention Collection System. Vote Leave, very ambitiously, decided to create its own software, because amazingly, there was 'no web-based canvassing system for the UK that allowed live use and live monitoring.' The development was done in-house and partly using an outside engineer, who sat in their offices for months. The point, according to Cummings, was to suck in and process data about voters 'from social media, online advertising, websites, apps, canvassing, direct mail, polls, online fundraising, activist feedback and . . . a new way to do polling.' And Vote Leave was to use 'experts in physics and machine learning' to do 'proper data science . . . far beyond the normal skills applied in political campaigns.'[28]

Information about voters was gathered centrally and locally. It was put into VICS, which then generated 'star ratings so that local teams could target the streets more likely to contain Leave voters.'[29] This was an iterative process: centrally

---

27 Dominic Cummings, 'On the referendum #20: The campaign, physics and data science', October 29, 2016.
28 ibid.
29 ibid.

organised initiatives and local canvassing, and there were 31,000 canvassers – of whom 12,000 were 'repeatedly active on a weekly basis'[30] – directed by what VICS calculated as being most effective; and this activity generated yet more data, which VICS then processed to improve the next round of canvassing and marketing. Cummings even claims that 'the models honed by VICS were used to produce dozens of different versions of the referendum address', such that the 'language and look' of a staggering 46 million leaflets were tweaked 'according to the most reliable experiments done in the world.' Vote Leave's plain and relatively unbranded 'the facts' leaflet was the most effective, he concluded.[31]

One especially clever idea was to gather information from a Vote Leave online football competition, which Cummings nicked from a PR stunt by the billionaire Buffett, who in 2014 offered $1 billion to anyone who could correctly predict the results of all 63 games in a US college basketball tournament. In Cummings' British version, contestants were invited to guess the results of all 51 matches in the Euro 2016 tournament, with the chance of winning a whopping £50 million, so long as they filled in their phone number, email address and home address, and also rated themselves on a scale of one to five in respect of how likely they were to vote for staying in the EU.

Cummings remains frustrated that he could only persuade an insurer to underwrite a £50m jackpot, even though the chances of anyone winning were infinitesimally small, because he ideally wanted the prize to be the £350m promised by Vote Leave for the NHS. But the data gathered in this way was

---

30 Dominic Cummings, 'On the referendum #22: Some basic numbers for the Vote Leave campaign', January 2017.
31 ibid., p. 88.

gold: Vote Leave acquired the contact details and voting intentions of hundreds of thousands of people, many of whom would never have participated in conventional surveys. VICS used the information to direct door-knocking and social media lobbying towards those who had revealed they were susceptible to the Brexiteers' arguments.

There is no ambiguity about the importance of social media to Vote Leave. That is where so much of its money went – especially to and via a specialist digital agency based in Canada, called AggregateIQ, whose expertise is in targeted Facebook advertising. In the list published by the Electoral Commission of beneficiaries of referendum spending by all participants, including Stronger In, what Vote Leave paid to AggregateIQ tops the list, by a country mile. The top three payments, of £852,981.52, £715,409.93 and £655,206.43, all went from Vote Leave to Aggregate IQ. In total, AggregateIQ received £3.5 million from Leave campaigners – including £675,315 via a twenty-three-year-old fashion student, Darren Grimes, and £100,000 from Veterans for Britain. Some £625,000 of the money spent by Grimes was a transfer to him from Vote Leave, which thereby avoided breaching statutory limits on what it could spend under its own name.

The total that Vote Leave spent directly with AggregateIQ was £2.7 million. Cummings uses dollars in his calculations, presumably because so much of the money channelled to AggregateIQ ended up with North American social media companies, including $1.7m to Facebook for 146m paid impressions. In total, Vote Leave delivered 309m online ads during the ten weeks, and an impressive 890m Facebook impressions between October 2015 and 23 June 2016. Cummings claims that during the ten weeks of the official campaign there were a billion targeted digital ads from Vote

Leave across all channels (including half a million text messages sent right at the end at a cost of just £9,000 plus VAT).

This represents communication with voters outside mainstream media on a mind-boggling scale. And unlike some political campaigns, Vote Leave preferred to pay for Facebook ads rather than go for a so-called 'organic' campaign of encouraging followers to distribute its messages, because it identified that Facebook's algorithm had been changed to favour paid ads in newsfeeds over posts shared by people being followed or liked. Cummings is characteristically savage in his criticism of those who spent considerable sums acquiring Facebook followers, rather than taking the direct route with ads. And to save money, Vote Leave targeted very few ads at residents of London and Scotland, because it rightly assumed that simply living in those places was a pretty strong signal of a propensity to want to stay in the EU.

But if Facebook was the medium of choice, what was the message? Well, what is perhaps counterintuitive is that while Vote Leave did do 'micro analysis' – or breaking down the electorate 'into small groups for analysis by using new tools not on the market' – it concluded that sending these small groups different messages tailored for their circumstances would not be effective.[32] Instead, and this will make some of you rail and rend your clothing, he says 'we discovered that essentially all relevant demographics responded best to £350m/NHS.' And as for video ads, 'most of the money was spent on persuading a group of about 9 million people defined as between 35–55, outside London and Scotland, excluding UKIP supporters' and 'the most successful with almost all demographics all the

32 Dominic Cummings, 'On the referendum #22: Some basic numbers for the Vote Leave campaign', January 2017.

way through was a variation on £350m/NHS that AggregateIQ did early on and we never could beat it.'[33]

Now before assessing the impact of social media on the 2017 election, it is worth exploring one other troubling feature of the referendum, identified by Cummings and not properly understood. He has observed that in the course of the campaign, betting markets always priced in a victory for Remain. The odds on the outcome typically implied a two-thirds probability of a vote to stay in the EU, and sometimes an 83% probability. Now in recent years, journalists like me have been wary of predictions made by opinion polls, because they've been a bit flaky – as they were in the 2015 general election. But we have tended to set greater store by what money was saying about the outcome of votes through bookies' odds. So it is interesting that betting markets called the referendum so wrong.

But it does not take a vast amount of money by the standards of the City, or indeed expertise, to manipulate betting odds. And Cummings also points out that for a hedge fund that felt it 'knew' the result would be for Leave, there would be a huge incentive to rig the betting markets to make it look as though Remain would triumph – for that would give it more opportunity to gradually and stealthily take a short position in sterling in currency markets (or gamble on the pound falling), and also make bigger eventual gains, because sterling would have further to fall after the vote. As he puts it, 'if you know the probability of X happening is much higher than markets are pricing, partly because financial markets are looking at betting markets, then there is a strong incentive to use betting markets to send false signals and give competitors an inaccurate picture.'

What makes this analysis more than theoretically interesting

---

33 ibid.

is that Cummings says he knew of at least two quantitative or 'quant' hedge funds that had conducted private polls showing Leave and Remain neck and neck on the one hand and Leave winning by 52 to 48 on the other. He says he has no reason to assume they did actually try to maximise their eventual profits by 'gaming' betting markets, but adds, 'Why would intelligent, well-resourced agents not do this?'

Here is the thing. A number of hedge funds made a killing on the fall in shares and the pound that immediately followed the vote for Brexit. One of the few to swank about this was bon viveur Crispin Odey of Odey Asset Management, who had bet on the stock market tumbling if that happened and was supposedly more than £200 million richer in the hours after the historic decision. '*Al mattino ha l'oro in bocca* – the morning has gold in its mouth,' he told the BBC. 'And never has one felt so much that idea as this morning, really.'

This appeared to be an extreme case of profiting from politics, because Odey had given money to research that supported the case for quitting the EU. The Electoral Commission shows he donated £423,000 to the Democracy Movement and £233,000 to Global Britain, both of which are lobbying and research groups that for years have made the case for taking the UK out of the EU. There is no reason to believe Odey's help for the Democracy Movement or Global Britain had any significant impact on the outcome. And I am not suggesting that Odey tried to manipulate betting markets in the way Cummings says is possible. Also, other hedge fund managers, such as David Harding, founder of Winton, provided support for the Remain campaign – and if they had profited from a Remain victory, I would feel equally perturbed.

The fundamental point, relevant here, is that our shaky confidence that democracy yields equal benefits for all is tested when very wealthy people both finance political campaigns and become enriched when those campaigns succeed. It creates the impression – perhaps mistaken, but hard to dispel – that the system is rigged in favour of the rich and powerful. That said, and some would say there is poetic justice here, Odey ended up poorer by the end of 2016, in part because he was too pessimistic about the UK economy and misjudged how much share prices would be inflated by the Brexit-induced fall in the pound, which boosted the sterling value of the revenues of the many multinationals listed on the London market. He seems to have been the one Leave supporter who believed George Osborne's doom-laden prognostications that Britain's prosperity and the value of British-based assets would be immediately and savagely wrecked.

The great thing about politics and business is that they run more on cock-ups than conspiracies. And what was particularly striking about the 2017 general election is that neither Tories nor Labour learned properly from what Vote Leave achieved on a small budget with a simple message and ruthless social media campaign. Labour came closest, by offering to wipe out the £9,000-a-year fees for students, its equivalent of £350m for the NHS, and with a smart online campaign to get the vote out. But Labour's biggest social media advantages were probably the accident of Jeremy Corbyn's personality, which plays well on Facebook, and the support for him of the Momentum movement and its many digitally savvy young members.

Theresa May and her then senior advisers, Fiona Hill and Nick Timothy, knew the rules of the political game have been changed by Facebook and Twitter, although they underestimated by how much, and they lacked Cummings' knowledge of it and passion. May agreed to do a Facebook Live interview with me – her first ever serious commitment to this brave new world – at 3 p.m. on Monday 15 May. For fifty minutes I directed questions

from viewers at her, and in a conventional sense, she performed
well. She answered questions on why she supported foxhunting,
legalising cannabis use, the shortage of affordable housing for
young people, cuts to disability benefits, the future rights of EU
citizens living in the UK and much more.

I did my best to give her a fair sample of what people wanted
to know, out of the more than 40,000 questions that flashed
up on my screen. She was articulate, straightforward and – for
once – eschewed those terrible catchphrases. There were no
obvious gaffes. So as a toe in the social media water, it was a
success, with around 2.5 million people reached by it.

But her Facebook Live foray also exposed how far behind
the Tories are in the battle waged on social media, which is
partly to do with the age-profile and numbers of party
members, but also to do with the savvy of officials. For
example, in the emoji battle during the interview – over which
of those Facebook icons were most clicked while she talked –
there were 4,300 'thumbs up' and 9,900 'angry faces'. This
probably reflected that Labour has half a million members,
and the Tories are thought to have considerably fewer than
150,000. And although the average age of members of both
parties is over fifty, according to the ESRC Party Members
Project, enthusiastic support from young people, who are
much more active on social media, is dramatically greater for
Labour than for the Tories.

It was in the response of Labour's office to the Facebook
Live event that Corbyn had a modest coup. His young social
media manager, Jack Bond, sent in a question using Corbyn's
own Facebook account. For reasons of balance, I felt I had to
put the question to May (though a few weeks later I ran into
Bond, who said he was amazed I read it out). It was a predictable and rather ponderous list of complaints about tax cuts

for the rich, cuts to the NHS and police and inadequate numbers of affordable houses being built, culminating in a demand for her to reconsider her refusal to debate with him live on television.

The longish question worked for Labour, because her face was a picture of annoyance. But her answer was reasonable: here she was facing questions from hundreds of thousands of British people; where was he? But within the dynamic of the election battle, Bond for Corbyn reinforced one of Labour's most powerful lines of attack – that even though May was running a presidential-style campaign, she was too frightened of a head-to-head, old-media TV debate. Bond told me that when it was clipped up and put online, this was their second most successful social media video of the campaign, watched well over 5m times, including 4.8m on Facebook itself.

The measure of how far behind the Tories were in techno-logical knowhow came on 31 May 2017, when YouGov published a poll showing the Tories on 42% and Labour on 39%. This was a little over a week before the election, and was remarkably close to the final result. The verdict on Twitter of perhaps the most distinguished of May's election campaign team, Jim Messina, who had been President Obama's deputy chief of staff and had managed his 2012 re-election campaign, was 'spent the day laughing at yet another stupid poll from @ yougov'. And Mark Textor, the right-hand person of Sir Lynton Crosby, both of whom were at the heart of the May team, concurred that 'it was quite bizarre'.

What they both seemed to have either missed, or underrated, was that YouGov was employing a very similar data-gathering technique to the highly successful model deployed by Cummings and Vote Leave. During the course of a week, it was getting data from a sample of 50,000 people, vastly more than opinion polls typically use (by a factor of 50 in some cases). And, like Vote Leave, YouGov's model was dynamic – the model 'learned' and was refined as information from a whole variety of sources was processed. Messina's dismissive tweet demonstrated how far the Tories were behind the political technological curve.

That said, Labour's approach to social media was slicker and more impressive than the Tories, but it did not have the simplicity and ruthless professionalism of Vote Leave's in the referendum. And we should not forget that for much of Corbyn's two years at the helm of Labour, many of their leadership's social media forays were, well, a bit worthy and naff. But what the crucible of the election demonstrated was the relative power on Facebook of his 'authentic' personality.

According to Labour's own stats, 'likes' of Corbyn's page rose 31% during the campaign, to 1.2m – with the number of people he reached every week soaring from under 4m to more than 24m. And his videos were seen 22m times in the first week of June, up from 2.5m in April. Which probably means that on social media Corbyn personally outperformed May in impact by a factor of more than two to one. As for the Labour Party as a social media player in its own name, it also punched through to far more people than did the Tories: according to the social media agency We Are Social, Labour increased its social media following by 61% to 868,000 in the first six weeks of the battle, compared with only 6% to 596,000 for the Tories.[34]

Of Corbyn's followers, 24% were under twenty-four and 55% under thirty-four. That points towards one of the most

34 Andre van Loon, 'Labour is winning the election on social media', We Are Social for *Campaign*, 7 June 2017.

astute digital initiatives taken by Labour, which was to encourage young people to register to vote and then more or less walk them to the correct polling station. Astonishingly, Labour's and Corbyn's partnership with stars of British Grime music was not the car crash suffered by the previous Labour leader Ed Miliband, when he tried to appear cool, hip and funny – with Russell Brand, for example – in 2015.

Corbyn seemed surprisingly natural when interviewed by the rapper JME in a North London pub, when JME's main aim was to persuade people to sign up to vote. A video endorsement by a Grime MC, AJ Tracey, was credible. And presumably because Corbyn has more than a little of the ageing rock star about him, there was not the cognitive dissonance I would have expected when Corbyn took to the stage of Tranmere Rovers' football ground on 20 May, before a Libertines gig, to shout that 'the election is about you'.

Here are the numbers that show why all this was not the vanity of an old geezer pretending to be down with the 'yoof': via text messages and Snapchat, Labour generated 1.24m visits to a special webpage the party created from public data and crowdsourced information that would direct people to where they were allowed to vote (more than 675,000 of these visits came from Snapchat). More than a fifth of these were under twenty-four and 61% were under thirty-five. They were a significant contributor to Labour's surge.

Labour's greatest advantage over the Tories, however, was probably that it is part of a broader movement, much of it on social media. There are lots of closed Corbyn-supporting Facebook groups that share pretty much anything he puts out. And then there is Momentum, a movement created explicitly to support him. Its social media activity complemented Labour's – and the Tories had no equivalent. One of its videos – 'Daddy, why do you hate me?', a conversation between a little girl and her dad set in 2030, about why he had voted for Theresa May and ruined her life prospects – was watched 5.4m times in just two days.

Momentum also fomented 'WhatsApp cascades' on polling day, or messages shared on WhatsApp with an estimated 400,000 young people designed to get the vote out. For what it's worth, all the successful digital media players – Momentum and Vote Leave, for example – have noticed that WhatsApp and text messages are vastly more efficient ways of communicating important stuff than emails, which tend to be treated by recipients as junk and ignored.

Labour was also helped by the phenomenon that we increasingly mistrust the established media, and naively perhaps, instinctively place greater trust in what we read via Facebook and Twitter, especially if it has been shared with us by a friend or contact. The act of sharing is a personal endorsement, which lends the article or video greater credibility. Throughout the campaign it was clear to me that this was massively help ing Labour, in that all I could see in my own newsfeeds was people angry about the government failing to provide adequate resources to schools and hospitals, or furious about its proposal to make old people pay more towards their own social care.

Labour was a passive beneficiary of the fact that millions of its supporters are younger and living their lives on social media, in the way that the Tories do not. This represents not only a weakness for the Tories, but a structural flaw that, in not many years, could make it almost impossible for them to win an election. They have to recognise that their current debate about the policies and ideas they need to make themselves relevant will not stand a chance of succeeding if it takes place outside the digital forum that is reinventing democracy.

In a future not very far away – and it may be as soon as the next election – campaigns will be won and lost in the way that hedge funds such as the multi-billionaire Jim Simons's Renaissance Technologies have beaten the market for years, with data gathering and self-learning algorithms. Cummings and Vote Leave got close with the way they used their VICS program and the expertise of AggregateIQ to gather information about voters and then targeted their marketing in a more laser-like way. A party's values and messages matter. But in today's digital Babel, they are probably less important than how the message is presented and to whom it is communicated.

A billionaire who seems to have worked this out early is – as it happens – Simons's colleague at RenTech, Bob Mercer. He invested $5 million in Cambridge Analytica, a firm that trawls the internet for data on all of us, and combines this with psychological expertise, so that when working on a political campaign, it supposedly knows exactly which of our buttons to press to get us to back the candidate or issue. Trump employed Cambridge Analytica on his presidential campaign and is close to Mercer, who is also with his daughter Rebekah a co-owner of the influential alt-right, pro-Trump, online news-and-views service Breitbart (whose executive chairman Steve Bannon was in the White House as Trump's chief strategist until August 2017).

According to the *New Yorker*: 'Mercer, having revolutionized the use of data on Wall Street, was eager to accomplish the same feat in the political realm. He screened many data-mining companies before investing, and he chose Cambridge

Analytica, in part, because its high concentration of accomplished scientists reminded him of Renaissance Technologies.'[35]

There is a huge amount of mystique and rumour around what Mercer and Cambridge Analytica have actually achieved (including that it was somehow involved in helping Nigel Farage's Brexit campaign, Leave.EU, but no payments to it have been reported to the Electoral Commission, as they should have been if it was employed). Assessing quite how effective they have been is hard to assess with empirical precision. But there are plainly dangers to the integrity of our democracies when one side in a political campaign is deploying massively more effective techniques than the other.

There should be concern that the available technologies are now a million miles ahead of the rules we have to enforce the fairness of elections, and the watchdogs do not seem to know what to look for. It is not so much Big Brother who will be bossing us, but Big Data. There is a realistic prospect of a deep-pocketed tech billionaire fixing the outcome of an election, by dint of his or her ownership of a self-learning model that gathers and processes data about voters' preferences and susceptibilities. Future elections may not be battles of ideas, but contests to scrape the internet for precious details about our hopes, fears and vulnerabilities, so that tailored messages can be sent to us that we find irresistible. It will be a war to find out who each of us thinks we truly are.

---

35 Jane Mayer, 'The reclusive hedge-fund tycoon behind the Trump presidency', *New Yorker*, 27 March 2017.

CHAPTER 5
WHO ARE YOU?

When I was a young reporter in my early twenties, a posh public-relations man was sitting next to me in the wood-panelled waiting room of a distinguished merchant bank. He was accompanying me to a chat with the chief executive. Exasperated that they were late for the meeting, he blurted out, 'Bloody Jews, caught them with their trousers down.' I had never encountered such overt or angry anti-semitism – although I was not exactly comfortable with the tenor of conversation about my people when I was a (hapless) English language teacher in a Catholic school run by priests in Normandy during my gap year.

'What kind of Christian exactly are you?' was the first question the head asked me, when I turned up in September 1978.

'Quite a British one,' I replied.

This was a time in my life when I had an ambiguous relationship with my Jewishness, partly because when I spent a couple of months on a kibbutz in Israel aged nineteen, I was made to feel not Jewish enough by the Israelis. The point, of course, is that as soon as the idiot PR made his racist slurs, my Jewish identity suddenly became the most important part of me. I told him what I thought of him, walked out of the waiting room and never spoke to him again.

Under attack or siege, we all suddenly discover where our loyalties lie and who we are. And it is human nature to want to rally round and protect the groups and communities to which we belong – especially when, as happened to the Jews of Germany in the 1930s, our membership of that group is defined by others' hatred of us, rather than it being our choice to be seen as a particular race or religion. Differences between faiths and communities add to the joy of life. But in times of economic and political instability, it is very easy to be made anxious and feel threatened by them, which is why it really matters that we strive for mutual understanding.

There is a particular responsibility on the media and politicians to be careful with what we say about race and religion, and how we say it. I agree with the Board of Deputies of British Jews that the *Sun*'s senior columnist Trevor Kavanagh was wrong to end a column about sex crimes committed by Muslim men and about Islamic extremists by asking, *What will we do about The Muslim Problem then?* (It was the *Sun* that used the italics and capital letters for emphasis.) Kavanagh's inflammatory question was directly related to the opportunity given by Brexit of putting us 'back in charge of immigration', which he sees as overwhelmingly popular because of 'heightened anxiety' over terrorist attacks and 'mounting anger' over 'the way some young, single migrant men treat Western women.'

The Board of Deputies, a conservative group that has been the main representative of Jewry in the UK since 1760, said it was 'horrified' and demanded a retraction and apology from the *Sun* (it coordinated its complaint with two Muslim groups, Tell MAMA and Faith Matters). But Kavanagh and the *Sun* were having none of it. He wrote a second article claiming that he had been 'walking on eggshells' and the attacks were a 'ludicrous, offensive and perverse distortion of the truth'. In this response to the criticism, he belatedly said that 'the vast majority of Muslims in Britain are decent, generous, hospitable and law-abiding men and women, who add to the fabric of this nation' and who are 'as appalled as the rest of us by extremism'.

Now having known Kavanagh for more than twenty years, I am surprised he does not see the contradictions in his state-ments. If he believes that the vast majority of Muslims are good people, which of course they are, there is no general 'Muslim Problem'. What there may be is a problem about some Muslims subject to specific influences in specific social and economic conditions. And it would have been reasonable for Kavanagh to have written an article looking at why Muslim men in some communities have done terrible things. But that is not what he did. He took specific instances of crimes and extrapolated to a 'Muslim Problem' (remember they were the *Sun*'s capital letters). That connection is no more reasonable than linking the historic role of Jews as moneylenders to the idea that Jews are mean – and indeed to the racist phrases I used to hear as a child, such as 'he Jewed me'.

What is particularly distressing is that Kavanagh's language is likely to achieve the precise opposite of what he presumably wanted to achieve, because if Muslims in general start to believe that important British institutions such as the *Sun* newspaper see them as 'a Problem', then they are much more likely to feel alienated from Britain, and susceptible to toxic extremism. By the way, the former Labour shadow minister Sarah Champion was equally misguided in writing, also in the *Sun*, that 'Britain has a problem with British Pakistani men raping and exploiting white girls.' Which is not to say that she is wrong to highlight that British Pakistani men committed vicious sex crimes on 1,400 children in Rotherham. There may be something about their Pakistani origins that is relevant to understanding why they behaved so disgustingly. But again, to leap from that to Britain as a whole having 'a problem' with British Pakistani men is a huge – and ignorant – leap.

Getting the balance right between generalisations that help our understanding and those that breed fear and intolerance is ferociously difficult. Arguably Labour under Corbyn has got that balance badly wrong in relation to Jews, in that it is extraordinary that the former London mayor Ken Livingstone was not expelled from the party, only suspended, for saying that in 1932 Hitler 'was supporting Zionism', and then consistently refusing to concede that he had done anything wrong.

To be crystal clear, worrying about the language we employ when it comes to issues of race, nationality and faith is not the stuff of political correctness gone barmy, or the hypersensitivity of the Snowflake generation. It will determine whether we can properly face up to the constructive and important identity questions thrown up by the Brexit and Trump votes – or whether we fuel hatred and mutual misunderstanding, and find ourselves on the streets of Charlottesville, in Virginia, confronting stupid white men doing Nazi salutes.

Among this book's many flaws, perhaps its greatest flaw, is that I find the concept of 'identity politics' challenging. It is not that I have difficulty defining myself: I am a North London, Arsenal-supporting, secular Jew, who loves the singing of Janet Baker and Ian Dury. It is just that I find it difficult to understand why anyone would vote in a particular way primarily because of how they identify themselves, in a racial, national or regional sense. Naturally I would find it challenging to support a politician who is anti-semitic, or indeed racist or intolerant in any way. And, of course, I would probably give more of a hearing to a candidate who seemed to share some of my more important life experiences and affiliations (maybe it is Corbyn's love of Arsenal that persuaded me to take him seriously before many other hacks did).

But what is alien to me is the notion of identity being the primary and overriding spur for how I should vote, other than perhaps in the circumstances of civil or extra-territorial war. So although I was aware that millions of people wanted Brexit in order to reinforce the sovereignty and independent power of the Westminster parliament, this was an odd idea for me. I could not conceive that I would somehow feel better about myself if I told Brussels to hop away from influencing our laws and regulations. As for Donald Trump's 'Make America Great Again' – oh my goodness, you have no idea of my contempt for him and a sentiment that defined the rest of the world as 'other'. He has made America grate again.

But more fool me. All I am revealing is that I am as obsessed with self-image as the English or Scottish nationalist. In fact, it is possible I care more than they do about how my peer group see me. The difference is that I am a fully paid-up member of the community of internationalist liberals – and we are as intolerant of those who challenge our convictions, which we arrogantly take to be universal truths, as the nationalists we hatefully and wrongly see as being small-minded.

So the distinction between 'anywheres' and 'somewheres' made by my former *FT* colleague David Goodhart is useful for understanding an important tension in today's politics. 'Anywheres' are content to live and work anywhere, thanks to their skills and outlook, and 'somewheres' are people who derive their sense of identity from the community in which they live and work.

But it is not the whole story, a sufficient explanation for why we chose Brexit and America chose Trump, because most of us sit on a spectrum somewhere between extreme internationalism and pure localism; we are a bit of both.

One reason why my identity is not for me a reason for voting in a particular way is that my sense of self does not feel threatened by the great economic and social shifts in the world – globalisation, immigration, the movement of capital and skills to anywhere on the planet where they can best be deployed. In a way, that is because, as Goodhart would say, I am lucky enough to have skills that have become more valuable, if anything, as markets have become more international. And it is also because my and my family's story is that of the Wandering Jew, though not as the curse of walking the earth forever never finding a home, but of seeing the whole world as a potential home.

My Jewish antecedents came from Austria, Poland and Russia at the end of the nineteenth century and early twentieth century, to escape persecution, but I suspect also as what today would be called economic migrants looking for better employment – and they built good, fulfilling lives in a welcoming country. My consciousness of being more immigrant than native stems from my grandpa on my mum's side, Joe Cohen, who was a jazz drummer, a tailor, a fireman in the docks when they were ablaze because of Hitler's bombs, a minicab driver, and an exceptionally kind and gentle man.

Not long before he died in his nineties in 1998, he told me about leaving Warsaw to arrive in a boat at London's docks as a little boy before the First World War. He never knew his own age or real birthday, because his parents had lied to immigration officials about his date of birth, so that he would be classified as older than he really was and could work as soon as possible. The last time I talked with him, he cried about siblings left behind by his parents in Poland, whom he never saw again, and who presumably went to the gas chambers.

From my Jewish émigré ancestors, I inherited a pathological contempt for anyone with a sense of entitlement that this country owes them harbour and a living. We are all guests. And what we take from this country we earn, from our good and social conduct, paying taxes and helping others. Joe is also why I have a visceral horror of putting up the barricades to immigration, and profound unease when politicians argue passionately for that; I would not have the life I do, I would not be here, if it were not for the generosity of Britain in letting Joe (and Solomon, and Abraham, and Herschel) into the country.

Funnily enough, I have always been desperate to be a 'somewhere'. Most of my teen years were characterised by the normal adolescent angst of worrying that I did not belong and looking for home. Eventually I found it as a 'somewhere' with deep roots in a part of London characterised by huge cultural and ethnic diversity. And I would argue that the way to prevent the politics of identity descending into ever more racially fuelled hate is to promote the idea that we are all immigrants, that almost none of us come from stock that has stayed tied to a single patch of land for centuries.

Where I do feel challenged, and a bit guilty, is that although I think of myself as properly British I have never felt 'really really English'. Here are the subtle contradictory shades of my identity: I become morose when England is humiliated (as usual) in a football match, but not nearly as upset as when Arsenal loses. And when Andy Murray plays, I have a greater sense of identification with him than I had when Tim Henman was on court, because Murray is British and seemingly a bit tortured, which I can connect with, whereas Henman was very English and clean-cut, which is not me at all. I am pretty sure this would pass the test of empirical proof, since I am confident that different bits of my brain would light up on a scanner in varying degrees when Arsenal or England go a goal down.

Here is the paradox, though. I am passionate in my support for Murray because my allegiance to the UK trumps my allegiance to England. But there is a bloody good chance that Murray himself feels more Scottish than British, because the British Social Attitudes survey says most Scots value their Scottishness as more important than their Britishness. It is the Murray factor, probably, that almost more than anything else makes me feel sick at the idea that Scots may one day vote to leave the UK. And my claiming of kinship with him is probably a reason why so many Scots are desperate to secede.

As it happens, I am not untypical of English Britons in having fairly lukewarm English identity: in the latest survey in 2012,[36] only 17% of the English saw themselves as English not British, and 12% more English than British. By far the largest number, 44%, thought of themselves as equally English and British. That isn't me, of course. Just 8% are like me in thinking of themselves as more British than English.

Now it is reasonable to assume that the rise of UKIP is a proxy for a growing pride in Englishness. And I don't mean that in a derogatory way. It is simply that UKIP made a direct appeal to characteristically English values. Nothing wrong with that, so long as it stayed the right side of racism, which for most UKIP supporters and leaders it did. But to quote the Grime star Joseph Junior Adenuga, AKA Skepta, that kind of Englishness, well, 'that's not me'. What I would never do is denigrate England or Englishness – or try to talk anyone out of that version of patriotism. The reason I raise this at all is

---

36 'British Social Attitudes: The 30th Report', NatCen Research, 2013, p. 148.

that those who think of themselves as very English tended to vote for Brexit – as of course did UKIP supporters! According to the British Social Attitudes Survey, 72% of those who identify themselves as 'English, not British' voted for Brexit, and 57% of those who are 'more English than British'.[37] By contrast just 38% voted for Brexit who call themselves 'British, not English'. And a poll by Professors Paul Whiteley and Harold Clarke[38] showed that only 36% of those defining themselves as Scottish intended to vote for Brexit.

There seem to be two nations within England itself: the nation of the self-classifying English, who feel threatened by the EU, and the nation of English Britons, who feel less hostile to, or even positive about, the EU. And in Wales, Scotland and Northern Ireland, this kind of national identification either has little bearing on attitudes towards the EU or operates in the opposite direction (Scottish Scots are fans of the EU). Why does patriotism for Scotland and for England play out so differently when it comes to attitudes towards the EU?

One probable reason is that proportionately more Scots feel more confident in their Scottish identity than the English do in theirs, and may therefore feel less threatened by a parallel European identity. Also, for some Scots membership of the EU is widely seen as making independence for the country a more economically viable option than it would otherwise be; they see it as potentially reinforcing their national sovereignty, whereas the English see the EU as encroaching on the sovereignty of their (our) nation.

For someone like me, Scots' uncomplicated pride in their

---

37 'The Vote to Leave the EU' in 'British Social Attitudes: The 34th Report', NatCen Research, 2017, p. 12.
38 Paul Whiteley & Harold Clarke, 'Why did older voters choose Brexit? It's a matter of identity', The Conversation, 25 June 2016.

Scottishness is something of a slap in the face. It makes me uncomfortable about my reluctance to claim my Englishness. It suggests that I am projecting on to 'England' values and characteristics that are not intrinsic to it. Of course, the English flag, the cross of St George, is often seen as associated with illiberalism, social division, protest by the dispossessed and those left behind by globalisation, even British National Party-style racism. But these are circumstantial. They are not what England or its flag mean in any fundamental sense. What they more properly represent, I fear, is that people like me have not fought enough to claim England for ourselves.

There was perhaps no clearer manifestation of how confused many English liberals are than when Emily Thornberry was forced to resign from Ed Miliband's Labour shadow cabinet in November 2014, for tweeting a picture of an unpretentious house decked out with English cross-of-St-George flags. Thornberry, who grew up on a council estate, did not write anything derogatory in the caption. But it was widely assumed that the mere publication of the picture was some kind of sneer, or indeed smear. What a messed-up nation we are!

So the onus is plainly on people like me to become more comfortable in our English skin and to marginalise the racist thugs who wave the St George's flag as bogus patriots. Which is why I resist Lord Patten's patrician denigration of the Brexiteers: 'So what is Brexit's message to the world: two fingers? Or maybe as Ferdinand Mount, the former head of Thatcher's policy unit, says, we'll catch the Brexiteers belting out that Millwall chant, "No one likes us, we don't care." Like the football team, they'll sing it all the way to the third division.'[39]

---

39 Chris Patten, 'Two fingers to the world: is that your message, Brexiteers?', *Guardian*, 7 June 2016.

As I have said, it is important that we all attempt to make a success of the way we leave the EU. Whingeing from the sidelines is self-destructive. Part of being constructive is to make common cause with Leave voters. But for liberals like me, this is tricky, because of the thread that goes, 'Proud Englander who has authoritarian values and is hostile to immigration votes for Brexit.' To be clear, this characterisation of those who voted to leave is not a liberal, elitist smear. The British Social Attitudes survey showed support for quitting the EU from 72% of those with 'authoritarian' views (defined as a conviction that those living in Britain should accept a common set of mores and cultural practices, usually of a socially conservative sort) and 73% of those worried about immigration.[40] And, as you'll recall, 72% of those who see themselves as English and not British were hostile to EU membership.

That said, I cannot overstate how important it is to recognise that the immigration debate is not a simple one between the anxious self-defining English on the one hand and those more conscious of being immigrants or being descended from immigrants. Many recently arrived migrants are wary of immigration and are opposed to EU membership. During the referendum campaign, time and again I met Asians planning to vote for Brexit, largely because – they said – they were concerned about the impact on their livelihoods of immigration. On a working visit to Leicester, I could barely find any member of an ethnic minority – from Indians to West Indians – planning to vote to remain.

I was shocked. But, of course, this is their country as much as anyone else's now, and it is completely understandable that they would want to preserve what their hard toil has won for

---

40 'The Vote to Leave the EU', NatCen Research, op. cit., p. 2.

them. For me, immigration enriches my life, because immigrants are not coming for my job – or at least not obviously. But my sense of income security is not widespread. That said, it is not only about job security. A friend said: 'I think you may be being a little too charitable to some of my fellow Asians. Plenty of wealthy, secure Asians I know have an odd sense of contempt towards Eastern European migrants and some Muslim migrants, too. It cannot solely be a product of concern for their own economic security as so many run successful businesses that do not seem under palpable threat. There is a weird cultural drawbridge effect going on among some and I have tried innumerable times to tear some relatives away from their copy of the *Daily Mail*.'

Contempt from one group of immigrants for those arriving after is nothing new. When my Ashkenazi Jewish antecedents arrived here in the late nineteenth century and turn of the twentieth century, they were greeted with resentment and desperate snobbery by the Sephardi population, who had arrived in a much earlier wave and become assimilated here. There was a shameful, if understandable, fear that the foreignness of the Ashkenazim would give Jews a bad name. Of course, anxiety about the economic effects of immigration is as old as migration itself. And the picture is mixed and complicated: immigration spurs growth, but the impact on living standards and the public finances is not always benign.

An influential paper written in 2014, by Christian Dustmann and Tommaso Frattini,[41] showed that immigrants from the rest of the European Union who have arrived here since 2000

41 Christian Dustmann & Tommaso Frattini, 'The fiscal effects of immigration to the UK', *Economic Journal*, Vol. 124, Issue 580, November 2014, pp. 593–643.

made a net contribution of £20 billion to Britain's public finances between 2001 and 2011 – and 'they have endowed the country with productive human capital that would have cost the UK £6.8bn in spending on education.' In other words, they paid into the state more than they took out. This makes sense, since many of those who arrive to work here, from Poland, Romania, the Czech Republic, Slovakia and so on, come on their own, either by leaving their families behind or as unmarried people. And it is only when any of us start a family, whether we are indigenous or a migrant, that we tend to be a significant drain on the state – either in respect of benefits and tax credits received, or use of schools and hospitals.

As it happens, over the same period, there was also a positive contribution from immigrants coming from outside the EU, of around £5bn. While those of us already here were a net cumulative drain on the state of £617bn. In other words, to employ the rhetoric of the anti-immigration lobby, it would seem that it was the indigenous population who were parasites.

Except, of course, that is mad. The reason British natives were a net cost to the state is because – unlike immigrants – we are typically not young working people: we may have children, we may be retired, and so on. The point is, according to Dustmann and Frattini, that immigrants who arrived since 2000 were 43% less likely than natives to receive state benefits or tax credit, they were 7% less likely to live in social housing and they are typically better educated than natives and have higher employment rates.

Now over a longer period, from 1995–2011, the picture of the net contribution of migrants is a more mixed one. All immigrants, and not just new arrivals, from the countries of the European Economic Area, which largely equates to the EU, made a positive contribution of more than £4bn. Which reinforces the idea of EU migration being largely good for Britain. But those from non-EEA countries – and this attracted a good deal of attention when it was published – thus from Asia, Africa and all other parts of the world, were estimated to have been a net drain on the state of £118bn.

Now in a way that's not surprising, because many of those non-EEA immigrants were older, with families, and some were retired. Their age profile was much more like that of the native population than the EU immigrant population. So inevitably, they would have used more resources than the EU migrant population. But controversially, Dustmann and Frattini estimated that the non-EEA net contributions to the state were almost 9% lower than for natives.

So the argument of the great cheerleaders of immigration, that it is always a net positive in fiscal terms, that immigrants always pay in more than they take out, was difficult to sustain. On the other hand, the Dustmann research does tend to show that the immigration debate – especially during the EU referendum – was muddleheaded, in that if there is a problem with immigration, it is not with immigration from the EU. Dustmann and co. suggest that migration from the EU, which was the migration that the Brexiteers are desperate to limit, has been good for Britain, whereas if there is a net cost it is in relation to migration from the rest of the world. And you will presumably remember that, usually to prove they are not in any way racists, Brexiteers would argue that all they wanted was for immigration from the EU to be controlled in the way we control immigration from other countries, which may prove they are not racist, but may also suggest a degree of, well, irrationality (or you might call them something else).

The big point is that immigrants become expensive when they tend to stay here for longer than the prime of their working lives. If all migrants left their spouses and children in their home countries, and then returned full time to their home countries when they were about forty to be with their families, the UK would be in clover. And it will not escape you that this fiscally benign pattern of migration is much more likely to happen with EU migration, because home countries for them are so nearby, and job prospects for them in their home countries are improving all the time. Which is another reason why it might not become so brilliant for Britain if we were to become relatively more dependent on immigration from the rest of the world.

This differential picture, of the costs and benefits of immigration from EU and non-EU countries, does complicate matters for the prime minister as she seeks to impose new controls on immigration that damage neither the British economy in the round, nor the public finances in particular. As she knows only too well, slamming the door shut would be disastrous for the many businesses and public services, especially the NHS, that depend on migrant labour.

Right now, whenever I run into anyone in the construction or housebuilding industries, they complain that their costs are going through the roof, because so many East European builders are going home. That exodus stems partly from a sense among migrants that the mood of the country has become hostile to them, in the aftermath of the Brexit vote, and also because the collapse in the value of the pound means that working here for them is much less financially attractive than it was (the point, as you know, being that many of them send their earnings back to their families who are still living in their home countries, like Poland and Romania).

This concern about Brexit leading to employment shortages and rising labour costs – and I hear the same in all companies who prefer to recruit from a worldwide pool rather than just from UK natives – does give the lie to one argument of the pro-immigration lobby, namely that immigration does not damage the wages and living standards of indigenous Britons. If you were a British bricklayer or electrician, it is simply implausible that there was no impact on your earning power when large numbers of Polish bricklayers and electricians initially turned up. The influx of all this migrant labour also made it much easier for companies to employ people on the shortest possible and least secure contracts – zero-hours contracts, agency contracts and so on – and this has been harmful to the welfare of the indigenous British workforce, too.

However, and this is important, immigration gives businesses access both to a larger pool of skilled and unskilled potential employees and to a larger pool of potential customers – and those improvements both in the supply of labour and in demand for goods and services help businesses to generate bigger profits, which should encourage them to invest in new capacity. That creates more jobs and, of course, native Britons benefit from the creation of those new jobs as much as anyone. It is extremely relevant that the unemployment rate in the UK has been falling consistently in the years of record migration from the rest of the EU and is now at its lowest level for more than forty years.

So it is quite difficult to argue that immigration destroys the employment prospects of natives. In fact, the opposite may be the case, if we have the kind of immigration, which we seem to have, that magnifies the dynamism of this place. And that again is another reason why Theresa May has to tread very carefully indeed imposing new immigration controls. Also, with our population ageing so rapidly, we are going to be in deep doo-doo if we staunch immigration too soon and too much, because we would then have far too few younger working people, who pay the taxes to finance the health services and pensions that are desperately needed by the retired population.

There is no contradiction in saying that immigration can be good for the economy as a whole, and for pretty much all of us in the long run, while also pointing out that it can be very painful indeed for many hundreds of thousands of native Britons, especially those with lower skills, such as cleaners and care workers. It is all very well for many employers to say they can't get Britons to do these jobs, which is often so, but that work-shyness is as much to do with how badly paid and insecure these jobs are as with the innate bolshiness or putative sense of entitlement of the natives.

The government has responded by increasing what it calls the National Living Wage, or the minimum wage all employers must pay. And it is also trying to reduce the number of Britons who only have the lowest skills by fostering apprenticeships, encouraging training at all career stages and creating new technical equivalents of 'A' Levels, called 'T' Levels. What it hasn't done is empower the many exploited workers – British people and migrants – to hold bad employers to account, to name and shame them and to force companies to pay compensation to employees they abuse. Immigration has shifted the balance of power between company and worker too far in the direction of the boss.

That said, most British people have been persuaded that the problem with immigration is not a purely economic one. Again, looking at British Social Attitudes data,[42] 40% of people

42 'Immigration' in 'British Social Attitudes', NatCen Research, op. cit., p. 7.

see immigration as good for the economy, and 22% see it as neither good nor bad – only 36% say it is bad for the economy. The balance is slightly tilted the other way when it comes to the impact on employment, with 32% saying immigration creates jobs, 36% believing it takes jobs away and 30% saying there is no impact.

Presumably most would therefore guess that Britain's problem with immigration is how it dilutes British or English culture – particularly after the shock for many of hearing Polish routinely spoken on buses and in shops, as hundreds of thousands of Poles came to Britain to make them the biggest community here by far of EU citizens. But again, that is not what the poll shows: 43% says immigrants enrich cultural life, 38% that they undermine it. Only with law and order are attitudes to immigrants strongly negative, with 50% saying crime problems are made worse by them, and just 13% that crime is made better. What is particularly worrying is that there is no empirical evidence that immigrants are in fact more likely to be criminals than natives – and I can think of no theoretical reason why they should be.

This popular concern that immigration may be linked to crime may stem from a natural instinct to distance ourselves from those who commit acts of terror or sexual grooming on an industrial scale, of the kind that took place in Rotherham. Such atrocities are so appalling that we may have an emotional need to believe they must be committed by newcomers to this country, when in fact they are typically committed by those who are the children and even grandchildren of immigrants, and are rarely committed by first-generation immigrants from the rest of the EU, or the only people whose rights of entry to the UK would change after Brexit. But the perception that immigration is in some way dangerous is important, because it implies that larger numbers of people feel threatened by it than the other survey answers would suggest.

Perhaps it is another way of showing that liberals like me, when making the theoretical arguments in favour of immigration, were too deaf to people's anxieties and the Chinese whispers in communities that felt threatened. Putting it more bluntly, people like me (well, me) have been far too ready to condemn as borderline racist any concerns anyone might have about the pace or impact of large-scale immigration from the rest of the EU. We were not merely wrong about this, we were self-defeatingly wrong.

There was a meeting in 2010 at the BBC, where I worked for a decade, when the penny finally dropped that the BBC's coverage of immigration – or should I say almost total news blackout about it – was a serious dereliction of a duty to report on what really mattered to viewers and listeners, and in a language that made sense to them. Simply telling them, as we did, that immigration is great for growth was an insult. And the BBC was in this case a proxy for the entire liberal establishment.

We made a serious category error in the arguments we made in favour of immigration. It is all very well to argue that immigration makes the nation richer in the long run. But that is irrelevant to a British family in Kent or Lincolnshire when immigration is increasing their cost of housing, is in some instances reducing their earning power and may be putting pressure on local GP practices and schools. However, this pressure should not be exaggerated, partly because immigrant doctors, nurses and cleaners are the backbone of hospitals, and also because even the government's Office for Budget Responsibility assumes that immigration increases net tax revenues – though it admits there is no certainty these revenues are deployed where immigration eats into public-service capacity. For many indigenous households, the putative long-term benefits of immigration are meaningless. They want help now.

Nonetheless, and this is depressing, immigration was cited by some as a reason for voting for Brexit in depressed towns like Stoke, where EU immigration is half the national average. Which does not mean that Theresa May – or indeed Donald Trump – are wrong to promise to control immigration. But it does mean that even if they succeed, and that is by no means certain, fractured nations will not suddenly find themselves healed. What is wrong in Britain and America is not immigration, and certainly not just immigration.

For example, clear majorities of those who greatly distrust government and greatly distrust parliament – 65% and 62% respectively – voted to exit the EU (according to British Social Attitudes). In other words, many Leave voters, who cast their ballot to 'take back control from Brussels', have no confidence in our parliamentary system of government. Which somewhat reinforces the idea that for many the vote was simply a 'fuck you' to the entire ruling class.

What is extraordinary is that it seemed coherent to stick up those two fingers by voting for the mega-tycoon Trump in America and the quintessential posh buffoon Boris Johnson in the UK. Both are great bulging bags of contradictory influences and values, most conspicuously that they talk a fabulous anti-elite game, while living and breathing the elitist dream. Johnson, for instance, had the greatest influence over people's decision to vote to leave, and yet is descended from Turks and is the son of a European Commission official – and he is also a super-posh Old Etonian, part court jester, part quintessential member of the establishment.

Whiteley and Clarke, together this time with Matthew Goodwin,[43] calculated the degree of warmth felt towards him by any voter and the associated probability of casting a vote for Brexit, and they say that 'feeling about Johnson had very strong effects on the probability of casting a Leave ballot.' Those who like him a good deal were almost 100% likely to vote for Leave. And since more than half the electorate like him at least a bit, Goodwin et al. say the evidence showed 'his ability to tip the outcome in the Leave direction.'

Anecdote is never scientific proof of anything. But one from a Labour MP perhaps goes some way to explain the Boris effect. She says her husband, who she describes as a 'White Van Man', or a member of the slightly angry, white English, self-employed working class, 'loves Boris because although Boris is posh, he seems just like him, by always getting into scrapes, falling on his face.' The MP adds: 'My husband and millions like him identify with the way Boris is always getting into trouble, but dusts himself off and starts again.'

In many ways, the appeal of Trump to white Americans on middle-to-lower incomes – including women – is similar to Johnson's to white working-class English Brexiteers. Joan C. Williams, in her *tour-de-force* book, *White Working Class: Overcoming Class Cluelessness in America*, says they spurned the Democrat party of Hillary Clinton because it was seen to be too cosy with a professional elite – whom they defined as lawyers and teachers, and not motormouth billionaires like Trump – that was thought to be ignoring their interests and sneering at their values. These important swing voters were not people on social security, not the very poorest – who did

---

43 Harold D. Clarke, Matthew Goodwin & Paul Whiteley, 'Why Britain Voted for Brexit', University of Kent, September 2016.

vote for Hillary Clinton. And they weren't the African Americans and Latinos, who also backed her.

More than 50% of Americans earning less than $30,000 voted for Hillary. But those on incomes between $50,000 and $100,000, not by any means a fortune in America, backed Trump. Meanwhile those earning more than $200,000 also went for Hillary. Voters on the middling incomes who abandoned the Democrats and switched to Trump would have once been thought the core of their support as the hard-working backbone of America. They used to work in factories before many of them were closed down, their greatest ambition is to own a home, they feel ashamed at the thought of unemployment and going on benefits, they resent those who do live on benefits, they admire the very rich, they are proud to go to church every Sunday, they hate the moral pressure for both the woman and man in a marriage to work and they had no doubt that Trump, not Hillary, spoke their language and understood them.

Perhaps most important, their incomes have stagnated, often for decades – though their expectations of a better life were set by parents and grandparents whose experience was much closer to the American Dream. Although they still enjoy higher living standards than many in the black and Latino communities, they hate how the Democrats seem to value immigrant communities more than them. It is an affront to what they see as the natural order of things – and if voting for Trump was one manifestation of how angry they have become, another was the hideously ugly face of white supremacism seen in the white nationalist rally at Charlottesville, Virginia, in August 2017. Whether Trump is the lightning conductor of racism or its facilitator is yet to be determined, but probably he is both.

The equivalent of many middle-income Trump supporters are the English authoritarians who are wary of immigration and voted for Brexit. In Britain, they did not like posh David Cameron. In America, they felt that Hillary Clinton actively disliked them. Many of them took it personally when she decried 'half of Trump's supporters' as being 'in the basket of deplorables'. And amazingly, the white women on middle incomes still preferred Trump – even after they heard his hideously sexist swagger about grabbing women 'by the pussy', which may simply mean that oafs who are disrespectful to women are everywhere in their communities and very familiar, and they would rather have the oaf (Trump) than the snob (Hillary).

At least, they would say, they recognised Trump; he was in that sense authentic, where Hillary was a phoney. And over here it is perhaps equally extraordinary that two products of elite schools and a privileged upbringing, Boris Johnson and Nigel Farage, were seen as more authentic and in touch with the white working class of the Midlands and North than two other products of the same upper middle class and posh schools, David Cameron and George Osborne. The really gripping though fatuous question is what impact Jeremy Corbyn, Labour's leader, would have had on the referendum outcome if he had been more committed to the Remain campaign, more visible and more conspicuously enthusiastic to stay in the EU. Because Corbyn is seen as the most 'authentic' of the current breed of leading politicians (in spite of being a lefty from a privileged rural background; he was brought up in a spacious Shropshire manor house with large grounds, and went to a selective school, Adams' Grammar School, founded in 1656).

What Corbyn, Johnson, Trump and Farage have in common is they don't appear to be the usual suspects – they are not

Blair, or the Clintons, or Cameron – even though they are just as privileged as the rejected 'establishment'. If at least a part of voters' concern about immigration is emotional, a fear that somehow home is not what it used to be, the three right wingers won their respective historic votes because they have the ability to suggest they share that sense of regret for a lost country. But even if we find a way to control the flow of immigration that does not destroy our public finances, cause staff shortages in hospitals and limit our companies' capacity to expand, we are not suddenly going to be reborn as a wonderfully unified United Kingdom.

The far better road to post-Brexit *entente* is to help shy Englanders like me become more enthusiastic about England, nudge loud Brexit-loving, self-proclaimed Englanders to embrace their place in European history, encourage Scots to be proud of how they have always been the brains of Britain and Empire and persuade migrants to steep themselves in the culture of their new home. This requires all of us to engage in a kind of collective therapy, a very public recognition that we all live in the same home and that it is time to acknowledge that, culturally at least, far more unites than divides us. Voters for Brexit and Remain, for Trump and Hillary, are like estranged couples in a failing marriage, frightened of examining why they feel betrayed by the other. But in the absence of admitting very publicly that we should all have made much greater efforts to understand each other better, our nations will continue to fragment, and possibly not without violence.

CHAPTER 6
THE GREAT BRITISH KAKONOMY

Pretty much whenever anyone writes about productivity these days, they quote the American Nobel prize-winning economist Paul Krugman. And I am disappointed with myself that I am about to do the same, because although he is right considerably more often than Trump, he gives Trump a wonderful run for his money as a big head. Krugman's aphorism that 'productivity isn't everything, but in the long run it's almost everything' just about sums up the great economic challenge faced by the West, because unless we can restore growth in productivity to its pre-Crash rates, we can abandon that central assumption of our way of life that we're all going to become progressively richer.

A less pretentious economist, Andy Haldane of the Bank of England,[44] points out that living standards in the United Kingdom, as measured by GDP per capita, have risen twenty-fold since 1850 – which is the story of our industrial success – and that if productivity, or output for every hour worked, had not increased at all in that period, our living standards would only have doubled. Without productivity gains, we

---

44 Andrew G. Haldane, 'Productivity Puzzles', speech at London School of Economics, March 2017.

would still be enjoying (if that is the word) Victorian lifestyles. Please give me a moment to sharpen my quill.

Productivity is all about the efficiency with which we work – how we are managed, and our level of skills – together with the quality and capabilities of the capital or kit we use (it was looms and lathes, now it is networked computers and robots). Using data from Hills, Thomas and Dimsdale,[45] Haldane deconstructs all growth since the industrial revolution into the contribution from additional labour and capital and the efficiency with which they are used, or what's known as Total Factor Productivity. 'This suggests movements in Total Factor Productivity have accounted for the lion's share of both the growth and variation in living standards since at least the mid-eighteenth century,' Haldane says.

Which is another way of saying that – since the point of organising our economy in a certain way is presumably to make most of us richer – the priority is to organise it so that we produce progressively more for every unit used of labour and capital, people and kit. We can only earn more, or at least over the long term and in a sustainable way, if we get better at making and selling goods and services.

This goes with the grain of our daily experience. Most of us want a decent education in the first place and then strive to improve our skills as we move up in a company or shift from one employer to another, precisely because that is obviously the way to earn more. What is true for us as individuals is – for once – true at the level of the economy (unlike the widely held idea that the debts of a country can and should be managed

---

45 Ryland Thomas, Sally Hills & Nicholas Dimsdale, 'The UK recession in context – what do three centuries of data tell us?', *Bank of England Quarterly Bulletin*, Q4, 2010.

like the debts of a household). It is affordable to increase wages and incomes only when that increment is underpinned by higher productivity.

But here is why what has been happening to productivity and where it is going needs to be at the front of all our minds, and not only policy wonks and academics. The crisis in the West is at least in part a productivity crisis. Over the past few years, and especially since the Crash of 2008, the growth of productivity has collapsed. And that is a big explanation for why living standards have barely risen since then. That in turn goes some way to explain why millions of people have been rejecting mainstream politicians, have become so furious with multinationals that pay so little tax and have been turning towards a fairly new breed of populist politicians who offer simple seductive solutions to the problem of stagnating incomes (such as Trump's erection of barriers to trade and immigration, or Corbyn's increase in taxes on companies).

In Britain, what Haldane calls the productivity puzzle is more important to unravel than probably anything else for four reasons:

- the variations in productivity between different regions – high in London, for example, much lower in the North-East – are huge by international standards, and may go some way to explain why people in places like the North-East feel more alienated and angry;
- the shift in productivity growth at the level of the whole economy from pretty rapid progress to flatlining has been more pronounced in the UK than almost anywhere;
- the UK is seriously less productive than our main competitors, notably France, Germany and America;

- there is plenty of evidence that productivity tends to grow when companies are exposed to competition in larger markets, so one of the main reasons to fear that Brexit will make us poorer is that we are voluntarily withdrawing from the largest relatively frictionless market on the planet, the EU's single market.

Let's start by looking at what we think we know about British productivity. It is probably as well to begin with some ritual humiliation, which is that the UK's productivity record is pretty much the miserable equivalent of our performance in international football. Our productivity, or output per hour worked, is eighteen percentage points below that of the G7 average of big developed countries. More starkly it is thirty percentage points below that of America, thirty-one percentage points less than France and thirty-six percentage points inferior to Germany. Even Italy, which is usually seen as the sick man of Europe in an economic sense, is ten percentage points more productive than the UK. In respect of productivity, the UK is the equivalent of the England national football team, and Germany is the equivalent of – well, Germany (which may be less of a coincidence than it appears, when you think about it).

What has gone so badly wrong? Well, there is evidence that productivity is in part related to the quality and quantum of infrastructure in a country, from roads, to rail, to broadband. And French and German infrastructure is famously better than ours (as is much of the Continent's). In the case of America, there are also the benefits of its technological leadership. And there are the advantages of scale for companies – the greater efficiencies that flow from expanding, which come more easily when they operate in a huge, competitive internal market like America's.

Also, and a bit like what's wrong with British football teams, management doesn't seem all that it could be in the UK.

Britain has had lousy productivity for as long as I have been conscious of its importance. And what is particularly worrying is the performance has become worse. This is what the Office for National Statistics says:

> This recent weak performance relative to the UK's long-term average is a continuation of the subdued rate of productivity growth since the onset of the economic downturn ... Labour productivity growth has averaged around 2% per year through much of the past half-century, with notable deviations above (in the 1960s, early 1970s and mid-1980s) and below (in the mid-1970s) this benchmark. The UK's recent experience – since the onset of the economic downturn in 2008 – is highly unusual. On this basis, the weakness of labour productivity between 2008 and 2012 is unprecedented in the last half-century, and the UK's recent productivity recovery continues to be little stronger than the weakest recorded point prior to 2008.[46]

For the best part of a decade, our productivity growth has been consistently and remorselessly weaker than at any point since at least 1965. At the beginning of 2017, labour productivity was still 0.4% below its pre-recession peak at the end of 2007. An indicator of the gravity of what's gone wrong is that each of us would be on average almost a fifth richer today – because the economy would be that much bigger – if productivity growth had continued at the previous rate.

---

46 'ONS UK Productivity Introduction', Office for National Statistics, January 2017.

What matters as much as the national trend is the regional distribution. Reassuringly, productivity in London is equivalent to productivity in America and Germany – and is 32% greater than the average for the UK. That goes a considerable way to explaining why living standards, before inflated housing costs, are so much higher in London than elsewhere.

But the gap between North and South in output per working hour (in this case what's known as 'gross value added per hour') is jaw-droppingly huge. Productivity in the West Midlands and Yorkshire and Humberside is 35% lower than in London. In the East Midlands and North-East it is also roughly a third below London. It was these regions that delivered the vote to take us out of the EU. And if those north of Watford happened to believe that membership of the EU disproportionately helped London and the South-East (where productivity is almost 10% above the national average) that would not be wholly unreasonable: the UK's huge and highly productive finance industry, together with associated services (law, accountancy and so on), is concentrated in the City of London and Canary Wharf, and has been a great beneficiary of EU membership. London is Europe's financial centre, the site of the market-leading and cutting-edge cluster of all financial and related businesses.

Regional patterns of voting in the EU referendum are by no means perfectly correlated with regional variations in productivity. It is lowest in Wales, where opinion on whether to leave the EU was only mildly tilted in favour of Brexit, and also in Northern Ireland, which voted strongly to remain in the EU. Productivity is more or less at the national average in a Scotland that voted by a massive margin to stay in the EU. As I have already explored, and will again in later chapters, decisions on how to vote in the referendum reflect a hotchpotch of cultural, social and economic factors. Low productivity is not a necessary and sufficient cause of Brexity sentiments, though it may be a contributory factor, nor is the strength of pro-EU feeling directly matched by high productivity.

But regional variations in productivity within the UK are greater than for pretty much any country in the world. And that must have an impact on regional variations in confidence that the economy works for people – and therefore in confidence in the establishment, or in mainstream politics and politicians. I am tempted to see the low productivity of the North-East, and detachment there from a sense that we are all in it together, as an explanation for why fewer people watch my ITV politics show, *Peston on Sunday*, in the North-East than in any other part of the UK. But this may be self-deluding. Surely Geordies cannot still be holding me personally responsible for the collapse of Northern Rock, as they once did? Or perhaps they simply have better taste than the rest.

Why is low productivity such a very British problem? Well, the place to start is the historic nature of our inferiority, that it is nothing new. Research by the innovation think tank, Nesta,[47] shows that even before the Crash and recession of 2007–8 there was what it calls 'insufficient business dynamism', which was acting as a drag on growth. It calculates that in the decade from 1998 to 2007, productivity was 7.4% below potential, at an annual cost to our national income of a whopping £96 billion.

Nesta identifies three flaws in the structure of the economy.

47 Albert Bravo-Biosca & Stian Westlake, 'The Other Productivity Puzzle: Business dynamism and productivity growth before the crisis', Nesta, October 2014.

First is that the most efficient companies were not finding or perhaps even seeking the financial support necessary to grow as much as they could have done. It says the economy 'became significantly worse at allocating resources to the best businesses'.

Second, an unexpectedly large number of good businesses, ones with superior productivity, consistently failed to survive and prosper. And lastly it thinks that lots of new businesses were mediocre.

All this is another way of indicting our financial services industry, our banks, the City of London, which are world class at serving big multinationals and governments, far too good at the financial engineering that creates toxic investments, and simply not good enough at providing what is known as the 'patient' or long-term capital and support to help proper businesses generate proper wealth. It suggests that banks and investors are hopeless at distinguishing between better and worse companies, when deciding which to back.

None of which is desperately surprising: our financial system is notoriously weighted towards short term speculative gains rather than longer-term sustainable wealth creation. It is also possible that regulatory conditions are too harsh for the more innovative start-up businesses, that red tape may give an unfair advantage to stodgy larger incumbents. But if this is so, it is difficult to explain why Germany's medium-size businesses, its *mittelstand*, thrive in a country where the regulatory burden is arguably greater than in the UK.

Here's the real conundrum: why should productivity have worsened since the Crash – when history would suggest that the reverse should have been the case, albeit with a lag? One initial cause was that as the recession took hold in 2008 and 2009, companies in the UK did not lay off people on the scale they had done in previous recessions. The reason they 'hoarded' labour was because they were under enormous social and political pressure to behave in a more humane way, and it had also become so much cheaper and easier for them to hire and fire over the previous twenty-five years, that they could take the risk of waiting to see how the economy progressed.

Even so, normally in an economic downturn the least efficient companies go to the wall, which is horrible for owners and staff, but for the economy it is cathartic, a useful purge. The survivors are the most productive, and capital is released from dying companies for investment in better and younger ones. So recessions tend to lead to at least a temporary acceleration in productivity growth. They are often seen as a painful but useful cleansing of an economy, when the irredeemably weak are flushed away, leaving only the better businesses to build a brighter richer future.

After 2008, this folkloric 'creative destruction' seemingly did not happen.

There is debate and controversy about why this latest downturn was so significantly and seriously different from previous ones. One plausible explanation, when the economy does not perform as we would expect it to do, is that for some reason we are not seeing the economy properly, that something has gone wrong, not with it but with the way we measure it. Some economists have wondered whether the so-called fourth industrial revolution we are experiencing, the growth of the digital and robotic economy, may mean that statisticians are no longer counting the right beans. But if that is so, and it may be, that would have been happening before the Crash, too. So although it would mean that in reality productivity and the size of the economy are a bit higher than official figures would show, that would not explain the lack-lustre trend.

For what it's worth, research by Goldman Sachs, the investment bank, calculated that consistent failure to capture the quality of IT output led to an underestimate of annual GDP growth to the tune of 0.7 percentage points in the US and 0.5 percentage points in Europe. Which would be significant, but in the words of Sir Charles Bean – a former deputy governor of the Bank of England, who was asked by George Osborne as chancellor to carry out a review of UK economic statistics – it 'seems most unlikely that quality mismeasurement can fully explain the productivity slowdown in many advanced economies.'

It was the very nature of the crisis that caused the recession – a near-total breakdown in the banking and financial system that the developed world had not experienced since the 1930s – that has made the aftermath of that recession different from those whose origins were eye-wateringly high interest rates or exchange rates (the recessions of the early 1980s and 1990s, for example). The reason is that, for a period, banks have been constrained in their ability to lend, which has meant that good companies were deprived of the finance they required for investment and expansion. Equally, the collapse in asset and property prices caused by the 2008 crash closed off another funding route for many British companies, which use their properties as collateral when raising finance.

Also, during a recession, when there is a rise in insecurity, there may be a slowdown in the churn of good people, technology and knowhow between bad and good businesses, with a consequential knock to productivity growth.

Then there is the mother of all economic paradoxes, which is that the Bank of England's response to the crisis had the effect of keeping mediocre companies alive as zombies, as the living dead: its decision to cut interest rates to almost zero kept lousy companies just about viable. Equally many banks may have felt under social, regulatory and political pressure not to throw struggling businesses to the wall (though many business owners say they experienced the opposite – banks ruthlessly seizing their assets).

Putting companies on the financial equivalent of life support may seem benign, but it can undermine wealth creation in the longer term, by locking up vital resources in chronically lame businesses.

A degree of 'creative destruction' is vital to any healthy ecosystem. The public policy question is what kind of immediate social price can we tolerate for the putative Darwinian benefit of encouraging the survival of the fittest? Haldane has estimated that if the BoE had held its Bank Rate of interest at 4.25% rather than slashing it to 0.5% at the start of 2009, an additional 10% of companies would have gone bust and 1.5m jobs would have been lost. This might have boosted productivity by 2% relative to what actually happened, which is not immaterial. But most of us – other than the more extreme right-wing ideologues – would have calculated the social cost of that much more unemployment as too great.

Another and more apocalyptic argument made for why productivity is rising weakly in most of the West is that two centuries of productivity-enhancing technological progress is over. This claim comes in a few versions, from the idea that the ICT revolution is somehow less powerful than the steam revolution or the electro-mechanical one, or that digital change has passed its moment of peak impact. Maybe there is something to this, but it seems counterintuitive at a time when the evidence of our eyes is that robots and algorithms are becoming so sophisticated and clever that they can do all sorts of work we thought only humans could ever do. By definition, this would be the ultimate in productivity-enhancing technological breakthrough. And I will return in Chapter Ten to the question of what jobs robots will soon be doing (and whether you would be better informed if this book had been written by Robot rather than Robert).

Probably the apt point is that technological breakthroughs that raise productivity and benefit all of us in the longer term can be very disruptive initially, and have been in the past. Large numbers of workers lacking the skills to exploit the new technologies and opportunities created by them experience a slump in their earnings. This happened on a huge scale in the early nineteenth century, when the share of national income captured by workers in aggregate fell; they became poorer. And even if today's technology shift eventually makes us richer, it is the short-term dislocation, the depressing impact on earnings of those whose jobs are and will be made redundant by robots or computer programs, that boss the social and political climate. Painful change, even for a minority, is a far more compelling influence on how we vote or whether we riot on the streets than the comforting notion that in the long term, technological change helps the average person. Improved living standards for the average person disguises abject misery for millions.

In the government's quest to learn what companies could and should be doing better, Liam Fox, the international trade secretary, successfully wound up his critics in the soft centre of politics when he told the Conservative Way Forward group, in September of 2016, that:

This country is not the free trading nation that it once was. We have become too lazy, and too fat on our successes in previous generations . . . We've got to change the culture in our country. People have got to stop thinking about exporting as an opportunity and start thinking about it as a duty – companies who could be contributing to our national prosperity but choose not to because it might be too difficult or too time-consuming or because they can't play golf on a Friday afternoon.

This was widely seen as an unfair attack on the professionalism of Britain's management class. But Fox was right. As someone who has spent thirty years in the company of chief executives – not for the sheer pleasure, but because it was a living, in its eccentric way – I am clear that they are less amateurish than they were when I first met them in the 1980s (though a lot less entertaining). But there is a strong element of 'kakonomics'[48] in the structure and organisation of British business, a tolerance of mediocrity. A culture of mutual acceptance of second best is so much less stressful than striving for perfection, and it is hard to come up with a more compelling explanation for why so many British companies are sub-standard than that their respective bosses are inferior compared with their overseas rivals.

Now it is extraordinary that this should be so, given that for twenty years the centrepiece of British industrial policy – if that isn't dignifying benign neglect as a cunning plan – has been to put up almost no barriers to foreigners buying our businesses and assets, with the avowed purpose of exposing British industry to the putatively higher management standards and superior managers of the rest of the industrial world.

---

48 A phrase established in the work of Italian academics Gloria Origgi and Diego Gambetta, drawn from the Greek *kako* (meaning bad).

This worked for the companies actually owned by foreigners, like the famous Nissan plant in Sunderland. But it does not appear to have rubbed off enough on indigenous businesses.

Do not take my word for it. The thesis that our big problem is the bosses is supported by a thoroughly depressing analysis by the Bank of England of the distribution of productivity across British firms. It shows that the British economy is characterised by a small number of high-productivity firms, which it styles 'frontier firms', and a vastly larger number of low-productivity firms. Another way of putting this is the productivity of a typical British firm, the so-called modal value, is half the mean average (whose value is swollen by the very high productivity of a small number of superstar companies). Our economy is only kept from the knacker's yard by a dangerously small number of world-class companies.

What is particularly unsettling is that the gap in productivity performance between good firms and bad firms is much greater in the UK than in other countries. And that gap has been increasing more here. As Haldane says, there is a worldwide trend of top companies pulling away from the pack, and there is a much worse British problem: 'The dispersion of services sector productivity is more than 50% higher in the UK than in other advanced economies. It has also widened by materially more in the UK. Even in a world of long and lengthening tails of low-productivity companies, the UK is a striking outlier.'

This apparently uniquely wide productivity gap between the best and worst of our service companies is especially worrying, given that we are, largely, a service economy; some 80% of our entire national income is contributed by services, as opposed to manufacturing, or farming. And, what's more, we tend to pride ourselves as world class in services. To rework an infamous chant of Bristol City FC, 'We're crap, and apparently we don't really know we are.'

Britain's poor productivity performance in recent years is almost all down to the vast number of sub-standard firms. The technological revolution is real and spectacular for the minority of superstar companies: annual productivity growth is an eye-watering 6% for one in a hundred British firms. The rest are trapped in a clunky analogue world, pondering during their tea-breaks whatever happened to Teletext. A staggering third of British companies have seen no productivity increase since 2000, says the Bank.

For Haldane, building on work by the OECD,[49] the inescapable conclusion is that the productivity calamity in Britain – and to an extent in the West – is not that innovation has slowed. It is that the normal process whereby leading companies gradually share their innovation and prowess with laggard companies, the dispersion of knowledge and best practice, has slowed, or perhaps even ground to a halt.

Why are so few of our businesses on the medals podium? It really would be imaginative to the point of naiveté to look much beyond the quality of their managers. But there are contributory factors. And before we give the hapless bosses the going over they probably deserve, it is as well to show the broader picture.

First of all, this pattern of an elite class of super-efficient firms pulling away from a mob of mediocrities is repeated all through the nations and regions of the UK – although London

49 Dan Andrews, Chiara Criscuolo & Peter N. Gal, 'Frontier Firms, Technology Diffusion and Public Policy: Micro Evidence from OECD Countries', OECD Productivity Working Paper No. 2, November 2015.

has relatively more of the stars, because of the magnetic power of the capital, and the well-observed global phenomenon of information-sharing between firms in large industrial clusters, such as the City of London's financial services hub, that drives productivity higher for all.

This long tail of below-average corporate performers is, according to the Bank of England, observable in many different industrial and service sectors. That said, exporting firms 'have systematically higher levels of productivity than domestically oriented firms, on average by a third,' says Haldane. And the average productivity of foreign-owned firms is twice that of indigenous ones.

Why would this be? Well, exporters and foreign-owned firms are both likely to be exposed to global competition that would force them to up their game, to adopt best practices or die. And they are also more likely to acquire components in a more efficient way, through use of global supply chains. Thus the Bank estimates that every ten-percentage-point increase in a company's export share of turnover is, on average, associated with a three-per-cent increase in productivity.

In this context, you can presumably see why anxiety about the risks of leaving the EU is not irrational. The point is that Brexit would – beyond any scintilla of doubt – increase the costs and friction of doing business with our most important market, which is also the world's most important unified market, viz the EU's single market. And that means, everything else being equal, that Brexit would put a brake on a much-needed productivity revival in Britain, and therefore make us poorer than we would have been.

But the links between our prosperity and political deals that give market access are hard for most of us to see. How else to explain raucous cheering on the Nissan production line in

Sunderland as each regional vote in favour of Brexit was announced when night became morning on 24 June? I asked a local politician why these workers were so chuffed to be leaving the EU, when so much of what they produce is intimately entwined with suppliers and customers all over Europe. 'They believed that their success was everything to do with their productivity, their efficiency, the investment in the site, and that this was all about them, and nothing to do with the circumstances of Britain being in the EU's single market,' said the politician. It is human nature to assume our success is all about our brilliance, and not the lucky break of being in the right place at the right time.

I am not trying to detract from the great achievement of Nissan in Sunderland in sustaining world-class performance over many years. But if the UK were to tumble out of the EU, the UK and Nissan would then face tariffs on trade with the rest of the EU, expensive customs checks on goods moving in and out of the EU and higher costs of doing business with fifty-odd nations that have trade deals with the EU. The cost of doing business for Nissan would rise significantly. And the rational response for Nissan would be to employ fewer people or pay its people less.

In other words, it matters to Nissan – and it matters to all of us – that Theresa May succeeds in her aim of replicating most of the benefits of membership of the single market, while also cutting free-trade deals with other important economies.

If she fails, we would all pay a high price.

As we saw earlier, the relationship between higher productivity and pay is not one for one. In recent years, owners of capital and those at the top end of the income scale have taken a growing share of productivity gains, while those on average earnings have enjoyed less of the incremental fruits of their work. The decline in what is called labour's share of income is another way of saying that rising productivity does not enrich all of us equally, or indeed fairly. But it is impossible to improve living standards for all in a sustainable way, unless and until productivity improves. Productivity matters.

Apart from anything else, those working for more efficient firms are demonstrably paid more: 1% higher productivity translates into 0.2% higher pay, according to the Bank of England. A one percentage-point faster rate of productivity growth drives a 0.5 percentage-point faster rate of wage growth.

But, and this also matters, the gap between the pay of workers in high and low productivity firms is much narrower than the gap between their respective rates of productivity, because frontier firms bank a good chunk of higher productivity in lower prices for customers, or higher profits for their owners.

So, as I have discussed, along with the challenge of improving productivity, another great task is to force companies to share more of their productivity gains with their employees, to increase the bargaining power of staff, to end the relative underpayment of people working for outstanding companies.

To recap, there is a connection between the massive regional productivity variations and the fracturing of the unity of the nation. It is not healthy for less productive nations and regions, where companies and people have lower incomes and pay less in tax, to have their public services permanently and substantially subsidised by transfers from the rich South. And improving productivity is never a bad thing, in any case. But even if we understand what has gone wrong with productivity in Britain, fixing it is nightmarishly difficult. If productivity were simply a matter of government policy, as opposed to deep-rooted cultural problems, the UK would not be so laggardly compared with France, Germany and America.

But government can help, and this one may be doing so a bit. The chancellor, Philip Hammond, rarely opens his mouth without saying 'it's all about improving productivity' or words to that effect (though if he said, as Labour does, that 'it's all about productivity and workers getting their fair share,' the government might be more popular). In his 2016 autumn statement, Hammond allocated significant recurring sums to new infrastructure investment, and in the 2017 spring budget he announced the launch of new technical equivalents to 'A' Levels called 'T' Levels. Investing in infrastructure and skills are the Emerson, Lake and Palmer of improving national competitiveness.

But whether enough infrastructure money will go to the regions that need it most, notably the North-East and Midlands, is moot – and that has become a greater concern after Theresa May pointedly dropped the clever regeneration brand, the 'Northern Powerhouse', coined and popularised by her nemesis, the former chancellor George Osborne.

More encouragingly, the government has asked the private-equity plutocrat, Damon Buffini, to conduct a review of why British businesses have so little access to 'patient' capital, that all-important finance for long-term investment.

It will all help. Though none of these government initiatives will yield tangible returns for many years. There are no quick fixes.

The value of any fix at all, whenever it comes, could be immense. Here is one way of seeing this. If all companies are divided into four groups, or quartiles, according to their productivity levels, Haldane calculates that if each group or quartile became as productive as the group or quartile just above them, aggregate British productivity would rise by 13%, and the nation as a whole would become 13% richer. And the point is that in the absence of such a productivity leap, it would take seven years for the economy to expand that much.

If only companies could learn from rivals just a bit more productive than themselves how to become better.

Perhaps that is not an impossible dream. A Productivity Commission, chaired by Sir Charlie Mayfield, also chairman of John Lewis, thinks there could be an app for it: a digital channel for companies to measure their productivity and working practices against benchmarks for their industries, and then learn from each other. The challenge, of course, is to persuade businesses that sharing experiences is not handing over precious competitive information, that it is part of a mutually beneficial conversation. Mistrust between businesses is the natural order of things.

But the example of the City of London, which became world class precisely because of its combination of co-operation, knowhow sharing and cut-throat competition, shows how all could be winners. Also, Haldane is considering the possible development of a 'virtual environment which would enable companies to simulate changes to their business processes and practices', similar to digital tools already used by cutting-edge firms to assess the benefits of new processes and technologies.

What matters is that boosting relatively low productivity, especially outside London, would probably do more to mend our fractured country, to restore some sense of shared purpose, than any other initiative. There is nothing more important for any of us, as individuals, as members of institutions, to feel we are paying our own way. And there is nothing more cancerous and divisive within family or nation than the sense we are being propped up by our richer cousins or neigh-bours. There is an important facilitating role for government, after decades of mis-starts. But companies have the power and duty to do much more for themselves, in particular to harness digital technologies, to collaborate and share wisdom, short of sacrificing commercially sensitive secrets. And in helping themselves, they will help all of us.

CHAPTER 7
TIRED OF WAITING

In the summer of 2007, after investors suddenly baulked at buying bonds made out of mortgages and a vital source of finance was switched off for banks, I had two thoughts: if banks can't borrow, they won't be able to lend, and we'll be in the mother of all recessions; and if we're all in the shit, there'll be riots in the streets.

The pain was felt throughout the world, with the economies of rich countries hurt most. And for a period, people did take to the streets. There was civil disturbance and various forms of direct action, from the conflagrations of Greece and Spain, to the Occupy Movement that briefly took over New York parks and the space around St Paul's Cathedral in London, to the looting all over England sparked by the police shooting of Mark Duggan in Tottenham. They all felt scary, but – arguably – they changed little. Politicians promised to listen. There were modest reforms to the regulation of banks and the financial system, to limit the risk that the next banking crisis would wreak as much havoc as the last one.

But these reforms would have happened anyway. And in respect of the operation of the global economy, of globalisation, nothing much was done. If 2007–8 was the moment when millions of people concluded that globalisation was not working for them, but only for the hated bankers and the unloved bosses of multinational companies – along with the rest of the burgeoning plutocratic class – it was also the moment when most mainstream politicians showed themselves dangerously out of touch with the wants and needs of their voters.

The real revolution was slow in coming. It arrived in the summer and autumn of 2016. But it was so much more serious than what happened on the streets. Because it happened via democratic votes, through the ballot box, first in Britain and then in America, which meant it was impossible for the establishment to ignore the truly fundamental challenge to their way of life. A vote on 23 June ended four decades of membership of the European Union, against the wishes of most of Britain's political class, its rich and those who run big businesses. And on 8 November came the humiliation of mainstream politicians in America, when a right-wing, evangelising, TV-star, billionaire demagogue became president and the most powerful man in the free world – again against the wishes of almost the entire American establishment, from Washington, to big corporations, to conventional media and Wall Street.

It is a challenge to the way the world is run like none we have experienced since the tearing down of the Berlin Wall on 9 November 1989, and the collapse of Communism and the Soviet Union. We will be living through the consequences for many years. But they have already included the eviction from power in France of the parties and politicians that have run France since the Second World War – by a former banker, Emmanuel Macron, who created his new centrist party, En Marche, from scratch in a matter of months. As president, and together with the chancellor of Germany, Angela Merkel, Macron may turn the eurozone into the kind of European superstate that – by transferring important economic powers from national capitals to Brussels – would at last restore to the EU a sense of purpose and direction. Or he may be the last gasp of the banking elite, as they try to resist vainly the siren voices of populist demagogues reasserting the claims to self-determination of the nation state. That battle is yet to be resolved, especially in Europe.

In British party politics, something very different but as important has happened. The Labour party has moved further to the left than it has been more-or-less since its creation a hundred years ago, under its sixty-nine-year-old leader Jeremy Corbyn, who spent his entire life as a left-wing agitator with no hopes or aspirations to actually assume power until he accidentally found himself at Labour's helm in the summer of 2015. And in June 2017, on a platform of mass nationalisation of transport, power and mail service, of trans-ferring huge rights and freedoms back to trade unions – such as to set pay for entire industries – and of raising tens of billions of pounds from higher taxes on companies and the rich, Corbyn's Labour won more than 40% of the vote in Theresa May's impromptu general election.

Corbyn may not have formed the new government. May just about clung on, by way of a desperate alliance with ten MPs from Northern Ireland's Democratic Unionist Party. But he deprived May's Tories of their working majority in the House of Commons. And he increased Labour's percentage share of the vote by a staggering ten percentage points, the party's greatest surge since its historic accession to power in 1945.

What we are witnessing is the delayed political reaction to the most important economic event, the Crash, since the 1930s. It caused an appalling recession and, equally bad, acute disappointment when the recovery revealed itself to be so anaemic. But the Crash was not the whole story, the sole cause. The political earthquake was caused by the conjunction of two economic phenomena: stagnation overlaid on a system that discriminated against whole regions, generations and classes. If we had voted for Brexit just because we had been made a lot poorer by the Crash and we were angry that no politician had properly said sorry, the result would not have been as close as it turned out to be, 52% for Brexit, 48% against: it would have been a landslide for Brexit. And Trump would have won a majority of the national popular vote, which he failed to do, and not merely majorities in important individual states and therefore in America's electoral college, the eccentric institution that ultimately chooses the president.

The votes were not only important for the way the establishment was given a bloody nose. They also mattered for demonstrating how fractured our countries have become. Looking at that Brexit vote, there were three regions, London, Northern Ireland and Scotland, that voted strongly to remain in the EU. And there were five regions, the East, Yorkshire and the Humber, the North-East, the East Midlands and the West Midlands, that voted decisively to leave.

What kind of correlation is there between their respective economic performances, especially in relation to living standards, and this differential pattern of voting?

As you would expect, growth in living standards has been negligible or non-existent everywhere. According to data from the Office of National Statistics, between 2008 and 2014, gross disposable household income per head – a proxy for individual prosperity – rose a little in London, by 2%. But in EU-membership-supporting Scotland and Northern Ireland, living standards fell a little over 1% and by a savage 6% respectively. Similarly, in one of the EU-Leavers strongholds, the North-East, living standards rose very slightly, by 2%, in the post-Crash years – whereas in other Leave regions, the East Midlands, West Midlands and Yorkshire and Humber, disposable incomes all fell around 1%. And in the Leave-backing East they flatlined.

These regional variations are so small as to provide an implausible explanation for why people in different parts of the country voted differently.

Much more important than the incremental differences are the absolute differences in living standards between regions. And if the Crash was a trigger – albeit with a lag – for the revolt over Brexit, it was that many people, and especially those in regions characterised by sub-par incomes, got tired of waiting for things to get better. There is a paradox here, of course, which is that many of those very same people who backed Brexit – especially the older ones – rejected Corbyn's Labour in the general election and backed May. And it was another group disproportionately hurt by the banking crisis and subsequent recession, the young, who were attracted to Corbyn and came out to vote on a scale not seen for decades. In other words, that great economic disaster of a decade ago has generated aftershocks that have altered the political landscape in so many different ways. And, appropriately, the establishment is paying a price for the gutless response to the crisis of their representatives who were in government at the time.

Here is why a limp recovery is so much more damaging in Sunderland than in London. Gross disposable income per head in the capital at £23,607 is a staggering 55% higher than in the North-East, 52% more than in Yorkshire and Humber, 51% greater than in the West Midlands and 46% higher than in the East Midlands. Also, there are far more people on very low incomes in these relatively low-wage areas than in the south: in the North-East, Yorkshire and Humber, the West Midlands and East Midlands, more than a quarter of all workers earn less than the living wage, compared with just 13% in London (according to the Resolution Foundation).[50] And of course, where there are lower incomes there is much less financial security. Around 50% of all adults in the Midlands and North have savings of less than £100, whereas in the South-East, fewer than a third have as little put aside as that.[51]

With the disparities between North and South so stark, it is extraordinary they have been tolerated for so long.

It also matters that living standards in Scotland, where 62% voted to remain – more even than in London – are above those in the Midlands and North of England. And it has far fewer, just 21% of workers, on very low pay. But the referendum vote was not all about the money; as I have been banging on about, it was also about identity and expectations. How else to make sense of Northern Ireland's vote to remain, given that disposable incomes there are the lowest of any UK nation or region and it has the worst savings performance in the UK? The determinants of the vote were more subtle and complex than London envy, or a sense of unfairness about regional economic performance.

There is acceptance throughout Ireland, and in the Republic especially, that EU membership has brought vital investment, that it has been good for them. Many in the province also have positive feelings towards the EU, because it is an important pillar of the Northern Ireland peace settlement. Strikingly,

---

50 Stephen Clarke & Conor D'Arcy, 'Low Pay Britain 2016', Resolution Foundation Report, October 2016, p. 37.
51 'Closing the Savings Gap', Money Advice Service, September 2016.

Orange communities near the border voted overwhelmingly for Remain, having had personal experience of the smuggling, other crime, violence and hatred fomented by a militarised border. And it may also be relevant that surveys show Northern Ireland's people are happier than those in the rest of the UK.

According to the ONS's annual population survey, Northern Ireland is by far the least anxious part of the country, and Northern Irish people also say they are much more satisfied with life than those in England, Wales and Scotland. I am not sure why those in Northern Ireland are so content with their lot, but it may simply be that material prosperity feels less important than peace, after years of living under the dark shadow of terrorism.

As for Scotland, its relationship with the EU is also complex – and may be connected with the nation's centuries-old affinity with France, and a long-standing nationalist identity that defines itself as anti-English rather than anti-European (in stark contrast to UKIP). For many in Scotland, the notion that London holds them back from fulfilling their potential is far more powerful than the equivalent charge made against Brussels. So maybe Brexit and Scoxit are two sides of the same coin – the currency of self-actualisation – but a viable Scoxit would almost certainly require Scotland to somehow stay part of the EU, or at least its single market (it is the idea of Scotland as a Sweden or a Norway).

What about regional variations in social mobility? If the Brexit vote was a protest against the status quo, it should have been greatest where it is hardest to break free from the shackles of birth. There is evidence for that. For example, the very strongly Leave areas of Yorkshire and Humber, the North-East and the West Midlands have no areas where social mobility is significantly better than average, zero so-called social mobility hotspots, according to the Social Mobility and Child Poverty Commission.[52] And equally the areas where people are most likely to be trapped on low incomes, those with the greatest concentration of so-called cold spots, are also in Leave-supporting places, the Midlands and the East of England.

The seeds of the Brexit vote may therefore have been planted more than thirty years ago with the decimation of heavy industry, much of manufacturing and even coal mining by Thatcher, because this meant the loss of work that delivered a sense of pride and place. But it is important not to overstate this: deindustrialisation in a city like Stoke may have reinforced its Leave vote, but Warwick just down the road voted to Remain, and probably more because of the presence of a world-class university promoting tolerance of other cultures and peoples, rather than because of any great industrial or economic superiority.

A malaise in manufacturing also does not explain why the ten towns that voted for Leave by the biggest margins are all in the strongly agricultural East of England and East Midlands, with Boston in Lincolnshire the most Leavy of all. In Boston, more than three-quarters of voters opted for quitting the EU, seemingly because of opposition to unfettered immigration from the rest of the EU. To be clear, it appears to have been the rate of influx of new people from abroad that mattered, not the absolute or relative number of them,[53] because what is

---

52 'State of the Nation 2016: Social Mobility in Great Britain', Social Mobility Commission, November 2016.
53 Sunder Katwala, Jill Rutter & Steve Ballinger, 'Disbanding the tribes: What the referendum told us about Britain (and what it didn't)', British Future, July 2016.

striking about Boston, for example, is that foreign EU nationals were less than 1% of the population there in 2001 and more than 12% by 2011. Those arrivals may have depressed the wages and living standards of some indigenous Bostonians. But the much more conspicuous impact was on the spare capacity of public services and the culture of the town. Although living standards, social mobility and economics matter; so, too, do culture and identity.

Arguably what drove the vote was a combination of living standards and the ability of an area to adapt to and thrive from change, especially the population change that comes from immigration – or what is often called institutional resilience. A town or community's history of openness, flexibility and robustness seems to account for a great deal. Drawing on the work of the anthropologist Sandra Wallman, analysis by Katwala, Rutter and Ballinger[54] shows that places suffering in a similar way from economic malaise voted very differently, depending on their respective capacities to cope with the intrusion and upheaval of immigration.

For instance, the number voting for Leave was eight percentage points higher in Braintree than in Chelmsford, in spite of these towns having comparable population sizes, levels of educational attainment, average wages, rates of employment and numbers of EU immigrants. The important difference is probably that Chelmsford has a longer history of immigration from the rest of the world, a more open culture, mixed neighbourhoods and superior transport links. Chelmsford people feel less threatened by change.

It is the relationship between our resilience as individuals and the resilience of our communities that counts. 'Groups

---

54 ibid., p. 19.

in Britain who have been "left behind" by rapid economic change and feel cut adrift from the mainstream consensus were the most likely to support Brexit,' say Matthew Goodwin and Oliver Heath. 'While their lack of qualifications put them at a significant disadvantage in the modern economy, they are also further marginalised in society by the lack of opportunities in their low-skilled communities.'[55] As we've already seen, where you live is significant, and especially who your neighbours happen to be: people with higher skills were more likely to vote Leave if they happened to live in a low-skilled area; and those with intermediate skills were more likely to vote for Remain if they lived in high-skill areas.

Even so, in both Britain and America the strongest predictive factor about how people voted seems to have been whether they went to university. As Goodwin and Heath say:[56]

> Age, income and education matter, though it is educational inequality that was the strongest driver. Other things being equal, support for Leave was 30 percentage points higher among those with GCSE qualifications or below than it was for people with a degree. In contrast, support for Leave was just 10 points higher among those on less than £20,000 per year than it was among those with incomes of more than £60,000 per year, and 20 points higher among those aged sixty-five than those aged twenty-five.

---

55 Matthew Goodwin & Oliver Heath, 'Brexit vote explained: Poverty, low skills and lack of opportunity', Joseph Rowntree Foundation, August 2016.
56 ibid.

And according to the British Social Attitudes survey, a staggering 78% of those with degrees voted to remain, whereas 72% with no recognised qualifications voted to leave. Older and poorer people tended to vote for leaving the EU, but those with fewest academic qualifications overwhelmingly voted for Brexit.

This pattern was to an extent repeated in the general election. Voting Labour was seen by many as a proxy for a vote for a closer relationship with the EU, and therefore it is predictable that 49% of those with university degrees voted Labour – while just 32% voted for Theresa May's Tories. And the proportions were almost precisely inverted for those educated to no higher than GCSEs: 55% voted Tory, 33% for Labour, according to YouGov. The more highly educated middle classes voted for the most left-wing Labour party perhaps ever, because of their conviction that May would deliver an abrupt rupture with the EU and that this would be a disaster.

The shift to Labour also captures disillusionment with the Tories of many with degrees working in the public sector, from doctors and teachers to civil servants, who were sick to the back teeth of cuts and austerity. But probably only the minority voted for Corbyn having discovered they had more red in their souls than they thought. It is not ridiculous to see the election result of just over 42% for the Tories and 40% for Labour as analogous to the referendum's 52% to 48%. Labour's gradual shift to a more pro-EU position than the Tories is rational and inevitable, because that is where their supporters are.

The capture by Labour of the university town of Canterbury from the Tories, the first time Labour has won that seat since it was created in 1918, was perhaps the totemic election result. It was of a piece with what happened almost a year earlier in the referendum, as David Runciman pointed out:[57] 'In England and Wales, many university towns emerged from the referendum as isolated outposts of pro-EU sentiment in a sea of Brexit. Newcastle, York, Nottingham, Norwich, Cambridge, Brighton, Warwick, Exeter, Bristol, Reading, Oxford and Cardiff all voted Remain.'

Nate Silver, the feted American statistician, comes to a similar conclusion about Trump's victory. 'It appears as though education levels are the critical factor in predicting shifts in the vote between 2012 and 2016,' he writes.[58] He looked at the fifty US counties where there were proportionately the smallest number of people with undergraduate degrees and he found that 'Clinton lost ground relative to Obama in 47 of the 50 counties – she did an average of 11 percentage points worse.' Working people, Rustbelt America, really did not like Clinton. Silver: 'These are really the places that won Donald Trump the presidency, especially given that a fair number of them are in swing states such as Ohio and North Carolina.' In America, too, educational attainment was the strongest predictor of how people voted, more than income, more than age, more than ethnicity.

Now I imagine you expect me to point out that less-educated people voted for Trump and Brexit because they are thick. But funnily enough, I don't take that view. Their votes were rational, because their jobs and living standards are more at risk from immigration, and from the ability of companies to move where people and capital are cheapest. And without the means to go private, it is a total pain for working-class families

---

57 David Runciman, 'How the education gap is tearing politics apart', *Guardian*, 5 October 2016.
58 Nate Silver, 'Education not income predicted who would vote for Trump', FiveThirtyEight, November 2016.

when there are more migrants in a community than local schools and doctors' surgeries can service.

By contrast, the competitive, fast-changing global economy, for which the EU became a proxy in some voters' minds, is less daunting for most graduates than for the unskilled and semi-skilled. And immigration for those with better educations and higher incomes delivers growth opportunities for their respective businesses, through access to a broader talent pool, and also a better quality of life at home – through the ability to hire the proverbial builders, cleaners and nannies more cheaply.

But there is also a laziness and cowardice in the group-think of graduates that liberalism is always for the best. Runciman suggests that graduates are embarrassed to challenge ideas such as that we are safer and richer for being in the EU, for fear of being ridiculed by other graduates. Paradoxically, those who have been to university may be more closed to intellectual challenge than those who have not; the prejudices of graduate communities may actually be harder to challenge than those of working-class groups. For graduates, voting for a sexist billionaire star of reality TV, or for a rift with Germany and France, is the equivalent of farting in public. It's not done.

Going to university is a powerful cultural experience at a formative period in our lives, especially in respect of shaping our political views – frequently views that we retain till death. This is how Laurence Knight, a BBC journalist who collaborated with me on my last book, *How Do We Fix This Mess?*, puts it: 'Young people come together from all over the country, and all over the world, and are exposed to all kinds of new ideas and cultures. And most importantly this is a shared experience, leading directly to a shared identity. And because universities are becoming increasingly globalised, that is an identity that is itself increasingly globalised.'

Young people's shared global identity, usually acquired at university, helps to explain why their anger about the shrivelling of their economic prospects has not turned them into nationalists – and why they continue to love what have come to be known as mega-cities, like London, even though for many of them it has become prohibitively expensive to actually own a home in one of those cities. There is a powerful idea here, about how our instinctive yearning to be part of what Benedict Anderson called an 'imagined community'[59] is bringing people together in important new ways thanks to digital communication. Laurence Knight:

> The rise of the internet and social media, and of English as a global lingua franca, especially in Europe, is creating global imagined communities, especially among younger people. This doesn't just mean left-leaning types who care about alleviating global poverty, breaking down borders, or addressing climate change. It also means, for example, the rise of white nationalism as an increasingly international phenomenon. When people are able to communicate with a global audience then they can also create a common mythology for that audience, can tell them a common story, and that leads to a common identity.

Many more people than just the less-educated and the left behind voted for Brexit, or indeed voted for Trump in America. Both results are manifestations of a desperate

---

59 Benedict Anderson, 'Imagined Communities: Reflections on the origin and spread of nationalism', 1983.

yearning for more control of their lives and for a clearer sense of who they are, especially in a national sense, as we have seen – at a time when globalisation seems to have shunted power further and further away from us, and a media revolution makes it increasingly hard to know who to trust.

Remakings of the world, of the magnitude we are experiencing, are rare and important events. They require underlying causes, such as our current and longstanding combination of low growth, poor social mobility and widening inequality. But they lead to revolutions, either on the streets or via the ballot box, only when accompanied by other changes in how we live and communicate. What makes the current world so unstable and unpredictable is how social media is challenging prevailing orthodoxy, especially in politics. And then there is the human factor. When we look back on this era, we will certainly see big personalities. But whether we will regard them as great men and women of history, or magnificent bunglers, is moot.

CHAPTER 8

WHO IS REALLY TO BLAME FOR AUSTERITY?

The Tories love to attack Labour's Jeremy Corbyn and John McDonnell for basing their ambitious public spending plans on money they would need to harvest from a magic tree. But it was not all that long ago that this country did seem to have cultivated that rare and precious magic money tree. Those years of largesse, in wages, in public services, may seem a world away. But extraordinary as it may seem, the years from 1992 – the end of the last recession before our Great one – to the beginning of 2008 were golden. Growth over fifteen years was unbroken and relatively rapid, around 2.6% per year. We had never had it so good, or at least not since the nineteenth century.

And that meant not only that living standards were rising in a highly satisfactory way, but also significant additional resources became available to spend on schools, hospitals and subsidies for work in the form of tax credits. In those years, average real disposable income increased from £14,913 to £27,370, rising 5.6% per year. House prices jumped from an average of £61,000 to £223,000. And over the same time period, the education budget increased 68% in real terms. The health service's budget for England more than doubled; it rose 117%. The tax credits introduced by Gordon Brown in 1999 became one of the most effective tools in history for lifting the living standards of poor and middle-income families, and were costing a fraction less than 2% of all UK national income (the annual value of everything produced in the UK) by the time Labour left office in 2010; only the state pension was a more expensive item in the welfare budget. Government was really making a big positive difference to the quality of our lives.

After decades as citizens of the sick economy of Europe, only able to enjoy modern fast trains and roads when on holiday in France, shamed by Germany's wealth-generating engineering prowess, we were suddenly in the vanguard of economic progress. The creaking, lumbering British economy was seemingly transformed into a model of international openness, employment creation and dynamism by Margaret Thatcher's invitation to the world's great companies to settle in the UK for access to Europe's huge market and her assault on the supposedly enterprise-crushing vandalism of the giant trade unions, which a remade Labour party under Tony Blair did little to reverse.

There were, conspicuously and egregiously, still parts of the country, the North-East and much of the Midlands in particular, that were struggling, left behind after their important heavy industries were devastated by her successive busts, booms and more busts from 1979 to 1992, caused first by an overvalued exchange rate, then by excessive interest rates. And industrial policy was insouciant, as the then Department of Trade and Industry indulged rapacious conglomerates like Hanson and BTR, which bought older manufacturers and remorselessly squeezed them for cash, rather than investing in them properly for growth.

But despite the valiant efforts of Michael Heseltine to turn regional regeneration policy into more than a fig leaf, a new orthodoxy from the Treasury ruled, which was that Britain could thrive on its world-class service industries, especially banks, hedge funds, private equity, insurance and other financial services. And that manufacturing really did not matter much any more, and by implication nor did the many parts of the UK outside London and the South-East that had formerly depended on manufacturing.

Treasury officials were almost religious in their faith that fifty years of being beaten economically by Germany could all be reversed if we simply played to our strengths in finance, media and other services, and realised there was nothing special about making stuff. The Treasury's other convictions were that anything that looked like a business owned by the government was by definition (and never mind the evidence) being badly run and should be privatised; and that British managers are so crap and useless (possibly true) that the only way to improve the efficiency of firms here would be to allow any or all of our businesses and assets to be sold to foreigners. This would bring in new and better managers, from whom our genial dunderheads – almost all of them men – could learn. And when our crown jewel companies, our airports, mobile phone companies, software makers, even most of the City of London, were flogged to foreigners, the capital so released would be re-invested here in new and exciting employment-creating businesses.

Those were the plausible theories. And they worked for a while, although they were primarily embraced by Treasury mandarins as a form of atonement for their and ministers' mismanagement of the economy in the preceding forty-odd years. In the 1960s and 1970s, industrial lame ducks were bailed out, at excessive cost, and inflationary pay deals conceded with too-powerful trade-union barons. But it was the disasters after 1979, and the advent of Thatcher, that really humiliated Treasury officials.

First there was the attempt to control the supply of money into the economy, which succeeded largely in causing the pound to soar, and led to a painful economic contraction and a rise in unemployment to criminally high levels. Then in the late 1980s, sterling became part of the European Exchange Rate Mechanism, a precursor to the euro, and involved fixing our currency once again at a too-high rate of exchange – although on this occasion it was the carnage caused by pushing up interest rates to maintain that rate of exchange that wreaked the most economic carnage.

The point is that the Treasury has a long and undistinguished history of always fighting the last war in its economic policies – of dumping one set of policies, which at the time it believed were founded on some eternal economic truths, only then to adopt with similar religious confidence another collection of dangerous shibboleths. So the fatuous monetarism of the early 1980s was supposedly the cure for rollercoaster Keynesian fiscal (taxing, spending and borrowing) management of economic demand. The mandarins are always convinced they have the true recipe for sustainable wealth creation, till the crisis they never expected proves to be the recession-causing exception to the rule.

When I talk about the Treasury, I am referring to both the brainy and influential civil servants, the mandarins, and also to their political masters. It would be absurd to absolve successive Chancellors of the Exchequer of responsibility for what went wrong. The balance of responsibility between officials and politicians ebbs and flows, depending on their respective confidence and competence. Officials adored Alistair Darling and George Osborne during their tenures as Chancellor, because they 'listened', which is code for 'they did what we told them to do' and 'we agreed on most things of importance'. Their relationship with Gordon Brown after he became chancellor in 1997 was more problematic, because he and his main adviser, Ed Balls, were determined to be the masters of the officials: it was a point of principle and pride for them.

This did not mean Brown and Balls were expansive, social-ist spendthrifts, or certainly not in their early period. They adapted the Treasury's cult of fiscal conservatism for their own purposes. In fact, during the first couple of years after Gordon Brown became chancellor in 1997, he engaged in fiscal hair-shirtism, or reining in spending and borrowing, with an effectiveness that George Osborne – for whom the word 'austerity' was seemingly invented – simply never managed. Brown had adopted spending targets set by his Tory predecessor Ken Clarke, which even Clarke regarded as too tight to be deliverable – as Clarke told me at the time.

Brown chose to accept these targets as a demonstration of fiscal virility, to prove that his and Blair's 'New' version of Labour could be just as controlling of public spending as the Tories, all history to the contrary. And unlike Osborne thir-teen years later, Brown undershot the targets. Also, for four successive years, from 1998 to 2002, he generated a surplus on the public finances; he raised more in revenues than he spent. This was a feat that Osborne did not achieve even in a single year, and which the current chancellor Philip Hammond now does not anticipate achieving till 2025 and, according to the government's Office for Budget Responsibility, could very easily be missed, so uncertain is the economic outlook.

Brown inherited a national debt that was 38% of GDP, our national income. However, by October 2001, according to official Office for National Statistics figures, the debt had fallen to 27.6% of GDP, which is the kind of low level that small-state, right-wing Tories have wet dreams over. Now in this period Brown benefited from a handsome £22 billion windfall from auctioning licences to the airwaves for mobile phone companies that wanted to provide faster 3G services. But nonetheless, he achieved something that seems incredible: not only did he reduce debt as a share of our national income, he cut it in absolute terms – from £364 billion in 1997 to £328.8 billion in 2001, or by far more than the dividend from selling 3G licences.

Here is the comparator that should make most traditional Tories retch with regret and envy: since the coalition of Tories and Lib Dems took office in May 2010, the national debt has risen from £1 trillion to £1.7 trillion. In other words, merely the increase in the national debt on their watch is more than double the total national debt after Brown's early years in 2001.

So was Brown a Billericay Dicky and Osborne a bleedin' thicky? Yes, in one sense.

If Brown was going to squeeze the public sector, this was the optimal time – in that he was keeping a lid on public expenditure when the global economy was motoring ahead, when growth in the private sector was pushing up wages, boosting living standards and increasing tax revenues for the government. This was a moment when the costs to people's lives of moderating the expansion of public services was bearable. Brown cut public spending as a proportion of GDP, or the value of what the UK produces, from 37.3% to 35.7% in 2000. But the squeeze was less than the reduction in debt: he allowed spending on public services and the public sector to rise a little bit slower than the growth of the economy. Brown was spending less than the government earned, living within his means – and his version of austerity, which he called 'prudence', was not a dampener on prosperity.

He was not doing this because of any deep-seated, ideological commitment to shrinking the state. Quite the opposite. He was doing it to prove that, as and when he started to enlarge the state, he could be trusted to do so in – to use his word – a 'prudent' way. Brown and Tony Blair felt they had to demonstrate they could be more Tory than the Tories in their fiscal management, in order to receive the permission of markets, media and voters to do some mildly socialist things. They were acutely sensitive – probably too sensitive – to the charge that whenever Labour had been in power, its steward-ship of public finances and economy had been defined by recklessness, incompetence and failure, with the nadir being 1976 and Labour's then chancellor Denis Healey going cap in hand to the IMF for a $3.9 billion bailout. Brown was deter-mined to show the City of London and its bankers that he really was on their side, as 'Prudence' Brown.

However, his parsimony really got up the noses of his Cabinet colleagues and Labour supporters, who became more and more bemused about what the party was supposed to be about, if not for rewarding public-sector workers and pushing up spending on schools and hospitals. The point is that by the standards of rich countries, the UK was spending relatively little on public services at the moment that Brown and Tony Blair took the reins: according to the OECD, there were twenty developed economies funding their public services much more generously than the UK, and some like Sweden and France spending half as much again as Britain as a share of the economy.

But within a couple of years of Brown becoming chancellor, the UK had an even smaller state; by 1999 there were twenty-one countries with larger public sectors than Britain's. For the traditional left, New Labour was proving to be utterly pointless. And the truth is that what Brown and his chief adviser Ed Balls were doing was a bit bonkers, because they were underwriting and validating the ideology of their bitterest opponents on the right.

Even Tony Blair was chomping at the bit for the Treasury to fund public services in a more generous way, as he told me in 1998, when we were 30,000 feet above the sea on an official prime-ministerial flight to the US. Blair was anxious to spend the reserves being accumulated by Brown and pronto. But when it came to economic decisions, and in fact to much of the domestic agenda, Blair was the least powerful prime minister of modern times; he had ceded extraordinary autonomy to Brown before they took office in 1994, as the price extracted by Brown for not challenging Blair for the leadership of Labour. So Blair and his colleagues were forced, by Brown, to bide their time till 2002, when the constraints on spending were finally relaxed.

The frozen winter in the public sector suddenly turned to balmy summer. From 2000 until Labour was ejected from office in 2010, public spending rose by well over a third, from 35.7% of GDP to 48% of GDP. And the UK rocketed up the international league table of big spenders among the richer nations, from 22nd place to 14th. The country was borrowing again, to splurge on schools and hospitals. Over the same period, the national debt shot up, more than doubling to 66% of GDP.

That level of debt was not in itself disastrous. But the rate at which the debt was increasing after the 2008 Crash was potentially disastrous. Brown – and his naive Treasury officials – had massively overestimated how much of the tax revenue pouring into Treasury coffers was sustainable. They failed to see how much economic activity in the City and property markets was a bubble that would pop, and therefore they did not anticipate that many tens of billions of pounds from income and capital taxes would vanish after the banking crisis. Government borrowing would not have ballooned quite as much as it did, if Brown had been less prudent in the late 1990s and more prudent latterly.

And he made another error. The longer he limited the flow of cash to schools and hospitals during his debut, the greater the pressure – from his party, from its trade union supporters – for a splurge. And when he relented and the cash started to gush into the NHS, its managers and doctors found themselves in the unusual position of receiving more additional cash than they could sensibly disburse. Inevitably, when they were throwing money at extra staff, equipment and drugs, the price of all these people and things was forced up. Quite a lot of the additional resource evaporated in inflation that was actually caused by the spending boom. So in that sense it would have been more efficient, and would have yielded better value for money, to give the NHS a little bit less each year, but to have started funding it more generously earlier than 2002.

But perhaps the more serious strategic mistake made by Brown was not to challenge properly the canard that austerity is appropriate for all seasons. Indeed, initially he underwrote this myth, in kowtowing to the economic illiteracy of the City of London by squeezing so hard (by the standards of the Labour Party). And, in order to create the illusion that he was not being spendthrift and reckless, he created a couple of fiscal rules that were supposed to impose a check on how much he could borrow, but in practice were not a serious constraint.

In other words, he gave unnecessary credibility to 'small c' fiscal conservatives with his rhetoric and rules; he reinforced the dangerous idea that government finances should be managed in the same way as household finances. And having asked to be judged in that misguided way, he eventually achieved the opposite of what he wanted: Labour's old reputation for irresponsible stewardship of the public finances came back to haunt the party, and haunts it to this day.

To repeat, it was not the spending spree *per se* by Labour that led to the explosive growth in the national debt. But the hapless regulation of the City, on Brown's watch, meant banks had to be bailed out and also led to a collapse in tax revenues when the financial crisis led to chronic recession. So those latter-year increments in health and education spending suddenly looked much less affordable. Brown's Treasury was also too keen on the creative off-balance-sheet financing of the Private Finance Initiative, which parked vast amounts of investment in schools and hospitals off the government's official books, but landed it with the huge long-term costs of servicing penally expensive contracts.

Arguably, therefore, Brown – and his long-term collaborator Ed Balls – were partly responsible for Labour losing the 2015 election, as well (of course) as the 2010 one, because they had failed to build a public consensus that austerity is self-harming, and especially so during a downturn caused by inadequate activity in the private sector. Right from the off, they had lent credence to the mad idea that borrowing is always an evil, and not even a very necessary one.

For the left, there was perhaps an even greater tragedy. Over thirteen years in office, the longest unbroken run in the history of the Labour Party, there was an opportunity to build a national commitment to a fairer Britain, one in which public services and the machinery of the state are always funded as generously as in places such as Sweden and Denmark, which are both highly successful as economies and as societies. Instead, the coalition government of Tories and Lib Dems cut spending as if they had won a mandate to shrink it back to levels not seen since before the Second World War – and their squeeze is proportionately more painful, because of the ageing of our population, which is making huge additional demands on the National Health Service.

This was a political and economic failure, whose roots were startlingly similar to Brown's and Blair's failure to restore and foster public confidence in the EU. Both were and are passionately committed to the UK's membership of the EU. But when in office, they too readily couched negotiations with the rest of the EU, over our contributions to the budget, or rules affecting financial services or pretty much anything, as a battle with the dreadful Eurocrats of Brussels, or with anti-British foreign politicians – and never as a rational, consensual exercise in establishing what is best for the EU and Europe as a whole.

In this case they reinforced the idea, nurtured by the *Sun*, *Daily Telegraph* and *Daily Mail*, of the EU as the eternal enemy. Little wonder that when it came to the Remain campaign in the referendum, many saw them as absurd when they argued that the EU has done more to bring peace, prosperity and stability to Europe than any other initiative on this troubled continent. The case for the EU was made too late and perhaps their only consolation is that David Cameron and George

Osborne looked even more ridiculous as born-again, pro-Europeans.

An approach to politics that New Labour tried to dignify as shrewd 'triangulation', or simultaneously facing in contradictory directions to woo *Daily Mail* and traditional Labour supporters, turned their party into a meteor, a soaring electoral success that crashed to earth, when both friends and enemies concluded they could not be trusted. And the true measure of Blair and Brown's failure is that – somewhat due to the relentless, partisan editorialising of a traditional media largely owned by Tory supporters – their appeasement of Euroscepticism and fiscal hair-shirtism delivered victory to both.

The point Brown should have made almost every day he was in office is that when companies and consumers can't and won't spend, because of their uneasiness about what the future holds, which is characteristic of most economic downturns, almost everyone will become needlessly poorer if the government does not increase its spending and borrowing for a period. He could and should have used his record time as chancellor to establish as a publicly accepted principle that while it is rational for you and me to try to spend and borrow less, as and when we lose our jobs or we incur a pay cut, it is almost always irrational for a government to spend and borrow less, when millions of us face pay cuts or unemployment.

He and Ed Balls would argue that in writing fiscal rules that allowed the so-called fiscal stabilisers to operate, they were managing the economy on precisely that principle, in that in a downturn they allowed benefit payments to rise and tax revenues to fall, to cushion the impact of the downturn. And that is true. But in characterising their policy as 'the operation of the fiscal stabilisers' – language that no one understands

– they were running away from what they should have been doing, which was to make the case explicitly and clearly for borrowing in bad times. Second, their use of PFI to fund investment was a disgraceful failure to recapture for government its legitimate role of borrower at low interest rates for public investment.

When Osborne and the coalition of Tories and Lib Dems slashed annual average increases in public spending to a paltry £10 billion a year between 2010 and 2014, and set unrealistic targets for rapid deficit reduction, it was legitimate to accuse them of taking a wrecking ball to our prosperity – of both damaging public services and holding back economic recovery. But since Osborne could claim merely to be wearing the clothes that 'Prudence' Brown had been desperate to wear, Osborne's economic message seemed coherent, while Labour's under the then leader Ed Miliband and shadow chancellor Ed Balls appeared weak and muddled; although it was in practice more sensible, for offering greater fiscal flexibility.

To be clear, the weakness of the UK economic recovery after 2010 was not all the result of decisions taken by Osborne and the coalition. He and the government inherited structural weaknesses, including a collapse in productivity, or output per worker, which had nothing to do with him. And the global economy was growing far less strongly than before the crash. What is more, it would have been irresponsible of Osborne to ignore the explosion of the government's deficit to the dangerously unsustainable ten per cent of national income that he inherited from Labour. But it was a mad mistake to cut spending on infrastructure and capital at the exact moment when the UK should have been investing to boost productivity. And as the health service and social care for the elderly are today struggling to keep afloat, and schools face crippling cuts, we are now seeing the toxic legacy of cuts that cumulatively undermined growth and therefore tax revenues in the longer term.

Austerity divided and fragmented a nation, rather than uniting it. It contributed to the Brexit vote and then delivered Corbyn's surge in the general election. Osborne and Brown are the parents of the jubilant Brexiteers and the Corbynistas, because they both have a share of responsibility for the long years of stagnating living standards – even if neither fathers nor offspring are happy to acknowledge the paternity.

Here are the big economic numbers that underlie the Brexit vote. They point to disappointed expectations among vast numbers of people. At the time of the referendum, the British economy was a little less than 8% bigger than it had been at the time of the onset of recession at the start of 2008, and it was just 1% bigger on a per-head basis. This was a much weaker recovery than after previous post-war recessions. Another way of calculating our disappointed expectations is that the typical income of those aged between twenty-five and fifty-five grew 26% in real terms between 1994/5 and 2004/5, but just 2% in the subsequent ten years. So on the basis of past experience, it would have been reasonable to expect us to be between 10% and 20% richer today than we are.

If it is any comfort, which it probably should be, because it shows our lacklustre performance is not uniquely our problem and our fault, our economy has in the round performed a little bit better than Germany's in respect of aggregate GDP growth since the crash, and much better than ailing Italy. But the US, and especially Canada, have outstripped us significantly.

The stagnation of our incomes is no less infuriating now we know that for much of that 1992–2008 golden era, growth was artificial and unsustainable. It was created by banks and a financial sector taking dangerous risks. It was phoney growth, though Gordon Brown and his colleagues wanted to believe it was real growth, because the City boom was generating a bulge in tax revenues that paid for at least some of his splurge in spending on schools and hospitals. The wholly inadequate regulation and oversight of the City by the now defunct Financial Services Authority and the Bank of England was not a deliberate aim of Labour's or Brown's policies, but it certainly suited.

It is literally an economic and social tragedy that the huge profits made by banks and other City firms were inflated, artificial and unsustainable, whereas the cash spent by Brown on public services and increments to our incomes with tax credits was real cash that millions of people enjoyed. Brown really did, for a while, improve our standard of living and quality of life. So the squeeze under Osborne when it came – after all those City-related tax revenues evaporated – was always going to be big, long and disappointing, even if it is bigger, longer and more disappointing than it had to be. Brown and Osborne may be an odd couple, but a couple they are.

Nor are those the only respects in which Brown and Osborne are co-conspirators in the past fifteen years of boom and bust, and of a prevailing sense that stewardship of the economy has a perverse and unfair impact on the distribution of wealth.

It was Brown who was responsible in 1997 for the biggest transfer of economic power from government to unelected officials probably ever, when he gave the Bank of England autonomous, independent control over the setting of interest rates and the creation of money. And it was Osborne who after 2010 reinforced the authority and powers of the Bank of England, by transferring to it the hugely important responsibility for monitoring and maintaining the health of banks and the wider financial system, and giving it all sorts of new powers intended to prevent financial bubbles being pumped up too much and too fast.

The point, which you already know (sorry), is that Brown in 2008, by then prime minister with Alistair Darling as chancellor, and Osborne in 2010, both felt highly constrained in their ability to use spending, borrowing and tax-cutting to revive the economy. The size of the deficit made this partly rational, but not wholly. Instead they expected the Bank of England to take on the duty of reviving the economy, through what is known as monetary policy, which it duly did. This involved creating £535 billion of new money, with quantitative easing, and reducing the interest rate it controls, Bank Rate, to 0.25%, lower than it has ever gone in the Bank's 323-year history.

The aim was to encourage investment, especially in houses, property, bonds and shares – collectively known as assets – so that asset prices would stop falling, or might even rise. The realistic hope was that owners of property, shares and so on would become more confident and would start spending again. Shoppers would shop, businesses would invest. And that way the economy would revive.

It worked. And because our economy is so unbalanced and so dependent on consumer spending, whose recovery took a while, the recession returned first to anaemic, almost negligible growth and then bounced to a bit over 2% a year. The post-referendum momentum in the economy also owed much to household spending, which in turn stemmed in part from the interest-rate cuts and additional quantitative easing that the Bank carried out in the summer of 2016, just in case we all panicked and stopped shopping after voting for Brexit. Since then the squeeze in our living standards from rising inflation, caused by a fall in the pound that captured investors' disappointment that we voted to leave the EU, has put the brakes on shopping and therefore growth again, and the medium-term trajectory for our prosperity is highly uncertain.

But the important point here is that relying on the Bank of England to revive the economy heightens the perception that the economy is run in a very unfair way. Interest-rate cuts and the creation of cheap money disproportionately reward those who own shares and houses, by increasing the value of those assets. To state the obvious, it widens the gap between rich and poor. And it also seems to rig the economy even more against the interests of younger people: houses and pension plans are largely the preserve of older people, and as these assets soar in value, they move even further beyond the reach of the young.

When chancellors abdicate responsibility for economic stewardship in this way, by asking the Bank of England to take the strain, the consequences are worrying for social cohesion. The Swiss investment bank Credit Suisse estimates that the UK in 2013–14 created more new dollar millionaires – that is people with net wealth greater than $1 million – than any other country, other than the US. It calculates that 478,000 joined their ranks, taking the total number of British dollar millionaires to more than two million.

Almost none of those new millionaires owed their additional wealth to the entrepreneurial prowess that creates jobs. Their additional riches stemmed mostly from a 10% rise in house prices, which was caused by the Bank's monetary stimulus. In fact, Credit Suisse says the UK enjoyed the biggest increase in household wealth, of almost 20%, on the planet. But it adds: 'It is interesting to note that only one G7 [or big rich developed] nation – the United Kingdom – appears in the list of 23 countries recording an increase in inequality this century.'

Now after the vote for Brexit, the value of the pound plunged, which had a serious negative impact on the value of UK assets as measured in dollars (a reduction of $1.5 trillion – no trivial sum). But Credit Suisse[60] reckons the UK still has 2.2m dollar millionaires – and the third greatest number in the world of so-called ultra-high-net-worth individuals, or those with net assets worth more than $50 million (it says the UK has 43 dollar billionaires, 84 people worth between $500m and $1bn, 1,454 worth between $100m and $500m and 3,112 with assets worth between $50m and $100m). Only the US and Japan have more of the super-rich among their residents.

The uneven distribution of rising wealth is reflected in significant concentration of ownership. So just 10% of British adults have 48% of all the wealth in Britain, and almost 70% is in the hands of just one in five adults. As for the bottom 30%, they have more debts than assets: they have negative wealth, in the jargon. There are serious levels of asset inequality in Britain – although, and this is not really a comfort, wealth inequality is significantly more extreme in the US, where the top 1% control 35.5% of all wealth.

When interest rates are cut, and economic activity is increased, everyone benefits to an extent – as employment and wages rise. But older people, with assets, benefit most.

---

60 'Global Wealth Report 2016', Credit Suisse Research Institute, November 2016.

And since they are concentrated in London and the South-East, the wealth gap between old and young is overlaid with the wealth gap between North and South. Relying on the Bank of England to save us increases the strain on the idea that we are one nation.

In fact, the Bank of England calculates that between 2006–8 and 2012–14, the change in the net wealth of a typical person in the North-East and Midlands – already among the poorer parts of the UK – was negative, whereas in London the rise was a stonking 50%. The Bank's chief economist Andy Haldane acknowledged in a speech[61] that although there was no evidence that the era of almost free money had worsened income inequalities between North and South, which none-theless remained as wide as ever, 'there is some evidence of the higher-wealth regions benefitting more than the lower-wealth regions over the period since the crisis.' Which is as close as you will get to a Bank official saying that monetary stimulus generates unfair consequences.

As for the intergenerational divide, because of the rise in house prices, which has made ownership of a house unafford-able for most young people and has driven them to rent, those born in the 1980s are spending more than a fifth of their income on housing – whereas at a comparable age, those born in the 1940s spent just 10% of what they earned on housing. And, according to the Institute for Fiscal Studies, only about 40% of those in their thirties today own their homes, which is 50% less than pretty much all other post-war generations when they were the same age. Today's young people are find-ing it as hard to get on the housing ladder as young people in

61 Andrew G. Haldane, 'One car, two car, red car, blue car', speech at the Materials Processing Institute, Redcar, December 2016.

the 1930s.[62] In other words, we have to go back to the Great Depression to find young people so challenged when it comes to buying a house and accumulating wealth.

There is something seriously wrong with both the structure of our economy – wealth concentrated in too few hands and disproportionately in property, rather than in employment-creating businesses – and with the tools we have to manage the economy, as they exacerbate the unfairnesses, the lack of balance.

With public services creaking, with young people struggling to find secure employment or affordable places to live, it was surely inevitable that a politician consciously and conspicuously distancing himself from the economics of George Osborne and Gordon Brown would attract support. Jeremy Corbyn's surge in the election reflected legitimate disillusionment with the status quo. But having come so close to winning, the question now is whether this was an anomaly, a freak – or whether he is on the cusp of rewriting in a credible way the rules of how the economy and state in this country are managed. Why Corbyn did so well, and whether he can now win, is the question for Britain.

---

62 Jonathan Cribb, Andrew Hood & Robert Joyce, 'The economic circumstances of different generations', Institute for Fiscal Studies, 2016.

CHAPTER 9

NOT THE MESSIAH, BUT NOT A VERY NAUGHTY BOY

Jeremy Corbyn is not prime minister and did not win the last general election. But it is understandable that his fans have been celebrating as though he did, because the contest took him to within a whisker of forming a government. He was supposed to be the hapless unreconstructed leftie who would lead his party to oblivion. But it was Theresa May who was on the verge of quitting during the three tense post-election days of 9–11 June 2017, after the debacle of the election she did not have to hold.

If David Davis, other senior ministers and Graham Brady, the senior backbencher as chairman of the Tories' 1922 Committee, had not persuaded her to stay on, Corbyn might well now be tending a vegetable patch in the Downing Street garden, in between deciding who to tax more and which businesses to nationalise – because constitutionally and presentationally, it would have been hard for a leaderless and rudderless Conservative Party to prevent Labour having a go at making a governing pact with the other minority parties.

May remains in office because her MPs are acutely aware that her resignation would be, for them, a collective suicide pact. They know their supporters are desperate for at least a few months of stability. So she will stay for precisely as long as it takes them to coalesce around a credible replacement, who is almost certainly someone not among the usual suspects or in her Cabinet, so neither Davis nor Boris Johnson. Her tenure, which could conceivably run to 2019, is more conditional than for any modern premier, and in that sense she is the weakest PM for decades.

Goodness, how different it all was on that sunny morning of 18 April, when she announced her decision to go to the country on 8 June 2017. Then she looked armour-plated, unvanquishable, as she declaimed the need for a personal mandate from the people for her vision of how to take the UK out of the EU – to neutralise what she called the 'game playing' of Labour, the Liberal Democrats and the Scottish National Party. May said:

> Division in Westminster will risk our ability to make a success of Brexit, and it will cause damaging uncertainty and instability to the country. The decision facing the country will be all about leadership. It will be a choice between strong and stable leadership in the national interest, with me as your prime minister, or a weak and unstable coalition government, led by Jeremy Corbyn . . . Every vote for the Conservatives will make me stronger when I negotiate for Britain with the prime ministers, presidents and chancellors of the European Union . . . It was with reluctance that I decided the country needs this election, but it is with strong conviction that I say it is necessary to secure the strong and stable leadership the country needs to see us through Brexit and beyond.

This was a ballsy decision, probably the ballsiest of the career of this unusually patient and cautious politician. One reason it was difficult to do is that she had consistently said since becoming prime minister the previous summer, both in her own voice and through spokesmen, that she would not call a snap election. Her explanations for eschewing going earlier than 2020 had been clear and compelling. So in July 2016, only a few days before her coronation as party leader, I put it to her (on *Peston on Sunday*) that surely she needed a mandate from the people, and that to be a strong PM she needed to win an election.

She could not have been clearer in disagreeing: 'No, if we just look at this, the Conservative Party was elected into government with a mandate on the basis of our manifesto only a year ago . . . I think it's important for us to continue to deliver on the manifesto on which we were elected. There's another factor for me in terms of a potential general election, an early general election. We have got this huge issue of nego- tiating the Brexit [deal], we've got the concerns about stability and the economy and the future of the UK, and I think if we were to have an early general election, it would just introduce another destabilising factor. I don't think that would be good for the economy, and I don't think it would be good for people and their jobs.'

Let us park the inevitable post hoc reflection that her judge- ment back then was spot on. The relevant point is that in changing her mind, she would be accused of going back on her promise – and that was dangerous for a politician whose supreme differentiating quality was that supposedly she was not like the other shallow, opportunistic mob who had been running the UK for almost twenty years, the Camerons and Blairs; she told it straight, she only did what she said, she kept her word.

So why did she go against her own cautious instincts and her cherished image as the honest politician in a world of crooks? Well, her personal popularity was almost off the charts for a serving PM. And her party was – as a result – riding high in the polls. And by the way, the Tory superiority was real, not the flakiness of surveys based on unreliable methodologies: the comprehensive British Election Study of 30,000 people showed the Conservatives with a lead of 41% to 27% in late April and early May.[63] This margin of advantage would have been irresistible to any normal politician. Indeed, one of Cameron's closest and most influential allies said to me: 'If we'd still been in Number 10 and faced Corbyn, of course we would have found a way to go to the country; it was too good an opportunity to miss.'

The consensus within the media and the entire political establishment, including most of his own backbench MPs, was that Corbyn was utterly hopeless, and was someone for whom no more than a small minority of blinkered or feckless people could possibly vote. Remember that only a few weeks earlier, on 23 February, the Tories had taken a seat, Copeland in Cumbria, held by Labour consistently since 1935 (either as Copeland or in its previous form as Whitehaven). This was the first gain by a governing party since 1982, the heyday of Margaret Thatcher and one of the post-war nadirs of Labour. There was a credible case that this was the most important gain for a governing party in a by-election since the late nineteenth century. May seemed invincible, Corbyn hapless and hopeless.

So May's two most trusted advisers, Nick Timothy and Fiona Hill, her joint chiefs of staff, advised her that calling an

---

63 Ed Fieldhouse & Chris Prosser, 'The Brexit Election? The 2017 General Election in ten charts', British Election Study, August 2017.

election to be held in June would be a sensible, calculated risk. They did not assume she would win the kind of 100-to 150-seat landslide that some in the media and punditry business breathlessly predicted. But they thought it reasonable to plan for a working majority of eighty or so, a significant increment over the slender and fragile majority of twelve won by David Cameron. Eventually, after much discussion and agonising with her most trusted confidant, her husband Philip, before and during a walking holiday in Wales, May agreed with them.

So, what went wrong? Well, two of their big judgements were correct, but another two went catastrophically wrong. As they hoped and expected, it was a Brexit election – even though there was remarkably little actual debate about Brexit during the election battle. But the most important factor determining how people voted was their attitude to the EU. And those who voted to leave the EU in 2016 then voted overwhelmingly for the Tories. Most importantly, more than half of UKIP's voters in the 2015 election switched to the Tories, with only 18% going to Labour. So as UKIP minus Nigel Farage collapsed, the Conservatives became incontrovertibly the Brexit party, and in the June election more than 60% of their share came from those Leave voters (according to the British Election Study).

The second judgement May got right was that the Tories' share of the vote would increase. It went up from 36.8% in Cameron's 2015 election to what would normally be a very healthy 42.3% – a proportion of the ballot the Tories had not enjoyed since Thatcher was in her pomp in 1983 and 1987. And remember, this 42.3% was greater even than the British Election Study was saying the Tories would win at the start of the campaign.

None of which is to argue that she was right to call the election, or that it wasn't a disaster for her and her party. But in the context of modern politics, it was a very unusual disaster.

So what May, Timothy and Hill called wrong was first that Labour would be seriously damaged if attitudes to Brexit and Europe were the determining factor in how people were to vote, and second that Corbyn would alienate and repulse vast numbers of potential Labour voters, and all but the most hardcore of Labour supporters.

Labour was seen – in spite of a manifesto position that was strikingly similar to the Tories' – as being less hardline about the necessity of a clean break with the EU's single market, and less religiously strict about the imperative of controlling immigration. So in the event, it picked up more than half of all those who voted to Remain, compared to just a quarter who went for the Tories and 15% for the Liberal Democrats. As the British Election Study puts it, Labour was seen, perhaps despite its best endeavours rather than because of them, as the party of 'soft' Brexit, a term that Theresa May loathes.

It was the degree to which Corbyn went from liability to asset that was most extraordinary. At the start of the campaign, May's likeability and competence ratings – the scores given to the leaders in the BES survey – were both about a third higher than his. By polling day, her likeability advantage had become de minimis and was only slender when it came to competence. The survey demonstrates that Corbyn's personal rating soared most among those who were not planning to vote Labour at the start of the campaign and then did vote for the party. In other words, it was his personal performance, rather than the party's policies, that seemed to have turned the tide for the party. Which, frankly, is what few among even his own

MPs had expected to happen. In fact, the greatest fear of May, Hill and Timothy before they pressed the button and announced the election was that somehow Labour would find a way to ditch Corbyn and replace him with an ostensibly slicker candidate early in the campaign.

Here is how Ed Fieldhouse and Chris Prosser of the BES sum up the magnitude of the misjudgement of Corbyn:

> Over the course of the campaign, Corbyn increasingly appealed to voters who had previously been unimpressed, helping them win new support for Labour, dramatically narrowing the gap to the Conservatives. Whilst this was undoubtedly the Brexit election, it was also a tale of two leaders and a campaign that mattered. The Conservative strategy to pin so much on their 'strong and stable' leaders appears to have been a spectacular mistake, which ultimately cost them an overall majority.[64]

Two scenes sum up for me what went wrong for May. One was towards the end of the campaign, at lunchtime on 1 June 2017. I was in a leafy, though baking, courtyard of a leisure centre in Pitsea, Essex, with my TV crew from ITV News and Corbyn. An opinion poll from YouGov had just indicated something quite extraordinary, which is that there could be a hung parliament, that the Tories could actually lose their narrow majority in the House of Commons. I did my duty as ITV's political editor and tried to pin down Labour's leader on where he actually stands on the biggest question of the age, namely how the UK should quit the European Union, and whether Labour was really committed to taking Britain out of

---

64 ibid.

the EU's single market and customs union, the institutional arrangements that provide frictionless, costless trade with the EU for British businesses.

Corbyn gave his stock evasive answer, which is that Labour wanted to retain the benefits of single-market membership after leaving the single market – an aspiration to have his cake and eat it grounded not in what might be realistically achieved from Brexit talks, but in not wishing to shatter the coalition of Brexiteers and Remainers who seemed to be supporting him. He was, and not for the first or last time, doing what Labour under Blair did routinely, and Corbyn's Labour was supposed to have rejected. He was facing in contradictory directions.

So I took a different tack, and asked him whether he was personally prepared for the madness and pressures of being prime minister, should it come to that. This time he surprised me. I had assumed he would swerve away from any suggestion that he expected to be PM, that he was in any way taking the votes of British people for granted. But instead he said he was 'ready for it' and took a swipe at critics who argued he would never get this close to 10 Downing Street. 'Look, never underestimate anybody,' he said.

But at the age of sixty-eight, did he have the energy and stamina? Yes, he replied, because he never drinks and leads a healthy life: 'I have a bowl of porridge in the morning and everybody should do that.' And what about his adored allotment, where he grows vegetables? Would he give that up if he became prime minister? 'Why would I give up my allotment? Listen, I think there is a need for everyone in life to balance what they do. However stressful and important their job is, it is important to do other things as well. I enjoy that ... And actually you do your job better if you give yourself time to collect your thoughts and do something else.'

At the time, the demands of being prime minister had rarely seemed greater: not only was there Brexit to steer in the most complex negotiations for any British government since 1945, but there had been two appalling terrorist attacks, at the Manchester Arena and in London's Borough Market, only days earlier. I assumed Corbyn would be savaged for not saying that he would be at the service of the nation every waking hour, rather than admitting that he would be tending his cabbages. But even the newspapers who loathe him, the *Daily Mail, Sun* and *Telegraph*, held back from poking fun or having a pop. And the reason, I think, is that he was being honest, relaxed and charming – in an era when most politicians come across as calculating and uptight (the generally hostile press had also been painting him as the dangerous friend of IRA and Islamic terrorists, and the image of him with a spade and watering can might have been too dissonant).

Corbyn is certainly not the messiah: there is plenty of evidence that he lacks the skills to manage the big and complex organisation that is government, given his struggle to unite even his own party. There are valid concerns he has been too soft on anti-semitism within Labour. And his reactions to human-rights abuses in states he regards as friends, such as Venezuela, look like appeasement. He is vulnerable to being seen by the likes of Putin as 'a useful idiot'. But whatever anyone thinks of his policies or leadership ability, he has an important virtue that few in public life seem to possess: he seems comfortable in his own skin. And Theresa May does not.

The private Theresa May, the one I have caught glimpses of when the cameras are switched off, seems almost as relaxed as Corbyn; she is more rounded, interesting and even fun than her painfully stiff public persona. Her preferred method of communication when the world watches is to adopt a catch-phrase – 'Now is not the time' for a Scottish referendum, 'Strong and stable' for how she sees herself as PM, 'Brexit means Brexit' for almost any situation – which she then uses as a bludgeon to prevent an interviewer or interrogator extracting information or opinions she wishes to keep stashed in her vault. She is desperately hard work for a journalist. She is evasiveness embodied; an anachronism in our social media age that puts such a high value on authenticity, or at least the appearance of authenticity.

So May is an extraordinary and unique politician. She has risen right to the top, despite apparently detesting the most important duty of any public figure, that of talking to people she does not know.

The second scene that captures May's electoral reversal was on the Virgin train to Leeds on the morning of 18 May. It contained most of the Cabinet, who had been summoned to flank the prime minister for the launch in Halifax of the party's new programme for government. Boris Johnson, the foreign secretary, strode down the aisle and summed up how he and his fellow ministers had been completely marginalised during the four weeks that had already gone by of the campaign: 'Has anyone actually seen the fucking manifesto?' he boomed. The answer was a resounding 'no'.

The only people who had the whole book were the hard-core of May's team: Nick Timothy, Fiona Hill, Lynton Crosby – the legendary Australian campaign guru who had worked for Johnson on his battles to become London mayor and for David Cameron on the 2015 election – and the cabinet office minister Ben Gummer, who pulled it together under Timothy's guidance. A senior minister told me: 'We had been sent the bits that related directly to our own areas, but none of us had seen the whole thing.' Little wonder that at midday, when May launched the manifesto in a converted industrial building in a town that symbolised the glory days of Britain's Victorian industrial revolution, May's ministers looked bashed up and bewildered. They were there as cheerleaders for policies that were almost as mysterious to them as to the rest of the world.

For what it's worth, I take the view that there is a decent argument in the manifesto, which is the one that Theresa May foreshadowed in her address to the nation from outside 10 Downing Street on becoming prime minister on 13 July 2016. This was when she said that her primary aims were to help those on lower incomes and to build a country that 'works for everyone' (one of the many Mayist aphorisms from her little blue book). In Timothy's more intellectual version, it was a rejection of 'pure social and economic liberalism'. And that is what he tried to develop in a manifesto that 'rejected "untrammelled free markets" and "selfish individualism", and declared that "our responsibility to one another is greater than the rights we hold as individuals".'[65]

There is a good deal of value in the slim, blue paperback that is the manifesto – such as unspecified protections for workers on the shortest, most insecure contracts, the appointment to each company board of someone who would represent employees' interests, much more investment in skills, transport and digital infrastructure, new technical qualifications called T-Levels for sixteen- to eighteen-year-olds, greater protections for the mentally ill in the workplace, a crackdown on the disproportionate use of force against black, Asian and other ethnic minority people in prisons and mental

---

65 Nick Timothy, 'Where we went wrong', *Spectator*, 17 June 2017.

health facilities, and a toughening and consolidation of the law on domestic abuse so that justice is more frequently served on those who commit it.

But while laudable in intent, none of those initiatives is populist, or even desperately popular. They did nothing to dilute the overall tone of the manifesto as about struggle and sacrifice. The very first words from the prime minister inside its sombre blue cover were: 'The next five years are the most challenging that Britain has faced in my lifetime.' And then the body of the Tory programme opened with: 'FIVE GIANT CHALLENGES'.

Now these challenges were all real enough: strengthening the economy, negotiating an orderly Brexit, healing Britain's yawning and painful social divisions, coping with the ageing of the population, harnessing the benefits and protecting against the real harm from the digital and robot revolution. Intellectually this was robust. Presentationally, it was a disaster, because Britain had already been living through a decade of challenges met with very personal sacrifices by millions of us, in the form of falling wages and the squeeze on public services. May's little blue book sounded like years more of collective belt-tightening – a message very hard to sell, when those at the apex of the system were patently making big money and doing very well indeed.

By contrast, Labour's manifesto was friendlier, chattier, less formal, more positive. Under the cover-page slogan 'For the many, not the few' – which was so much more welcoming than the Tories' almost Chinese-style militaristic 'Forward, Together' – it began with Corbyn saying that when he goes round Britain, 'it's a reminder that our country is a place of dynamic, generous and creative people with massive potential.' Corbyn started with a group hug, whereas May began with an instruction that we all had to roll our sleeves up and toil together.

And then Corbyn moved on to a description of what needed to be fixed, which described the daily reality for millions of families, rather than being couched – as Timothy had done – in respect of more general (though powerful) economic and social trends. Corbyn wrote: 'Faced with falling living standards, growing job insecurity and shrinking public services, people are under increasing strain. Young people are held back by debt and the cost of housing. Whole families are being held back from the life they have worked towards.'

The nutshell of the two manifestos would have been that while the Tory manifesto had a clear understanding of the problems faced by Britain, Labour had a much better understanding of British people. And this was a moment when Britons wanted to be understood.

Now I recognise and have sympathy with Timothy's frustration that his coherence was denigrated as dour, even – by the former Tory chancellor George Osborne – as the worst manifesto he could remember in history. And I felt Timothy's pain when he wrote, 'One of the criticisms is that, instead of offering voters giveaways and bribes, we spelt out where cuts would fall. While I accept that the manifesto might have been too ambitious, I worry that the implication of this argument is that politicians should not be straight with the electorate.'

But he was naive to think that there would not be damage to May if the only eye-catching new policies were those implying there would be considerable pain for vulnerable voters: namely the plans to means test the fuel allowance – the energy subsidy – that pensioners receive, and the proposal that all old people should pay something towards the costs of their care when infirm, up to the point that the value of their respective assets, which is normally their homes, had been depleted to a maximum of £100,000.

Timothy has since made two defences, first that it is unfair to tax poorer, younger people to pay for the social care of older people with assets, and often substantial assets; and second that the idea of using the inflated prices of older people's houses to finance care was not exclusively his, but had been worked up over many months by politically neutral civil servants (as I understand it, the plan was especially championed by the Cabinet Secretary, Sir Jeremy Heywood).

As it happens Timothy is right, that expecting the impoverished young to subsidise their property-rich elders is unjust. But it is odd that neither he nor May worked out that in the heat of an election, the policy would not be seen as they saw it – namely as an example of their sense of social justice. Instead it would be viewed through the prism of austerity, as a typically cruel Tory raid on life savings accumulated by hard-working people – and a raid whose magnitude would be determined in the cruellest way, by the lottery of whether an older person succumbed to dementia early in retirement and would therefore be faced with a humongous care bill. Hill and Crosby tried to warn them off this act of self-harm, to no avail.

What senior Labour strategists close to Corbyn recognised, almost immediately, was that even many younger people would hate what came to be known as the 'dementia tax'. Because in a world where the young could not afford to get on the housing ladder, their only hope of ever owning a home was to inherit the family property and convert it into a decent wodge of cash after their parents popped their clogs. Meanwhile parents saw it as shockingly cruel to undermine perhaps the most important feat of their lives, namely generating some wealth to pass on to the next generation.

As for the means testing of the winter fuel allowance, this wreaked havoc on May's hopes of winning Brexit-supporting Labour constituencies in the North-East and North-West. A number of northern Labour MPs told me that – after the winter-fuel announcement – wavering supporters returned to the fold to an extent they had never expected. 'There was a sense that this showed the heartless Tory party in its true colours,' said one. And the anger in the North was intensified after the astute leader of the Scottish Tories, Ruth Davidson, announced that there would be no such means testing north of the border. 'My constituents were outraged,' said one Northumberland MP. 'They all said that it's just as cold here as in Scotland, so why should we get less to heat our homes than the Scots.'

The Tory manifesto was supposed to be the written embodiment of May: sensible, serious and solid, not making promises she could not keep. But it was also too much like her in ways that weakened her cause. It was tremendously vague in parts, a bit dull and too worthy. It was the kind of agenda to change Britain of someone whose fear of exposing herself prompted the implausible claim that her naughtiest transgression was failing to ask the farmer before running through a wheat field. Her caution creates the impression that much darker thoughts and secrets are hidden.

By contrast, Labour's manifesto let it all hang out, just like its leader. What expensive goodies wasn't it promising us? There was a £49 billion increase in day-to-day spending on public services and welfare, including a £4bn softening of the Tories' planned £13bn of welfare cuts (the least generous of Corbyn's pledges), £5.3bn for early years education and care, £5.6bn for health, £6.3bn for schools and a whopping £11.2bn for university students, including the abolition of the fees they pay. Then there was a £250bn 'National Transformation Fund', for investment in housing, science, transport, communications, energy and so on. Oh, and for good measure the Royal Mail, railways and energy would be taken back into public ownership (although not in one big bang of nationalisation, but gradually).

Now because John McDonnell, the shadow chancellor, still believes that British people are signed up to the notion that a party seeking authority to govern has to at least pretend to balance the books, the Labour manifesto included plans to increase taxes by – you guessed it – £49 billion, for companies and those earning more than £80,000 a year. More coherently, he was also proposing to borrow £250bn for investment over ten years in all that infrastructure and so on.

In the round, if the Tories' manifesto was a dour, puritanical vicar, Labour's was a sharp-suited, smooth-talking, flim-flam man. As the impartial and respected Institute for Fiscal Studies pointed out, there was literally zero possibility of Labour raising that £49bn in the way it claimed, because the tax rises would inevitably encourage companies and the rich to change their behaviour and either forgo or hide revenues to reduce their tax bills. The IFS said he would raise £9bn less than he needed.

That said, the £9bn shortfall from what McDonnell wanted to raise was mainly an embarrassment, because of his claim to be aiming to balance the books on current spending. Had he not claimed that, the gap would have taken some explaining, but it did not blow up the entire manifesto in an economic sense. The failure of the taxing and spending numbers to balance should have made Labour more vulnerable politically. And what's literally amazing is that the Tory election campaign was so shambolic that it did not lay a glove on him.

It was also astonishing that the Tories failed to challenge in any serious way Labour's massive bribe to students and potential students, with its proposal to abolish the £9,000 a year of university fees and the associated personal debts. Clearly it was going to persuade hundreds of thousands of our children to vote Labour. They would have to be even dimmer than we think they are to turn down a gift of nine grand a year. But the progressive case for the abolition of these fees is hard to sustain, since it would represent a huge windfall for middle-class families. And there is clear evidence that the expansion of the university sector facilitated by the fees system has led to a significant rise in attendance at universities by those from disadvantaged backgrounds (although our elite institutions are disgracefully still favouring those from privileged families and schools).

What is more, our universities are one of our few world-class exporting industries: they attract students who pay them big fees from all over the world. And there is a danger that if they again became dependent on direct government funding to cover the costs of educating British young people, over time they would be deprived of resources generous enough to remain world class.

Finally, most sensible analysis of what is increasing poverty in Britain and widening the gap between rich and poor points to the Tories' freeze on working-age benefits and cuts to child tax credit, which reduce the incomes of poorer families by more than £8bn a year. The refusal of Labour to promise to cancel these cuts is obviously not something for which Theresa May could have easily castigated Labour, since she would be criticising herself at the same time. But it is slightly odd that Corbyn and his party did not seem to be at all damaged by what would appear to be a serious act of omission for a left-wing party.

Arguably both parties broke the basic rules of manifesto writing, Labour by being too feckless, the Tories by being too proper, and only the Tories paid a price. Perhaps the funniest joke about the campaign, unless you are a Tory, is that Labour convincingly claimed that it was being prudent and the Tories were being dangerously spendthrift, because only Labour had published estimates for what it expected to spend and raise from taxes.

Another joke at the Tories' expense is that they failed to gain any benefit when Labour's entire manifesto was leaked, something that has never happened in the history of British elections and was initially seen as proof that Labour's fighting machine was in chaos. Most of the press described the revelations of the nationalisation, spending and taxing plans as terrifying, which was probably the moment when newspapers showed most graphically how out of touch they were with a public so fed up with austerity.

In practice, the leak gave Labour front-page news for days longer than it expected for highly popular promises to give more resources to schools, parents of young children and hospitals. Even its plans to take into public ownership hated railways and energy companies appealed to millions of voters. And the incident showed how disconnected May was from reality. There was ample time between the leak and the finalisation of her manifesto for her to alter her proposals for public services to make them seem, well, a bit more generous. Instead she stuck rigidly to a policy of no giveaways – perhaps an honest approach, but one which failed to read the mood of the people.

Among the paradoxes was that May called the election, but Labour was at least as well prepared for it, perhaps better prepared. How could this have happened? One of the reasons is that May was not minded to go for it till a few weeks before she pressed the button. So there was a limit to how much preparatory work she could actually do, especially if she did not want it to leak.

By contrast, Labour officials always thought it probable that at some early juncture May would try to convert her lead in the opinion polls into more seats in the Commons. It was on constant election alert, and paradoxically it had a head start on pulling together policies that could form a manifesto, which was drafted from submissions by Andrew Fisher, a former trade union official in Corbyn's team (who had been temporarily suspended from the party in November 2015 for disloyalty to it, though not to Corbyn).

During the election battle itself, Corbyn and Labour had more time to devote to making sure they were sending out the right messages in the right way at the right time. The handicap for May was that she was still prime minister, still responsible for making the unavoidable decisions that are necessary in that role. Which is true, of course, for all prime ministers when they go to the country – and the disadvantage of being distracted by government work is normally offset by the campaigning advantage of simply looking experienced, prime ministerial and reassuring to the public.

But this time it was different, because of the two terrible terrorist attacks at Manchester Arena and at London Bridge. There were several days when May had to focus almost exclusively on national security. Which meant she had less time and intellectual capacity to take stock of why Corbyn and Labour were gaining so much momentum, and work out a way of dealing with it. She probably hoped that voters would reward her for being the person dedicating herself to keeping them safe from future atrocities. And that hope may well have been reinforced by the way much of the Tory press continued to paint Corbyn as untrustworthily friendly with those connected to terrorist groups.

But the problem for May and the Tories was that the more ferocious and personal they were perceived to be in their charge that Corbyn was unfit to lead and protect the country, the more they reinforced the idea – especially among younger voters – that they lacked any kind of positive plan for Britain. If voters wanted to talk about schools crying out for more resources, for example – which they did after thousands of head teachers wrote to parents warning of the impact of funding cuts – they were still going to want answers, even if they were in shock after the atrocities. Corbyn also made the brave but inspired decision to challenge the Tories on what would normally have been seen as their home turf, that of security, law and order, by attacking them for cutting police numbers and funding.

British people are stubborn and resilient in the face of attacks perceived to be on our democracy and way of life. And they won't be bullied or shamed into changing their behaviour by murderous assaults. Those planning to vote to leave the EU were not put off – they were not persuaded they were on the wrong side of the argument – after Thomas Mair shouted 'Britain First' when killing the Labour MP Jo Cox. Voters rightly rejected the notion there was any connection between his evil and their views on the EU. Similarly, many would have felt it was in some way a victory for the terrorists if they switched their vote because of the attacks linked to so-called Islamic State – and they were not going to do that.

What, if anything, could the Tories have done differently? One compelling question is whether Theresa May could, in the heat of battle, have been anyone but the 'Maybot' – as the journalist John Crace resonantly styled her difficulty with, or distaste for, engaging in an approachable and personal way when being interviewed by journalists, or wooing voters on the stump. Her insistence on resorting to the catchphrase of the moment – 'strong and stable, in the national interest' and so on – when interviewed or on the stump ultimately alienated not just the press. She came across as too limited and stiff, where Corbyn seemed friendly and flexible.

Possibly her aloofness would have mattered less if she had lived up to her self-claimed 'strong and stable' image. But when she performed the first ever U-turn during an election campaign on a manifesto pledge, announcing that there would be a cap as well as a floor on how much older people would be forced to pay for their social care, to make it clear that what people would have to pay if they were diagnosed with dementia would not be unlimited, she seemed anything but strong or stable (her tetchy and implausible denial that this was a U-turn did her no favours, either). In fact – and it is difficult to recover from such an image reversal – she became too much of a national joke.

What is incongruous is that those potential Tory voters – who were no longer quite so confident in her and her presidential campaign as they had been – did not transfer their allegiance in any great numbers to the parties nearest to hers politically, UKIP to the right and the Lib Dems to the left. What UKIP and the Lib Dems had in common is that they were led by individuals, Paul Nuttall and Tim Farron, who were regarded as less plausible even than she was becoming.

She is not the first politician to be resolute and clear headed on most matters other than how to realise her own ambitions. My unprovable hypothesis is that her head was for the snap election, but not her heart – that she never quite convinced herself she wasn't doing a bad thing by going back on her word not to call an election (a somewhat worse sin than running through a field of wheat without permission). What is profoundly unclear is whether the shock and humiliation of defeat can persuade her today that she has nothing left to lose, and therefore she can be more herself when engaging with the British public, which would mean taking the risk of allowing people to see her real limitations, not the phoney traits she puts on, and trusting them not to judge her too harshly.

The lesson of Corbyn is that virtues can be made of weaknesses. His consistent and stubborn refusal to change his personal opinions to match his party's official positions on renewing Britain's nuclear weapons capability or on limiting immigration – as just two examples – would conventionally be seen as a political disaster. But growing numbers of voters have seen it as a token of his honesty, a refusal to lie about his convictions. And they have probably been reassured, too, that Labour's party apparatus seems to have reined him in, so that his opposition to all nuclear weapons, for instance, has not become official policy.

It is certainly a novel kind of leadership when a leader disagrees with his own party. But it may be a model for an age when many of us are disillusioned with the slick spin of the Blairs and Camerons. What was communicated when Jeremy Paxman tried to humiliate Corbyn in a Channel 4 and Sky interview for disagreeing with important parts of Labour's manifesto was that the manifesto took precedence – and that did Corbyn a favour.

May's biggest mistake was not to take more seriously her own articulated reasons for going to the country. She said she wanted her position on Brexit endorsed. And then she failed to set the terms of debate in the election as being about the way we leave the EU. What is striking is that in the end, as I've pointed out, people's primary reason for voting one way or the other was because of their views on the EU – with Leave voters largely backing her, and those who wanted to remain going with Corbyn. Her error was to allow this choice for voters to be so black and white, so binary. She was so obsessed with killing UKIP that she never challenged the perception of herself as Farage in kitten heels. She should have worked much harder to persuade not merely those who were ardent Leave supporters to back her, but also those who voted to stay in the EU but now see exit as inevitable – and therefore want the best deal for Britain.

There was an opportunity to unite the nation around a shared vision for Brexit. This could have involved a much more nuanced and sensitive account of how immigration, when controlled in the right way, can enhance the living standards of almost everyone. It would have been a positive case for the kind of immigration that meets the country's very real needs for skills of all levels. Instead, she repeated a commitment to reduce net annual immigration to the tens of thousands, from the current hundreds of thousands, which sent a message to voters and to EU leaders that she would remain wedded to what they think of as a brutal rupture from the single market and customs union, at the possible cost of an impoverishing fall in trade and investment.

Where May could have formed a coalition of hope around her supposedly superior negotiating skills, she re-polarised views on Brexit. In a sense, the referendum campaign was run a second time – and it is not a desperate surprise that the result, a margin of victory of just over two percentage points for the Tories, was not a million miles from Leave's margin of victory.

May's other mistake – and that of her team of Hill, Timothy and Crosby – was not to learn the big lessons of Dominic Cummings' successful Vote Leave campaign: that obtaining intelligence from data analytics on how identifiable voters are likely to vote is the bedrock of everything; that targeting these voters with resonant and relevant messages is vital; and perhaps more important than anything, that hope massively trumps fear after our decade of belt-tightening gloom. The spurious £350 million for the NHS was so much more effective than Osborne's warning of economic armageddon. In May's election, Labour's 'For the Many' slogan was cheery, the Tories' 'Forward, Together' daunting and scary.

What is hideous for May is that her election achieved precisely the opposite of what she wanted, even though she managed to win more votes for her party than Tony Blair ever achieved for Labour (as Nick Timothy likes to point out, obvs).

Not only has she lost her majority in parliament, and made her ability to get legislation through parliament embarrassingly dependent on the support of ten Democratic Unionist MPs from Northern Ireland, whose limited and narrowly prescribed backing through a 'confidence and supply' arrangement was bought with promised investment of £1.5bn in the province. Which means her ability to pass any laws, let alone the hugely contentious laws necessary for Brexit, has been massively constrained and reduced.

But she has also legitimised Labour's opposition to her on Brexit, which we saw first as Labour's different and more emollient approach to negotiating a trade deal with the EU, including a demand that the UK remains inside the single market and the customs union during a transition to full exit of up to four years. May responded on 22 September 2017 by announcing in Florence of all places that she too would want a transition, of around two years, to prepare the UK for the rigours of life as a more independent state. Given that so much of Labour's support is from those who regret Brexit, Corbyn is coming under increasing pressure – perhaps irresistible pressure – to shift towards a promise to emulate Norway and stay in the single market permanently. That could eventually turn into a change of heart about whether we should be leaving the EU at all, though Corbyn might prefer to bite off his tongue than admit as much.

I am not saying that Labour will demand another referendum. I am arguing that May's election has turned the probability of the UK staying in the EU after all from zero to unlikely-but-not-impossible. And in respect of the backdrop for however long she remains as PM, that is a disaster. Because it means all the old EU battles will be fought again and again – especially in her own party, with its terrible vulnerability to self-harming civil war over our relationship with Europe.

The looming disaster for the Tories is that the penny is dropping for Corbyn and Labour that the reason the UK has returned to the kind of two-party politics we haven't seen here since the 1970s – the main reason why UKIP was almost eliminated as an electoral force, and why the Lib Dem and SNP vote shares both fell – is absolutely not that the country decided he is the messiah and not a naughty boy after all, even though voters like him much more than they did. It is that around half the population do not want either May's version of Brexit, which they fear will be too brutal, or any Brexit at all. They expect Labour to be their champion.

If Labour fails them, they will find themselves as far from power as they have ever been. As for Corbyn, having against all his own hopes and expectations over fifty years as a left-wing political activist found himself within a whisker of becoming prime minister, he will not stand in the way of Labour becoming the party of the 48% – even if he continues to make it clear that, in a personal sense, he is not completely comfortable with that.

CHAPTER 10
WE ARE TERMINATED

The question of whether technology is our slave or master has haunted us through history, which is why *Frankenstein* and *Terminator* resonate for every generation. The conventional view is that technology always makes us better off, because during the past 300 years of industrialisation, in what are normally regarded as the three industrial revolutions – the steam age at the turn of the late eighteenth and early nineteenth centuries, mass industrialisation of a century later and the IT era of the late twentieth century – technological shifts that altered the nature of work have eventually ended up making most of us richer.

But that is to dehumanise the many millions of people robbed of their purpose and livelihoods by invention. There's even a special word for those seen as stupid enough to want to stand in the way of technological modernisation of work, 'Luddites' – a nod to the English artisans around Nottingham in the early nineteenth century, who smashed relatively automated looms and knitting machines in mills that were doing them out of work.

The argument that technological change is always for the best has much in common with the associated one that immigration always makes us richer. It is made by people like me, who are typically winners from immigration and new technologies, rather than those whose livelihoods and security are put in jeopardy. But the Luddites weren't smashing machines as a piece of performance art to highlight the unfairness of nascent capitalism; they were not self-indulgent precursors of the Punk movement. They were struggling people, for whom the giant weaving machines were mechanical monsters that were taking the bread out of their children's mouths. These artisan weavers' intermediate skills became less valuable, thanks to the competition from the giant mills, and their living standards collapsed.

But mainstream economics tells an altogether happier story for other British people, for most British people. The great factory mills drove down the price of cloth and clothing, so the money earned by all workers went further; their real incomes rose. And they then used their spare cash to buy other goods and services, creating additional demand for other stuff, which in turn created new employment. New jobs in new industries were created precisely because the old jobs had been made redundant by the machines. And for economists it is almost an iron law that technological improvement first leads to painful 'displacement' of workers, but then there is 'compensation', as displaced workers end up making the things we didn't even know we wanted or could afford.

The happy ending is that our wages go further, because of the ever-more-efficient interplay between man and machine. And in the cases where machines replace us altogether, we find other productive things to do. Machines are always our slaves – or if we are feeling irrationally sentimental, our partners – but are never our masters.

But at the beginning of each new industrial revolution, the machines look anything but benign to those whose jobs face extinction or radical change. And even if in the past those raging against the machine have been wrong, who is to say that one day the rise of the machines won't end up making most of us – or at least too many of us – redundant? What if James Cameron's *Terminator* is not simply compelling fiction that captures one of our most basic fears, in its account of how the ultimate man-made neural network, Skynet, decides that humans are intrinsically inefficient and tries to phase us out in a war to the death? What if Cameron turns out to be an economic genius, who saw that technological changes that make us richer are the early-years exceptions to the more general law that the ultimate destination of so-called techno-logical progress is to phase out humans?

Here is probably the most important economic and polit-ical question of our age. Are we in a fourth industrial revolution that is somehow fundamentally different from the previous ones? Is this the one in which the machines, in the form of robots and artificial intelligence, Frankenstein's monsters all, really do get the upper hand, forever?

And even if such fears are the typical hysteria in the face of change, even if this industrial revolution ultimately turns out to be as benign as its predecessors, there will inevitably be massive amounts of pain along the way for many millions of people. So the minimum we should do – and we are not currently doing that enough – is ask whether we are preparing ourselves properly for a brave new world. And at a time of such shifts, the most important question is whether the educa-tion provided in our schools is even vaguely relevant for the challenges ahead.

When a cosmologist whose preoccupation is the creation and destruction of universes gets worried, perhaps we should be, too. Stephen Hawking:

The automation of factories has already decimated jobs in traditional manufacturing, and the rise of artificial intelligence is likely to extend this job destruction deep into the middle classes, with only the most caring, creative or supervisory roles remaining. This in turn will accelerate the already widening economic inequality around the world. The internet and the platforms that it makes possible allow very small groups of individuals to make enormous profits while employing very few people. This is inevitable, it is progress, but it is also socially destructive.[66]

If he's right, and he may well be, we need to start working now to tame the inevitable social dislocation – for fear that the rise of populists in our politics will be followed by something much worse.

Having said that – and with the explicit aim of seeking reassurance where I can – every time there is a technological shift, very clever people argue that it is the end of work as we know it. No less a genius than J.M. Keynes argued in 1930 that the working week would shrink to fifteen hours and we would all become civilised folk of leisure. If only. And when I joined the *Financial Times* in the early 1990s, the newspaper was filled with learned articles about how we should all prepare ourselves for new lives away from the shackles of employment, because computers, information technology and robots were all going to liberate us to give up work – well, that was the positive gloss, an alternative to describing us as expensive and redundant – and therefore the challenge was to make sure we found culturally enriching things to do in our days. In

---

66 Stephen Hawking, 'This is the most dangerous time for our planet', *Guardian*, 1 December 2016.

practice, for me – and I assume for you, too – every new tech-nological breakthrough has in fact made my working life busier, and has created new tasks and goals.

As a journalist, the internet speeded up the process of research, but it also massively increased the volume of infor-mation and data available to research. Do I spend less time researching than before the digital age? Well, I spend less time walking to libraries and looking for books and newspaper articles. And investigating a company's accounts or who owns a business is no longer a laborious paper trail. But I use the extra time to explore new digital avenues for facts and infor-mation. And there is a similar story of speed generating more activity in how I liaise with colleagues and contacts at work.

As letters and the telephone have been augmented with internal electronic messaging systems, emails, texts, iMessage, WhatsApp, Telegram, Facebook Messenger and so on, it has become so much quicker and easier than it was to communi-cate. But that just means that if in 1992, when I joined the *FT*, I would typically communicate with twenty people seriously in the course of the day, today I will communicate with 200-plus people – although not all of them in depth. More is obviously 'more', except sometimes not in a qualitative sense.

Finally, the advent of digital has massively increased the amount of work that I expect to do – or am expected by my employers to do – by creating whole new means of distribut-ing my journalism. So in a typical day, along with my television broadcasts (and when I was at the BBC, my radio broadcasts as well), I would expect to write blogs for ITV's website and for my Facebook Live page, I would record little video essays for Facebook and Twitter, I would do live broad-casts via Facebook and Periscope and I would put out maybe twenty-odd comments to those who follow me on Twitter. My output and productivity has increased enormously. But I work longer hours, and those hours are busier than they have ever been. If I make it to the Emirates to watch my beloved and maddening Arsenal, it is a little miracle.

Nor do I think my experience is untypical. That smartphone millions of us have in our pockets is part slave, part master. Although I am not complaining. I am lucky in that I adore what I do for a living, which is not true of everyone. But many of us have learned, through gritted teeth, that technological breakthroughs create work, as much as they displace some traditional jobs.

The scale of displacement since the 1980s caused by computerisation has been dramatic. The percentage of jobs lost or changed by technology is impossible to identify with complete precision, because this has also been the era of maximal globalisation – or the outsourcing of manufacturing, software writing and call-centre jobs to low-wage economies like those of China and India. But research by the US Federal Reserve Bank of St Louis gives us some idea of the extraordinary upheaval there has been in our lives.[67]

The St Louis Fed's economists categorise all work in four broad ways: 'non-routine cognitive', such as that of managers and computer scientists, who use their brains to solve less predictable problems; 'non-routine manual', done by nurses and carers, *inter alia,* who do physical and emotional jobs that again are less predictable; 'routine cognitive', such as bookkeeping, various forms of data processing and administration; and 'routine manual', which includes much of manufacturing and transport.

Even before the advent of machines that can think, learn and adapt, robots and computers have fomented tremendous

---

67 'Job Polarisation', Federal Reserve Bank of St Louis, April 2016.

changes in the nature of jobs available in the US – and by logical extension in Britain and Europe, too – according to this research. Back in 1983, routine manual work accounted for 26% of all US jobs. Thanks to robots on production lines and automated trains, for example, that has fallen to 20%. Equally dramatic has been a drop over this period from 28% to 22% in routine cognitive or brain work, as much admin, data processing and number-crunching has transferred to computers.

Numbers employed in non-routine manual work have risen a bit, from 16% to 17% – partly because as we become older and richer, we need and can afford more nurses, and android nurses aren't the finished article (yet). But the most dramatic change has been in non-routine cognitive work, which employs 40% of the workforce, up from 30%. A massive increase in managerial work, problem solving, all manner of intangible services – including media and journalism, for gawd's sake – are both a cause of and reaction to the soaring numbers in higher education: there are now 20 million at American universities, compared with 2.4 million after the Second World War; in Britain, the comparable number today is 2 million, up from only 130,000 in 1970.

Those who have lost their jobs or suffered severe pay cuts tend to be those who did not experience higher education; they are the semi-skilled, those in the so called intermediate group. We have been living through a hollowing out of the jobs market, with people in the highest-skilled and lowest-skilled categories faring better than workers in the middle.

Trump was right during his election campaign that manufacturing in the US is not the employer it was (hardly the most amazing of insights) – although he was wrong to single out supposedly unfair competition from Mexico and China, rather than the impact of technology, and even wider off the mark to suggest that America as a whole had been made poorer. Apart from anything else, America is still a very large manufacturing nation, although the politics is all about the numbers employed and the quality of jobs.

Research by the Center for Business and Economic Research shows that in the six years after 2007, manufacturing output in the US grew by 2.2% a year, or 17.6% in total, which was mostly driven by investment in labour-saving machinery, such as robots, and improvements in productivity or output per worker.[68] One way of understanding how the new machines displaced workers is its estimate that if US factories were only as productive in 2010 as they had been in 2000, there would have been 21 million Americans employed in manufacturing, when in fact there were just 12 million working in that sector (though it is worth noting that over the longer sweep of history, from 1983 to 2016, the proportion of jobs in routine manual occupations may have fallen, but the absolute numbers of people employed have actually risen, from 26m to 31m).

Manufacturing bosses were not gratuitously and maliciously depriving Americans of decent fulfilling jobs. They were modernising to remain competitive – in the face of intense global competition. And although Trump was right that much of this low-cost competition came from Mexico and China, there is no serious evidence that America and Americans would have become richer if Washington had put up barriers to trade and prevented factories from moving abroad. In fact, the reverse is almost certainly true, because

---

68 Michael J. Hicks & Srikant Devaraj, 'The myth and the reality of manufacturing in America', Center for Business and Economic Research, June 2015 & April 2017.

American consumers would have had to pay much more for manufactured goods. Even so, China's policy of running a huge surplus on its trade was deleterious for the US (and in fact the whole of the rest of the world), because if the Chinese had bought and invested more, there would have been more demand for what America produces and more jobs created there. Trump's critique of China could have been a lot dumber.

By the way, there is evidence that the problem with British manufacturing is not too much automation and too many robots, but too few. Analysis by Georg Graetz and Guy Michaels[69] shows that manufacturing employment fell pretty sharply in most developed countries between 1996 and 2012, but has fallen least where investment in robots has been greatest. That implies that the competitive advantage of using the new technologies outweighs the job displacement. And it is particularly striking that the country where manufacturing employment has shrunk most is the one where robots have been almost the least used, namely the United Kingdom. As for two more fearsome manufacturing economies, Germany and America, Germany installed far more industrial robots than the USA, but endured a 19% fall in manufacturing jobs, far less than America's 33% decline.

Before we look at what the fourth industrial revolution may mean for our way of life in the next twenty years, it is important to understand how these new digital companies are so different from their predecessors in their impact on the distribution of wealth. The kind of new machine age we are living through is creating billionaires at a speed we have never seen before. And that is one reason why in the income and wealth

---

69 George Graetz & Guy Michaels, 'Robots at work', LSE Centre for Economic Performance, March 2015.

league tables, the richest 0.1% and 0.01% are pulling away from us. According to Forbes,[70] the ten wealthiest tech billionaires are:

1. Bill Gates, $86bn, Microsoft, (computer software and hardware).
2. Jeff Bezos, $72.8bn, Amazon.com, (online commerce and tech hardware).
3. Mark Zuckerberg, $56bn, Facebook, (social media).
4. Larry Ellison, $52.2bn, Oracle, (software and cloud technology).
5. Larry Page, $40.7bn, Alphabet [parent company of Google], (internet services, software and hardware).
6. Sergey Brin, $39.8bn, Alphabet, (internet services, software and hardware).
7. Steve Ballmer, $30bn, Microsoft [former chief executive, now owner of the LA Clippers Basketball Team], (computer software and hardware).
8. Jack Ma, $28,3bn, Alibaba, (e-commerce).
9. Ma Huateng, $24.9bn, Tencent, (social networks, internet services, instant messaging and e-commerce).
10. Michael Dell, $20.4bn, Dell Technologies, (computer hardware and software).

And two of the three wealthiest people on the planet are tech billionaires – Gates and Bezos.

Now what is striking is that the oldest of the businesses founded by these tech plutocrats is Microsoft, which was created in 1975. The youngest is Facebook, created just thirteen years ago. Fortunes are being made in the digital world

---

70 Forbes Rich List, 2017.

both faster and in greater numbers than at any time in history. Powerful new dynasties, or philanthropists like Bill Gates with more clout even than Andrew Carnegie, are being born almost at the speed of light.

It is worth thinking for a second why riches for tech superstars are being amassed on such a colossal scale and so rapidly. The important contrast is with the big and patient investment over many decades, associated with the employment of tens of thousands of people on middling salaries, that characterised the wealth and power accumulated by the likes of Henry Ford. It is hard to overstate the significance of the industrial shift here: both in the vastly greater numbers employed by a Ford compared with a Google or Facebook, and the nature of the employment offered. The shift from Ford to Google is in a way the death of the working class. Often these digital businesses spawned their billionaire owners when they employed just a few tens or hundreds of people, and on the back of only a few million dollars of investment.

Lord (Adair) Turner has given a neat illustration of how this happens. He points out that the creation of a network like Facebook, which connects hundreds of millions of people across the world, is the equivalent of magic. Imagine, he says, that you invented a spell like 'abracadabra' – or my personal favourite the magnificent Sooty's catchphrase, 'izzy wizzy, let's get busy' – that allowed people to see and talk to each other all over the world for free. If Sooty could have patented his spell, and could have charged a tiny amount for each time we use it to speak to each other, he would today be the richest little bear in the world.

The point is that the likes of Google, or Uber, or Facebook are exactly like magic in that sense. Having developed their initial software, for a cost usually much smaller than building a Ford plant, each download of that software by you and me is essentially free for them. So even if they charge you and me only a penny for using their service, that is a penny of pure profit. And when you connect the world via this network, those pennies soon turn into billions of dollars or pounds.

So, if you can create a technological network that we all want to use, you are creating what the venture capital industry calls a unicorn, a business worth at least a billion dollars – and probably vastly more – and in the process hugely enriching the creators and those fortunate enough to have backed it early. And, although the most conspicuous of the new plutocrats are the famous founders, there are thousands of others who work with them in various capacities – some on the outside as venture capital providers of finance, some on the inside as assorted executives – who also become rich beyond most of our wildest dreams by clinging to their coat tails.

Is that fair? Life isn't fair, as I fear my mum is still occasionally minded to remind me. But I guess we begrudge these tech entrepreneurs their gazillions less than we resent the riches accumulated by bankers who gambled and lost with taxpayers' money, because at least they have given us services and products that most of us enjoy or use for gain. But the way that so much money accrues to the business founders is not wholly without its problems. The main one is that it confers on them massive, largely unaccountable political power, which they may or may not wish to exercise: the resources to lobby for pet projects, to fund politicians and their campaigns, to buy influence via the media – even to become president of the US. And it cuts them off from the rest of us in a bubble where they are immune to the normal concerns of the rest of us, where they can largely do what they want. Personal wealth on that scale, however generated, is rarely associated with happy, socially cohesive societies.

That said, most of us are less upset at how much relatively poorer we are than Bezos or Zuckerberg and more upset when we feel trapped and unable to improve our own life prospects. And here is where the huge and materially important uncertainties for all of us reside in relation to a fourth industrial revolution. Will it make most of us richer, sooner rather than later – by increasing our productivity and allowing us ultimately to receive the fruits of that increased output? Or will this be a revolution where for years or even decades most of the benefits will accrue to a limited number of business creators, owners and investors, leaving us to muddle through on stagnating wages, or handouts from the state?

Part of the answer rests on which further jobs are most at risk of being eliminated by robots and computer algorithms in the next few years and longer – and what that means for the human skills that will continue to be valuable. A framework for assessing this that I find useful is that of McKinsey, which analysed more than 2,000 work activities in greater than 800 occupations. Using official data, it quantified the time spent on these activities and their susceptibility to automation – and it found that currently proven and demonstrated technologies could automate 45% of the tasks people are remunerated for and also that 60% of all occupations could see 30% or more of their activities automated.[71] Now without wishing to labour the point, what is significant about the McKinsey approach is that it is only looking at the implications of technologies that

71 Michael Chui, James Manyika & Mehdi Miremadi, 'Where machines could replace humans – and where they can't (yet)', *McKinsey Quarterly*, July 2016.

exist and do what they are supposed to do, rather than engaging in more speculative futurology.

McKinsey argues that 78% of all predictable physical work, which in itself represents 18% of all labour in the US economy, can be automated 'by adapting currently demonstrated technology'. That implies there will be another huge wave of automation in manufacturing, food service and accommodation provision. It says 'within manufacturing 90% of what welders, cutters, solderers and braziers do, for example, has the technical potential for automation.' That said, food service and accommodation is even more ripe for humans being replaced by machines.

McKinsey cites Momentum Machine's hamburger-cooking robot, which is said to be able to assemble and cook 360 hamburgers an hour. This is what the San Francisco burger company, which employs roboticists from the electric car company Tesla and even from NASA, says about itself: 'Our first device makes gourmet burgers from scratch with no human interaction. These burgers are fresh-ground and grilled to order and accented by an infinitely personalisable variety of produce, seasonings and sauces. Serving a burger this great at such affordable prices would be impossible without culinary automation.'

So as the burger-bot company implies, the issue is not purely about what robots can do, it is also about what they can do better and cheaper than humans. And that is the source – or perhaps even the infinitely personalisable variety of sauce – of much uncertainty and anxiety.

Other activities with huge residual potential to be automated, even though many of them have already been changed hugely by machines, are data processing and data collection. By contrast, managing people and applying expertise to creative tasks, planning and decision making are still daunting challenges for robots. A bit less daunting for them, but still tricky, are unpredictable physical work and so-called stake-holder interactions (activities like advising people what to wear based on their shape and colouring).

Even so, McKinsey reckons more than half of all activities carried out by retailers – including gathering customer infor-mation, stocking the shelves and sending stuff out – could be automated. But for some time yet we will probably be wary if a robot advises us which foods are most delicious, so robots may take over the kitchen in a high-end restaurant, but may not (for a while) be serving us.

As for the sector least at risk of automation, that is educa-tion, because 'the essence of teaching is deep expertise and complex interaction with people'. Even healthcare is more automatable, with a potential of 36%, McKinsey argues, because it involves fairly predictable physical activities like cooking food and administering non-intravenous medicines. But we are probably not yet ready for the nurse or doctor bot who asks some direct and some subtle questions to elucidate our real state of health or mind – or who fits a cannula.

But it may well be, as Hawking implies, that the limits of what robots could eventually do is limited only by our imagin-ation. Breakthroughs are being achieved all the time with machines that can navigate through complex changing phys-ical environments, such as special delivery bots (I met one in the House of Commons the other day), construction auto-mata or driverless cars. And there is whopping investment by companies in trying to give computers the ability to learn and properly understand natural language. If they succeed, some version of Apple's Siri would then see shop assistants and financial salesmen facing obsolescence and redundancy.

So what scale of potential job losses are we looking at, as

more robots clock in? Well, the Bank of England has adapted a methodology similar to McKinsey's, by Carl Benedikt Frey and Michael Osborne, which assigns probabilities – low, medium and high – to jobs being automated over the next few decades in Britain and America. Like McKinsey, the Bank puts clerical, administrative and production jobs in the high-risk category. And jobs that require considerable non-cognitive human interaction, that involve what is often called emotional intelligence, are classed as least at risk. This is the gloss from the Bank's chief economist, Andy Haldane:

> For an accountant, the probability of vocational extinction is a whopping 95%. For a hairdresser, it is 33%. On these numbers, the accountant's sun has truly set, but the relentless upwards ascent of the hairdresser is set to continue. For economists, like me, the magic number is 15%. At first, I found that number disconcertingly high. But in fact, it puts me in the lower third of 'prone' professions.[72]

If he's right, my job is fairly safe for now (it's OK to share my joy). But according to the Bank, a staggering 15 million British jobs are at risk of automation and 80 million American jobs. To put that into context, that would mean 47% of all those currently in work in the UK could see themselves made redundant by Metal Mickey or Max Headroom.

It will not shock you that this prediction by the Bank is even less reliable than its normal forecasts – that, like most economists', are mainly defined by their unerring inaccuracy. But the Bank is correct about the direction of travel in the labour

---

72 Andrew G. Haldane, 'Labour's Share', speech at the Trades Union Congress, London, November 2015.

market, which means that governments should be agonising at breakfast, lunch and tea over what to do about robots.

The challenge is more acute and urgent precisely because it is the alienation, disillusionment and anger of those on lower pay that has been bossing politics all over the rich West, and putting the establishment on notice that its time in office may be up – and there is a close and toxic correlation between lowness of wages and vulnerability to being automated out of a job. Skilled trades, machine operatives, social and customer service are all at the top end of jobs that robots can do. And in recent years, many in those jobs have felt most at risk of being replaced by cheaper, harder-working immigrants. Would any of us blame them if they took to the street chanting 'Robots go home'? Highly paid bosses, however, not exactly the pin-ups of those who voted for Trump and Brexit, are pretty safe from being made obsolete by technology.

We need to go into this fourth industrial revolution acutely aware of the risks it brings of social strife, and also that it presents us with urgent choices. Our schools are teaching the wrong things, they are creating a generation of young workers vulnerable to being made irrelevant and unnecessary by the machines. Maths, reading and writing are vital for living, but not so much for earning a decent living, because machines can already do all basic information management and processing much faster and more accurately than us. What machines can't do – and quite possibly never will be able to do – is negotiate, build relationships, empathise, instil confidence, win trust, create great art, write moral philosophy, dream, or any of the other emotional and intuitive activities that are central both to highly paid careers and the sheer joy of being alive.

With schools ordered by governments to become sausage factories churning out students with the best exam grades, they do not spend enough time helping young people become more creative, better communicators or adept empathisers. In the UK, the recent remodelling of the system for measuring students' success, back towards exam prowess and away from project work, is especially nuts, because it disproportionately rewards ability to memorise and meet deadlines, and inadequately captures initiative and teamworking.

Exam skills are wonderful if you want to be an old-school newspaper journalist, which by chance was the formative career of the then education secretary, Michael Gove, who abolished project work in academic qualifications for sixteen-year-olds. But not quite everyone can be a hack, and those skills are precious little protection against obsolescence and redundancy for the vast majority of the coming generation in a world of robots.

Then there is the non-trivial question of how to make sure that the rewards of the robot era don't all go to the owners of the robots, rather than being shared with all of us. As I've pointed out, the founders and owners of technology companies are enjoying returns that would make a pharaoh blush. I am not doubting that they are brilliant entrepreneurs. But do they really 'deserve' all those gazillions for writing a marginally superior algorithm? There is often an element of luck about who gets first to market, whose service acquires the greatest acceptance and usage earliest, whose business becomes the monopolistic network.

So maybe it would not be an affront to natural justice, or indeed economic suicide for the developed world, to tax their wealth at a supernormal rate, to fund institutions providing permanent retraining (for example) to the rest of us. The march of capitalist invention would not be halted if the techies contributed a few tens of billion dollars more towards making the society – that gave them their living – more resilient to the economic earthquakes triggered by their inventions. And becoming much more vigilant and active in breaking up the new monopolies as and when they are created, to spur competition and growth, would be a counterweight to the destruction of jobs by technology.

The stability of the West is being shaken by a revolt of people fed up with the longest freeze in living standards in modern recorded history. As and when the robots properly take over, the unfair distribution of earnings would only become worse, because the rewards for capital would be infinitely large, and for labour pitifully small. A world combining little proper work and paltry earnings would be unstable, volatile, unsustainable.

This fourth industrial revolution may be a challenge to everything we know about how best to run the state. Keynes may finally be proved right (he normally is) that leisure is set to become the new norm for us. But if we fail to plan, it could be an impoverished leisure, anaesthetised by the opioids already tearing apart the fabric of depressed, low-income communities in the US. If under-employment becomes the new inescapable norm, welfare dependency – the undermining of incentives to work through excessively generous state handouts – will become not a problem, but an aspiration. One challenge would be to tax the owners of capital and the machines sufficiently to provide a universal basic income set at a high-enough level to guarantee a decent way of life for all. And life would then be about volunteering to make our communities more humane, caring and safer; and the enjoyment of culture. Failure to change our welfare safety net into a satisfying way of life would have only one outcome. We would all become Luddites – and justifiably so.

CHAPTER 11
THIS IS HOW WE FIX THE MESS

There has never been, in my lifetime, a more uncertain time. Or at least not in my conscious life. My mum says that the Cuban Missile Crisis felt as terrifying as the world today. In 1961, during the 'Bay of Pigs' invasion of Cuba by exiles backed by the US, who were trying to topple Castro, she and my dad were living with baby me in California. Dad was enjoying a short transfer from the London School of Economics to the University of California, Berkeley. 'Not quite one year old, you sat in your high chair in front of the TV while I watched as the announcer told us to contact our neighbours, as President Kennedy would be making an important speech,' my mum told me. 'It was all very scary.'

Today's standoff with North Korea, also involving a nuclear threat, may be chillingly analogous – two countries, Trump's America and Kim Jong-un's North Korea, so unable to communicate, so mistrustful of each other. But that is not the only locus of possible or actual conflict with the potential to harm all of us. There is the endemic instability in the Middle East: the power of so-called Islamic State to inspire or create terrorists who commit atrocities in our land and other rich countries; the chaos and wars gripping so much of the region, but notably in Syria and Yemen; and energy-rich Qatar accused and isolated by Saudi Arabia and its allies for allegedly giving succour to terrorism.

There is the perennial tension between Japan and China, especially over their respective territorial claims in the East China and South China seas. The mistrust of each other by their respective peoples, stemming from the mass killings of Chinese by Japan from 1937 to 1945, is the source of chronic instability between the two Asian regional super-powers. With China ruled by its most autocratic leader since Mao, Xi Jinping, the concern is that China could foment conflict with Japan if there were ever signs of unrest at home that he wanted to marginalise and waylay. This one-party state, the exception that prosperity requires democracy, has enriched its people – lifted hundreds of millions out of poverty – like no other country in history. But forty years of supernormal economic growth is slowing down and may judder to a halt. After the West's economies seized up in the 2008 banking crisis, China could no longer rely on us to buy all the stuff it makes. So Beijing re-engineered its economic model to be less dependent on exports and more on debt-fuelled domestic investment, by its State Owned Enterprises, and in every conceivable form of infrastructure and bricks-and-mortar, from roads, railways and airports, to homes and office blocks.

China's indebtedness has expanded too fast and too far. Much will never be repaid, forcing losses on banks and investors. Or to put it another way, China's recent growth has been generated by a debt bubble. And we all know what happens to prosperity when a debt bubble goes pop. So the expectations of tens of millions of Chinese that life can only get better and better may finally be disappointed, which in turn may make them question whether their sacrifice of democratic rights and freedoms we regard as basic is still worth it – even with China's skill in restricting the use of social media.

A lesson in how populist dictators cynically exploit nation-alist sentiment when the economy comes unstuck is Putin's Russia. He is another great fomenter of Western discombobu-lation, at least in part to distract his own people from the country's failure to lessen its dependence on its vast energy resources as the underpinning of living standards. Russia's invasion of Ukraine means the whole of the Baltic region lives under the shadow of Putin's expansionist ambitions. And Russia's engagement in cyberwarfare – hacking emails and websites to destabilise elections in the US and Europe, supposedly crashing parts of Ukraine's powergrid as a test of its ability to disrupt our vital infrastructure – is a threat to the integrity of all our democracies.

And then there is Trump, whose narcissistic impetuousness is testing the checks and balances in the US constitution to their limit. For Trump to be leader of the free world, when there is so much instability elsewhere, is perhaps unfortunate – unless, that is, the reasonable perception that he could do literally anything in a crisis prevents the maddest of the world's potentates from pushing their luck too far.

So we should count our blessings, I think, to have the sane and rational double act of Macron and Merkel in Europe, and their grand design to renew the confidence, strength and wealth-generating mojo of the eurozone and the European Union. But even in their case the risks and the stakes are high. If they fail, there will be a renewed surge in popularity of continent-dividing, right-wing populist demagogues such as the Front National's Marine Le Pen in France.

So the times they are unstable. And I mention this for two reasons. First, a world that is more dangerous than it has been for decades is hardly the optimal time to withdraw from the EU. Brexit would be a disaster for us – and for the rest of Europe – if in the process we distance ourselves from our EU friends and allies in relation to defence and mutual security. A Brexit that were to undermine our diplomatic, military and intelligence ties would be very foolish indeed. Such an estrangement is not inevitable, and it must be pre-empted.

Second, there has rarely been a time when our ability to control our own destinies has been more in jeopardy. Much of this book has been about what has gone wrong within our own borders, and what to do about it. But if a maniac dictator abroad were to lose the plot and unleash fire and brimstone, any plans we might have to make our schools fit for this millennium, for example, would feel less relevant.

There is a fear, of course, that the sheer number and scale of the global threats may be paralysing our leaders from fixing what can be fixed at home. That would be a terrible historic mistake, the harbinger of even more instability and chaos. The rejection by millions of voters of the way we have run this place for decades, the repudiation of liberalism and globalisation, is only a step or so away from a rejection of democracy. Populist proponents of social and economic nationalism are in charge to the west of us, in America, and to the east, in Russia, Poland and Hungary. It does not take a huge imaginative leap to see some of the new populist pretenders and leaders morphing into a Western version of Putin. The richer heart of Europe may not have fallen yet. And the 2017 elections in the Netherlands and France show that internationalist liberals are not down and out. But it was populist social and economic nationalists who secured victory in the UK's vote to leave the EU. And all over Europe the nationalists are regrouping, not surrendering.

It has never in our lifetimes mattered more than to demonstrate that our sui generis democracies can deliver prosperity at home and stability abroad. This generation of anti-extremist politicians has to renew its licence to govern. Our leaders need to remake the case for a market-based economic system, for relatively permeable borders for capital and people, for free expression and the freest market in ideas, for international co-operation. And they will only succeed if they have the confidence to argue what has not been fashionable – that the state must do more to lift up and protect all those but the richest and most privileged.

The priority is to reunite us as a people, to better face the internal and external challenges. So how do we fix this mess? Here are a few ideas. They are not intended to be a comprehensive programme for government. They are riddled with practical flaws. Obvs. But they're intended to spark a conversation, about how we can do things differently and better here. They consciously go with the grain of constrained capitalism, or liberal markets managed for a social purpose.

What concerns me most is how unfit for purpose our schools are. That is nothing to do with the quality of teachers and all to do with the lack of imagination in government about curriculum. Our children are being trained with military dedication to do jobs that robots and algorithms can already do. Obviously, everybody needs to be literate and numerate, simply to get the most out of life. But jobs that rely heavily on literacy, numeracy, processing and analytical skills now require almost no human involvement. Even if lots of those jobs – in administration, manufacturing and assorted services – are still done by humans, they won't be much longer.

Tasks that robots may never be able to do as well as humans are those that require creativity, emotional engagement, intuition. This is the stuff of management, the media, the arts, scientific research, caring, hospitality, even politics – and for a while, the creation of new algorithms and robots, although machine-learning is already empowering the robots to improve their own software.

What is profoundly shocking and harmful is that we have a school system almost entirely focused on compelling children to get the best possible grades in exams that themselves measure a very inadequate set of skills. There is too little focus on, and time for, encouraging creativity, flexible thinking, confidence, intuiting, empathising, the ability both to lead and work in a team, and acquiring the capacity to listen, observe and adapt. It is worse today even than when I was at unremarkable state schools in the 1960s and 1970s.

At least then the teachers really encouraged us to read widely and think independently. What shocked me whenever I spoke with my children's teachers was that they would look at me as though I was mad when I asked what additional books my boys should read. The priority, they said, was for them to take home and memorise worksheets handed out in class, not go on intellectual journeys that might be incompatible with the all-important mark scheme of those ridiculous exams.

This generation of students are being evaluated on the wrong set of criteria, and so are their schools. We need a revolution, in which outcomes are measured much more in respect of whether students have acquired the fundamental skills to thrive in a changing world, to remake themselves as and when they want or employment circumstances demand, to be more self-reliant. It is insane that we have an education system that would have been brilliant fifty years ago, when there were jobs for life in public and private sectors. It is almost useless when

even our biggest employers baulk at the idea that they might
be offering an implicit lifetime contract.

And by the way, in a rational world we would treble the pay
of teachers, because there is literally no economic imperative
greater than making sure the brightest and best are engaged
in preparing the next generation for life and work.

On the subject of schools, they are the best place to tackle
our mental health crisis. Extensive research shows that almost
all mental health problems developed by adults begin
unnoticed by parents and teachers in childhood and teenage
years. A system of sensitive early intervention, in schools,
would vastly improve individual lifetime happiness and would
reduce the cost to the state of an epidemic of breakdowns and
of self-medication through drugs and alcohol.

For what it is worth, I am a believer in the importance of
elite institutions, because it is good not bad to help everyone
make the most of their talents, from sport, to physics, to
pharmacology, to music-making. But they are cancerous – as
they are today – when they become the vehicles for an oligar-
chy of the rich and powerful to maintain their privileges
through the generations, and make it much harder for those
from poorer backgrounds to thrive.

It is little short of scandalous how useless Oxford and
Cambridge are at taking the brightest and best from under-
privileged backgrounds. They need to develop the kind of
close relationships with state schools, especially those with
disproportionate numbers of children from low-income
families, that they have enjoyed with the Etons and
Winchesters for centuries. As for the Etons and Winchesters,
they should be stripped of their charitable status and tax
privileges – and then be told they can earn those privileges
back if they prove beyond doubt that either within their own

walls, or in collaboration with state schools, they are really making a difference to the prospects of disadvantaged students.

Within government, the elite institution is HM Treasury. It raises all the money, holds the purse strings for all departments, often has the first and last word on industrial policy, welfare policy, financial-sector policy and, of course, economic policy. As such it is the great magnet for the brightest and best in the public sector. Which means that it has been consistently arrogant and over-confident. And other departments are starved of talent. The reason there has never been an active industrial policy here since the 1980s – unless you count as an industry policy the Treasury's obsession with privatisation and allowing foreigners to buy any and every possible British company and asset – is because even the phrase 'industrial policy' is heresy in the Treasury codex.

The hugely unbalanced structure of the British economy, its long-term over-reliance on the City and financial services, is the product of Treasury lore. The propensity of the British economy to swing from relatively extreme boom to bust is equally down to the Treasury's obsession with prioritising the control of inflation using the latest fashionable approach to monetary policy, and its rejection of taxing and spending as active levers of employment creation and growth management.

I agree with much of the critique of the Treasury made by the former head of the civil service, Lord Kerslake,[73] although I would go further than him in reforming it and cutting it

---

73 Lord Kerslake, 'Rethinking the Treasury: An independent review of the Treasury to consider how it should work to promote and manage more sustainable growth in a fairer and more equal society', February 2017.

down to size. The Treasury is an elite institution both too big for its boots and too powerful for the country's needs: too closed to counter-arguments on the questions that determine our prosperity. So it is time to do what no prime minister has dared try since Harold Wilson's failed experiment with a department of economic affairs in the 1960s. It is time to break up the Treasury. It should be slimmed down into effectively the finance department of the government, where it would concentrate on raising money as fairly and effectively as possible, assessing the spending needs of individual departments, and evaluating the efficiency and effectiveness of their use of scarce resources.

But policymaking – across the gamut of the economy, welfare and public services – would go to an expanded Cabinet Office, so that the prime minister in proper collaboration with ministers would have the tools to reshape how we generate and share wealth, and direct scarce money to the public services capable of making the greatest positive impact on our lives.

Now an empowered Cabinet Office should make its priority restoring dignity, security and rising living standards for those on average and lower incomes. One priority has to be to equalise the tax treatment of different forms of employment, so that there is no longer the massive tax disincentive for companies to hire people as proper employees. It is mad that national insurance payments for a self-employed person are 9%, compared with 12% for an employee, whose employer also pays 13.8% in NI for him or her. It means that for someone on average UK earnings of around £28,000, the national insurance cost of them being employed is almost £2,600 greater than if they were self-employed. And as Matthew Taylor's review for the government of 'Modern Working

Practices'[74] points out, the tax advantages are even greater for someone who hires themselves out through a company they have set up. This lack of uniformity in tax treatment goes a long way to explain why, when money is tight, and when new so-called platform technologies like Uber and Deliveroo make it easier for people to get work on a sporadic, piecemeal basis, there has been an explosion in the numbers classed as self-employed.

There may be good lifestyle reasons why anyone would prefer to be self-employed. What the tax system should not do, however, is provide employers with huge incentives to force workers to take insecure piece work. It should not favour one employment model over another. This is as wrong as when the tax system favours particular industries – except when there are demonstrable, wider economic benefits of helping particular sectors (which happens only rarely).

One of the most unedifying spectacles before the general election was in March 2017, when right-wing Tory MPs and the right-wing press went ballistic with the chancellor, Philip Hammond, for announcing national insurance for the self-employed would be raised two percentage points to 11% – still below the rate paid by the employed – to raise £2 billion. They were attacking him for reducing by £2bn this de facto subsidy for self-employment, because they feared this would cost them the votes of the owner-operators colloquially known as 'White Van Man' – even though Tories are supposed to believe that resources are allocated best by a marketplace undistorted by arbitrary tax differentials. If Hammond had offered £2bn a year to bail out our ailing steel industry, he

---

74 Matthew Taylor, 'Good work: the Taylor review of modern working practices', July 2017.

would have been accused of mad interventionist socialism. But raising NI for the self-employed was an attack 'on our people', and therefore had to be abandoned. Which it duly was.

What should happen is that there should be a wholesale review of all income and employment taxes – and the tax differences for different forms of employment should be eliminated, in a way that neither raises nor loses money for the Exchequer. So the tax and NI cost of employing someone should be cut, and it should be increased for being self-employed or selling services through a service company. Differential tax and NI costs should not cloud judgements about how we should be employed, which for both employer and employee should be about the degree to which we value certainty or flexibility.

But in this relationship so central to our quality of life, far too much power is with the employer. The rolling back of the ability of trade unions to organise and protest has gone too far. I would agree with Labour's manifesto that all workers should have an enforceable right to trade union representation at work, and that trade unions should have the right of access to workplaces to speak with members and those who might wish to become members.

I would also encourage trade unions, or public-spirited digital developers, to create platforms for workers and the self-employed that would be equivalent to profit-making, gig-economy platforms like Uber and Airbnb. At Walmart in the US, staff who find it difficult to find out their rights from the company now have access to an app, WorkIt, which was created by a group of workers, Organization United for Respect at Walmart. Also in America, coworker.org is an online tool for workers at any business to petition their employer for workplace improvements, such as providing sick leave or improving the food in a canteen.

It is useful, because most bosses are impressed when a demand for change is signed by hundreds or thousands of workers. But plainly it would be more effective if employers were compelled to make the changes when a majority of employees signed the relevant petition. These changes would be restricted to those that are not frivolous, such as a right to convert self-employment status into employment contracts. They would be subject to vetting and approval by a new employee rights watchdog, which I discuss below.

There is also scope for apps to offer many of the services of a traditional trade union, such as instant advice and help when an employer is withholding payment or cancelling at no notice the offer of a shift, or refusing to convert piece work into regular contracted work. It would link the worker to others working for the same platform, employer or industry. And so obviously it could be the digital presence of an existing trade union, rather than a wholly new workers' organisation.

In an ideal world, these apps would be endorsed and monitored by a new employee rights watchdog, equivalent to the Financial Conduct Authority (whose statutory role is to prevent the mis-selling of financial products to consumers, and punish transgressors). There is a palpable unfairness that there is no equivalent watchdog to ensure that employers are in fact paying the National Living Wage, or honouring rights to sick leave, maternity pay and so on.

The watchdog, which could be called the Employer Conduct Authority (ECA), would have as one of its most important functions making sure that companies that pay their workers as though they are self-employed, and therefore deprive them of all the benefits and security of proper employment, are in fact giving those workers the right and power to work precisely when they want.

If the workers really could clock on and off precisely as they choose, without facing punishment, all would be well and good. But if in practice the workers were instructed when to work and for how long, then the ECA would probably rule that the employer should convert them into proper employees, and offer them the rights and benefits of being an employee – from holidays to auto-enrolment in an accredited pension savings scheme. If a company hires its workforce as freelance, self-employed contractors, then it must be clear that those workers are making a clear and explicit lifestyle choice to work when they want, not when the company desires.

If the Ubers, Airbnbs, Deliveroos and others of the new generation of digital platform companies are only about gaming or arbitraging our tax and employment laws, they create no meaningful wealth in the long term, and only serve to undermine the security, earnings and quality of life of workers. If their technology really empowers us to sell our services and goods how we want and when we want, then they really are in the public interest. The ECA would separate the real gig-economy innovators and stars from the phoney, cynical, rapacious tribute bands.

But there is something else it would do, which would be more important: namely giving the most vulnerable workers – migrant workers in textile factories, for example – a champion, somewhere and someone cheap and sympathetic to turn to when they are being paid half the National Living Wage, and lack the confidence and the funds to launch a complaint in an employment tribunal. It was a truly wonderful moment at the end of August 2017 when the Supreme Court ruled as illegal the fees of up to £1,200 for claimants in tribunal cases, which were introduced by Chris Grayling when he was Lord Chancellor in 2013.

These fees were a licence for unscrupulous bosses to ignore the strictures of employment law in relation to their lowest-paid workers, because the cynical employers knew their workers would never have the money to launch a tribunal case against them. The decision of the Supreme Court to abolish the fees was probably the most progressive action taken by the state since Theresa May became prime minister, and it had nothing to do with her! That said, there should be no need to go to court, especially when small claims are involved. Instead there should be a simpler system, of complaining to an ombudsman at the ECA.

What we fundamentally lack, in Britain and all over the West, is a sense of shared purpose in the capitalist pursuit of profit. Too often employees feel exploited even when they are well paid. So what about a rule that said for businesses over a certain size – measured by some combination of number of employees, capital employed and income – there would have to be a distribution of profits to all staff after those profits have breached the minimum necessary for investment by the business from its own funds, and for raising capital from outside sources.

For instance, it might be reasonable to assume for a retailer that a 3% net return on sales is high enough for it to thrive and secure the financial support of banks and investors. There may be a case, therefore, that any profit over and above that threshold should be distributed between employees, shareholders and executives. For the sake of debate, perhaps the distribution should be in the proportions 45%, 45% and 10% (and before you fixate on the equity or iniquity of those numbers, I do not claim any scientific basis for them – they have been chosen merely to spark a conversation).

Mandatory sharing of profit with workers in this way would lessen the perception that all efficiency gains are for the benefit of investors and bosses. It would enhance solidarity in a business and help to restore battered confidence that the economy works for all. Of course, for a business such as a bank, where a return on capital employed is a better measure of success than return on sales, this distribution of profit to staff would be triggered when a minimum return on capital was surpassed.

For the avoidance of doubt, I know there is a risk that many companies would be tempted to increase bosses' pay or other costs to keep profits below the distribution threshold, and also that companies will hate the idea that the state will be keeping tabs on their profits and profitability.

But surely we cannot go on with a wealth-generating system that massively favours the few at the expense of the many.

And as for reversing the toxic long-term trend of workers receiving a falling share of what the economy produces, history shows that reducing the market power of firms works wonders. Governments should be bolder in breaking up domineering companies and blocking mega mergers.

The reason why some employers feel they can get away with treating staff in a high-handed and shoddy way is that – even at a time when the UK unemployment rate has fallen to a level we have not seen for more than forty years – some parts of the country have still not recovered from the 2008 shock. We need to do much more to stimulate the economy outside London and the South-East.

We cannot continue to ignore the massive income, wealth and business-activity gaps between different parts of the UK.

So there is a case for doing something that many conventional economists and government officials will see as heretical and insane, namely differentiating monetary policy on a regional basis. The Bank of England in London would still set its Bank Rate based on UK-wide conditions, and create new money through quantitative easing on the same basis. But a North-East Central Bank, a Scottish Central Bank, a Welsh Central Bank and so on, a system of devolved central banks that would be branches of the Bank of England and would cover the nations and regions, would use Bank Rate as a benchmark and then set their own Regional Bank Rate.

In other words, they would offer a marginally different borrowing rate to commercial banks, perhaps a maximum of 12.5 basis points in either direction (0.125%), on the strict condition that those banks would have to pass that interest-rate difference through to home buyers and businesses in the relevant region. Right now, it might make sense for the funding rate offered by the North-East Central Bank to be a bit lower than the UK's Bank Rate, and the funding rate offered by the London and Home Counties Central Bank to be a bit higher. This would help to correct what we have seen over recent years, which is an uneven and unbalanced economic recovery, with London and the South-East continuing to pull away from the rest of the country.

Central banking purists would argue that this devolved system of setting lending rates depending on regional economic conditions would make it harder for investors to assess monetary conditions in Britain, and could perhaps increase the volatility of sterling and therefore the cost of capital here (the fundamental cost of capital in a country, the cost of borrowing, reflects the views of global investors about the riskiness of the borrower). But if the maximum increment of difference for the regions was just 0.125%, I am not sure the integrity of the sterling area would be seriously impaired. And this decentralised system of central banking would have the advantage, I think, that decisions that really matter to people's prosperity and lives would be seen to be taken not by snooty technocrats locked away in their grandiose Bank-of-England fortress in the City of London, but by Scots for Scotland, the Welsh for Wales, and so on.

Just possibly this kind of devolution would serve to bind Britain together more, if it led to a convergence in house-price inflation between Newcastle and Islington, for example, or in rates of change in business investment between Liverpool and Swindon. Perhaps it would be a counterblast to the powerful forces pulling the nations and regions apart, especially Scotland, from the rest of the UK.

If in the end this reform were thought to be too risky and complicated, it is certainly not the only way to try to reverse the widening income and wealth gaps between different parts of the UK. An alternative would be for the state to set up regional lending banks. The Business Bank of Scotland, the Business Bank for the North-East, and so on, would be created for the sole purpose of providing medium-term (five- to ten-year), fixed-rate loans to small and medium-size businesses in their respective regions. The modest initial funding would come directly from the Treasury. But then they would package up the business loans they had made into bonds, which they would sell to investors.

Now in the initial years, the Treasury would have to provide a guarantee to investors that all or most of the bonds' face-value sum would be repaid, because without such a Treasury guarantee, these regional and national business banks would probably only be able to raise money at penal interest rates. Even so, this would be a relatively inexpensive way of spurring business investment in the parts of the United Kingdom that need it most. And again, it could and should help to bind us closer together.

Finally, there are the two related issues of how to address the most glaring source of inequality, which is wealth, and also how to fund the growing demands on our public services from the ageing of the population. Nick Timothy, the prime minister's former chief of staff, and Theresa May were savaged for their manifesto proposal that when we grow old and need to be looked after, some of the costs of that state-provided social care should be met from the wealth we've accumulated, including the wealth locked up in the value of our homes. But what they proposed was much fairer than the status quo, which is in essence to force hard-pressed working families to pay for the social care of their better-off elders through direct taxes. There is an analogous argument that with the economy having been managed for decades to suit the interests of those aged fifty and above – who own the vast bulk of properties and are almost alone in having decent pension savings – some form of annual levy on the wealth of almost everyone would correct part of the inter-generational and class unfairness in the allocation of that wealth and those assets.

Let us say, again for argument's sake, that there was a 1% annual levy on all those with net assets – that is gross wealth minus debts – greater than £500,000. The levy would have to be low enough to minimise incentives to dodge it, for instance by moving the ownership of assets offshore or transferring them to family members and trusts. The levy would be bonkers if it gave us a strong reason to enrich financial advisers and banks by paying them fees rather than shovelling tax to the Exchequer. Maybe 1% is therefore the correct rate. And to reduce grotesque evasion, it would probably require a national register of financial assets, a bit like the Land Registry for properties, along the lines proposed by the economist Gabriel Zucman. At 1%, the levy could potentially raise big sums, since the value of all assets in the UK, after the deduction of associated debts, is £8.8 trillion, including £5.2 trillion locked up in our homes and £3.7 billion in pension and insurance schemes.

In theory therefore, if there were minimal tax avoidance, such a levy would raise many tens of billions of pounds every year – less than income tax, but a serious sum. And for those who could not afford to pay the levy, maybe because they are elderly retired occupants of lovely houses, there would be an opportunity to defer payment, perhaps till death. The government would charge interest on the amount owed, but at a rate no higher than the average of the interest rates it pays when borrowing for up to thirty years, so maybe 1.5%. The point is that everyone, and not just the elderly, would have the right to defer payment, because deferring would not in theory deprive the government of upfront cash, in that the government itself would be able to borrow very cheaply against the security of the guaranteed future wealth-tax cash receipts.

This wealth tax would not be a bottomless purse. But it would go a long way to meeting the long-term needs of hospitals and schools. And as I have said, it would bind us, rather than fragment us, as a nation – in that a disproportionate amount of the tax would be raised in the asset-rich capital and South-East, but the proceeds would improve the lives and life chances of all British people. The liberal metropolitan elite would be paying their way. And about time, too.

CHAPTER 12
GRENFELL CHANGES EVERYTHING

Dear Dad,

It is fashionable to say that all the great uncertainties of our rich Western democracies are because of the rise of what is called 'identity politics'. Arguably our political behaviour, and especially how we vote, is being conditioned to an unusual degree by the badges we want to wear, especially the badges of nationality or regional identity. Obviously, there is something important in all that. Trump's 'Make America Great Again' resonated with a white middle class there. Sturgeon's appeal to Scottish Scottishness is powerful. Many of the English outside London and the South-East showed in the EU referendum that they saw the EU as a threat to the idea of who they are. Hostility to immigration, in Europe and America, is in part a complaint that our homes, our communities, our country are being reshaped too fast and without our consent.

But as your son, my response cannot be that politicians should respond by feeding the beast of nationalism or sectarianism. There is obviously far more that governments could and should do to give people more confidence that they control their destinies. But the world does not need more division based on local, national or racial identity. What it requires is more mutual understanding. And the lesson of history is that people tend to be more tolerant and accepting of change when they have hope that their lives will improve.

So having bequeathed me your conviction that economics matters and is about the pursuit of the good society, my response to the crisis of legitimacy of established politicians in the US, Britain and Europe is to see it as a manifestation of how millions of poorer people were stripped of their optimism that the economy works to give them better lives and livelihoods. Therefore, the imperative must be to come up with ideas that could make all of us more confident we can prosper in the mayhem of a world of intense technological and demographic change. That is why almost all the policy prescriptions of the previous chapters are about how we equip ourselves to stand a better chance of earning a decent living, how governments can share national income in a fairer way – including possibly guaranteeing a universal minimum income – and how businesses can become more productive, such that as a country we begin to pay our way in the world, and our living standards can rise in a sustainable way.

All of this is achievable, if we keep a clear head, and do not panic. Even the appropriate response in the UK to concerns about immigration is less nightmarishly complicated than people think. There is only a minority of Britons who are ignorantly and hatefully opposed to all immigration – that is absolutely clear both from how Vote Leave won, with its spurious promise of £350m for the NHS, and its narrow margin of victory. If asked, most would recognise that we all benefit when foreign doctors and software engineers come to work here. That is why the government's new immigration charge of £1,000 a year for skilled workers arriving from outside the European Economic Area is probably neither in the national economic interest, nor especially popular with indigenous Britons.

What is a greater source of concern to many is unskilled immigration, though the evidence is not that people want no such immigration, or even Theresa May's promised annual target of 'tens of thousands' for the skilled and unskilled. It is not about an arbitrary number. It is about the apparent lack of any ability by the British government to match numbers of people coming to Britain with the available housing, transport and public services capacity, and to prevent painful deterioration of job security for indigenous Britons in low-wage occupations.

So investment by government in housing and infrastructure would help, as would measures to increase stability and quality of employment. And if steps were taken to improve the fabric of Britain and cut insecurity of employment, the mere fact that at Brexit the government would have notional control over the immigration process may be all that matters. The heat at that point would probably go out of the debate. If grit was introduced into the immigration process, by migrants having to prove at the border that they have an invitation to work from an employer, or by legislating for a requirement that those coming could not stay if out of work for longer than two or three months, then numbers would decline – perhaps by more than would be healthy for the economy, but certainly enough to satisfy most of those who voted for Brexit. Apart from anything else, the net increase in migration to the UK is already falling.

Dad, when I started conceiving this book, it was in the immediate aftermath of the votes for the UK to leave the European Union and for Trump to become leader of the free world. I was depressed. And I was ashamed, because I had been so comfortable in my cosy, smug North London ghetto that I had not noticed how alienated millions of people, especially poorer people well away from the capital, had become with an economic and political system that suited only a privileged few of us.

My conceit was that it was largely the responsibility of the 48% of us who voted to remain in the EU to make a success of Brexit. How so? Well, all the evidence shows that we the 48% have the money and the power. And that means it is our fault that we did not clock how unfair the political and economic system had become; that it rewarded most of us, while trapping millions of others in a kind of economic purgatory, on relatively low and stagnating living standards, with precious little hope of escape.

In other words, we may have ourselves to blame that the 52% had become so despondent about their circumstances and prospects that the tantalising promise of taking back control, made by the leading Brexiteers, was simply too good to miss. This is to argue that Brexit is a symptom of long-running and global economic trends to which Britain was more exposed than many countries by our tradition of openness to the flows of capital and people – and to which we were more likely than many to baulk at some point, because of our national story as an island never successfully invaded and occupied since 1066.

As a journalist who both by instinct and the ordinance of the TV regulators could not campaign, I watched with growing frustration an In campaign that consistently missed the point, and was all about trying to raise the alarm over the economic cost of quitting the EU, for those who didn't feel they had much left to lose. But I am not sure a campaign more astutely couched in the patriotic language of what would actually make Britain and Britons safe and rich, in the face of economic and security threats stemming largely from outside the EU, would in the end have made a great deal of difference. Spilt milk. And as you lectured me more or less from the moment I could talk, agonising about spilt milk is as pointless when making economic and political decisions as it is in our personal lives.

So the imperative, especially for those in the 48%, is to make Brexit work even though – or perhaps because – if Brexit is as bad for the UK's prosperity as their prominent spokesmen warned it might be, they (and I) would not be the ones to suffer most or even at all, in that they have the skills, the drive and the money to go wherever gainful employment and opportunities are to be found. But presumably none of the 48% would want to live in a UK where we would turn to the 52% and say 'told you so' if they became poorer. That way lies madness and chaos.

I dearly hope that madness and chaos does not turn out to be our post-Brexit diet. I really fear, as you know, that it may be – in part because of the shambolic way that this government has handled negotiations thus far. As I have already ranted, one of the greatest ever acts of vandalism to the British national interest was Theresa May's decision to give her most Eurosceptic right wing at the Tories' autumn party conference in 2016 that sop of a commitment to trigger Article 50 by the end of March 2017. In her showy gesture that she really, really believed in Brexit – despite having been on the other side of the argument before 23 June – she stripped her country of any power it might have had to negotiate leaving the EU on terms that suit us. She made the terrifying prospect of tumbling out of the EU on 31 March 2019 without a deal – with all the accompanying costs for business, anxieties for EU citizens living here and Brits living in the EU and bottlenecks at our borders – a realistic possibility.

As I said to you, Dad, one of the reasons I gave Theresa May the benefit of the doubt for many months was because her first promise as prime minister was that in everything she did she would favour those 'just about managing' over those she styled the powerful, the mighty, the wealthy, the fortunate few. And in her Maoist Mayist way, she had that statement framed and hung on the wall all over Downing Street, so that her officials and colleagues would be in no doubt of the direction of travel.

For a while she talked a talk of reforms that might to some extent empower and enrich the voiceless and powerless: of giving workers more of a voice on boards, of giving greater employment protection to those not knowing from one day to the next whether there would be work on offer from an ostensible employer, of building more affordable housing. But progress was painfully slow, in some measure because she and most of her important ministers and officials were wholly bogged down in trying to work out what Brexit really did mean – from assessing its many technical and legal ramifications, fighting and winning the court-room and political battles that had to be fought before Brexit talks could begin, and then setting priorities and devising some kind of strategy for the Brexit talks.

Then three things happened that have forced me to re-evaluate where we should travel from here: Emmanuel Macron's election as president of France, May's snap election and the appalling fire at Grenfell Tower.

Macron and the UK election have made me rethink whether leaving the EU is inevitable. The point is that in partnership with a re-elected Angela Merkel, he may well at last push through economic reforms to the EU that would make the euro sustainable and would at last properly revive the eurozone's economy. It requires Paris to sacrifice more budget-making autonomy to central Brussels control, and

Berlin to use more of its wealth and income to support other eurozone member states. It would, in short, need significant progress towards the eurozone becoming a United States of Europe. This is the last and best opportunity for the realisation of the founders' dreams that their Common Market would one day become one seamless Europe.

If it is realised, the economic and political cost for the UK of leaving the EU would become much greater. A trickle of investment from British-based banks and manufacturers to a faster-growing, more confident European continent would become a torrent. The UK would – for who knows how long – become Europe's sick man again, as we were in the 1950s and 1960s.

Being weaker once more than the rest of the EU would feel like a social embarrassment for wealthier voters who voted to stay in the EU. And for the millions on lower incomes, their struggle would be more daunting. But would it be penurious enough to change their minds on Brexit? I am not sure. There is no certainty even that they would be convinced Britain's lower growth was linked to leaving the EU, rather than further proof of the incompetence of those who run this place. It is plausible that a significant proportion of those who voted for Brexit may at some point decide they are the victims of an 'affinity fraud' perpetrated by the Leave campaign – if the £350m a week for the NHS never materialises, or the cost of living continues to rise while wages stagnate.

But the thing about affinity frauds – or scams perpetrated within a community of likeminded people – is that the victims wilfully ignore warnings from outside their community that they have been done in, unless and until there is no ignoring the money that has permanently vanished from their bank accounts. If we want to avoid a devastating social disintegration and a perhaps irreversible collapse of confidence in the governing class, Brexit could only be transmogrified into Bremain – we could only stay in the EU – if it became palpably and unambiguously clear that most of us wanted that.

Any or all of the political elite, from Tony Blair to Nick Clegg to Ken Clarke, are at liberty to argue that we have to change our minds and stay. Which is fatuous to point out, because there will be no shutting them up. But if they were seen to be at the head of a conspiracy to keep the UK in the EU, they would kill the very thing they so dearly seek, because if there is a lesson to be drawn from the madness of the last year it is that Britons do not want to be in a gang where Blair, Clegg and Clarke are the conspicuous senior members.

There is no point lecturing the British people they have made a mistake in going for Brexit. They will either decide that for themselves, in a spontaneous awakening led by someone or some people a million miles from the current class of leaders – or they won't.

For public opinion to be shifted back decisively in favour of the UK staying in the EU would probably require an admission by the rest of the EU that accepting the principle of free movement of people is not a necessary condition of EU membership; that some degree of national control over migration from other parts of the EU is permissible. Given that the UK would never adopt the euro, such an exception could theoretically be granted to us without damaging the integrity of the eurozone.

But it is difficult to see why the UK would be granted that status of privileged associate or half member, in circumstances where the ambition of the rest of the EU is to persuade all European countries and their citizens that prosperity and happiness lie in closer integration. In the creation of a United States of Europe, why formalise for the UK what would be seen elsewhere as Britons having their cake and eating it? I cannot see why Merkel and Macron would proffer that.

Brexit still means Brexit. The presumption any rational person would make is that Brexit will happen, and to throw everything at trying to prosper both as individuals and as a nation outside the EU.

The prospect of an optimal Brexit has become more remote, because of the way May and her team have made a right old Horlicks of the process of getting there (my nod to a bedtime drink as traditionally British as fish and chips and Beefeaters is no coincidence, because its manufacturing plant in Slough is being closed, its UK brand is being flogged, but its owner GSK insists that anyone who sees a connection to Brexit is fantasising). Her snap election saw May surrender her party's parliamentary majority, and established a probable majority for MPs from across parties who hate the plans she announced at the turn of the year for a supposedly clean rupture from the EU.

So the Article 50 process for leaving the EU by the end of March 2019 is bound to be defined both by periodic crises in the talks with Michel Barnier, the chief negotiator for the twenty-seven remaining members, and in the vital parliamen-tary business of legislating so that the country can actually function on the outside. It is all so incredibly precarious that I hesitate to predict what form Brexit will take, or how long we will continue to be associate or half members during a period of transition to full independence.

My own preference would be for a long transition, and a final settlement that would involve the least costs and friction for our trade with the EU commensurate with our exercising control over immigration, plus maximum co-operation with the EU on security and economic issues. But that is to talk in platitudes – or the language of most senior politicians of all parties. I am not going to waste your time, Dad, by listing the many thousands of legal and practical preparations necessary to prevent a whole series of mini and major problems at the official date of Brexit – though it would seem sensible to organise enough road and warehouse space for new customs checks, put in place a system for authorising the use of new medicines and agree new rules for EU aeroplanes to land here, *inter alia*.

The devil will be in the detail. And although the detail is important, the truth is that it is displacement activity, a distraction from bigger challenges faced by this country and most of the rich West. In the great British tradition, we will probably muddle a way through to the door that takes us out of the EU. May's miscalculations have already significantly increased the toll we would pay as and when we go through that door; she has maximised the costs of leaving. But we will be alright in the end.

It is an illusion held by the entire government and most MPs that everything about Brexit is life and death. Brexit itself was the biggest decision relating to Brexit. Everything else related to Brexit – how we do it, over what time period and so on – is a second-order question. The priority is to fix the country's structural flaws, those that hobble us out of the EU or in.

If we have been in denial for many years about what we have done wrong, we were forced to confront our scandalous complacency in the early hours of 14 June, when public housing for 600 low-income and vulnerable people, Grenfell Tower, went up in flames. The conflagration seemed

Victorian both in its merciless killing of around eighty people, and the failure of council or government to give immediate and appropriate succour to the survivors. The charred skeleton of the building haunts us now, redolent of a war zone. It is visible from the back garden of our recent prime minister, David Cameron, who will be reminded daily that the lethal refurbishment of the block took place while he was in office.

One of the hallmarks of a civilised society is that it provides opportunities for everyone to prosper and enjoy the good things in life, while making sure that those lacking the advantages of people like you and me, Dad, are never put in harm's way. That is implicit in the social contract we all sign, regardless of our political affiliations, left or right, and our faith or creed. We can argue about the degree of active support that the state should give to those with least, or held back by disabilities and other disadvantages. But it is a given that we should never house them in a tower block susceptible to being engulfed in flames, of becoming an inferno, within a few short hours – after having given many of them the wrong advice to stay in the flat in the event of fire.

And to be clear, it may feel worse that Grenfell was state-provided council housing. But it would be equally scandalous if this was low-rent private sector housing. In a rich country like ours, there should be no place for landlords who lack the competence or compassion to make absolutely sure their tenants are not living in a deathtrap. And equally there is a minimum level of practical support that servants of the state – in this case those working for the Royal Borough of Kensington and Chelsea, and the Kensington and Chelsea Tenant Management Organisation (which managed the borough's public housing on behalf of the council) – should be willing and able to give to those devastated by losing their homes.

The local authority, Kensington and Chelsea, failed abjectly for days to meet the needs of the many made homeless, who were grieving for friends and relatives, who had lost all their possessions and precious touchstones of who they are, who were terrified by what they had just experienced and who were probably suffering from post-traumatic stress disorder. It was only through the work and compassion of volunteers, who poured into the borough, or donated money and clothes, that the victims had any sense they were part of a caring community. The state broke down, did not work – and in the function that matters most, caring for those who need it. At the time of writing, half of those who died had still not been identified, as if they had never existed. Grenfell shames us all.

The detailed pathology of what went so appallingly wrong is still being worked on. But there are conclusions we can already draw. One is that there was a deep flaw either in building regulations, or in the way they were enforced. We know that because of the initial results of tests ordered by Sajid Javid, the secretary of state for communities and local government. Cladding banned for use in other countries, such as the US, was routinely used and stuck on the side of high-rise blocks here, as a cheap alternative to knocking them down when they became weathered and tired. And more than 160 social-housing blocks have failed tests and been proved unsafe, because of the way they combined external cladding, insulation and internal fire-protection systems. Grenfell has exposed a systemic pattern of poor people being put at risk when the state houses them.

Here are the questions about how we run things in Britain that need to be asked in response to the Grenfell fire. Were corners cut in relation to fire prevention because of austerity, and the squeeze on council funding? That was not so for some of the buildings now seen to be unsafe, because work on them preceded the election of the Tory–Lib Dem government in 2010, but it may have played a role in the 2016 refurbishment of Grenfell Tower, and the council's lamentable initial response to the catastrophe.

Second, was regulatory failure – that led to unsafe materials being used in unsafe combinations – the consequence of a cultural shift that (again) came with the advent of the coalition government in 2010? At a time when the economy's potential had been undermined by the 2008 banking crisis, the response of David Cameron and his ministers, notably the minister for government policy, Oliver Letwin, was to launch a 'Red Tape Challenge' to reduce the burden on business of rules and regulations deemed to be unnecessary.

It was all about cutting costs for companies, to help them back on the path to growth. And Cameron claimed important successes. In January 2014, he announced that 800 regulations had been abolished or simplified, and that 3,000 in total had been identified for amendment or scrapping. Cameron estimated the potential cost savings for businesses as being 'well over' £850 million per annum. 'We will be the first government in modern history to have reduced – rather than increased – domestic business regulation during our time in office,' he swaggered in a speech to the Federation of Small Businesses.

The examples he gave of how companies were being helped were the 'slashing' of 80,000 pages of environmental guidance for them, the ending of 'needless health and safety inspections', plans to exempt a million self-employed people from health and safety law, the scrapping of the rule that companies are automatically liable for accidents and a pledge to housebuilders to fillet '100 overlapping and confusing standards applied to new homes to less than 10.'

This Red Tape Challenge, which culminated in the 2015 Deregulation Act, was the corollary or sinewy sister of austerity. A priority for the government was to spur the expansion of the private sector as it shrank the size of the public sector, because it feared that failure to do so would have made us even poorer. And reducing regulatory costs for businesses and public-sector institutions was an important way of doing this – or so Cameron believed.

Now to be clear, it was completely right to scrap some rules, because they were thoroughly bonkers, such as the right of employees to sue their employer if a customer insulted them, or ordinances for what 'No Smoking' signs should look like. Also, successive governments have underestimated how regulation can stifle wealth-creating competition: red tape is proportionately much more burdensome for small businesses than for big companies, because they simply lack the resources to comply easily with it.

But the entire history of capitalism shows that many wealth creators will take the short-term route to maximising profits by doing the absolute legal minimum to comply with safety and other official standards. And when those minimum standards are lowered, the risks of harm for customers or employees increase. What is extraordinary is that Cameron and his colleagues embarked on this wholesale deregulation for the entire economy when he and the chancellor, George Osborne, were determined – rightly – to do precisely the opposite for banks and the City of London.

They were both acutely aware that the economy-destroying banking crisis was in part the result of insufficient and inadequate regulation and supervision. And they ordered and legislated for much more onerous banking rules and oversight of banks. They were in no doubt about the harm that can be done when regulators turn a blind eye to excessive risk-taking, because pretty much their entire government programme, or at least the important parts, were a response to economic damage wreaked by banks' rapacious pursuit of profits.

All that said, I am not alleging or implying that Cameron's war on red tape in and of itself prevented proper fire-safety evaluation and fire prevention at Grenfell. What I am saying is that if the public sector is put under pressure to adopt a culture of assessing regulations to identify those that are unnecessary, if slashing and burning red tape is what generates rewards for officials, the chances are significantly reduced of those officials having the time or inclination to warn that regulations should be increased or toughened in some important areas – such as fire-safety rules for public housing, for example. And it is relevant that in 2016, the then housing minister, Gavin Barwell, who is now Theresa May's chief of staff, promised a belated review of fire-safety regulations, prompted in part by the 2009 fire at the Lakanal House block in south London that killed six people, and yet nothing has ever been published.

Nothing could therefore be more important right now than for the war against red tape to be slammed into reverse – and for ministers and officials to review where within their areas of responsibility there is the potential for catastrophic events, and to ensure there are no important lacunae in regulatory and supervisory structures. The culture introduced by the coalition government of deregulating for the sake of liberating business must be supplanted by a culture of putting the safety of people, and especially vulnerable people, first.

But in a pre- and post-Brexit world, the chances of this happening are depressingly slender; before Brexit, because most ministerial and official time has been captured by organising the immensely complicated institutional reforms necessitated by leaving the EU, including making sure thousands of EU rules are properly translated into British law – and after, because so much of the propaganda from the proponents of leaving the EU was that Brussels had imposed wealth-destroying red tape on us that now has to be put on the bonfire.

It is eye-catching that David Cameron's great champion of deregulation, Oliver Letwin, who as it happens backed the Remain side in the referendum, is now chairman of a 'non-partisan project', the Red Tape Initiative, whose goal is to 'identify the most important, least controversial opportunities for cutting red tape in a post-Brexit world.'

The other massive flaw exposed by Grenfell, as it was by the banking debacle, is the absence of effective chains of command and responsibility for decisions that have far-reaching consequences. Among the many scandals of the banking crisis is how few bankers were prosecuted, or indeed lost their fortunes, because under the law it was impossible to prove that any were personally responsible for what now looks like the most negligent stewardship in all history of organisations that underpin the economy and our prosperity.

In the case of Grenfell, the police have mooted the possibility of prosecutions for 'corporate manslaughter' against institutions, namely the Kensington and Chelsea council and the Tenants Management Organisation. But whether it will be possible to identify named individuals who were to blame is not clear. And that would be unsatisfactory. Because yet another general lesson we should have learned from the banking crisis is that people will take mad risks when there is a reasonable

chance they can trouser profits when things go right, and others
– taxpayers, us – pick up the bill in a disaster.

So the number one priority, I think even ahead of negotiating the sanest Brexit available, is to learn the lessons of
Grenfell.

One is that we require both more and less of the nanny
state. We need the right regulations, properly monitored and
enforced. That is the more nannying. But we also need deci-
sion-makers – councillors, landlord organisations, bankers,
chief executives – to be more accountable for their own decisions. If they do not follow the rules, they should pay an
appropriate price. That is the less nannying.

And perhaps more than anything else, we have to stop being
frightened of public borrowing to fund investment. We are
prisoners of two myths, which both stem from the UK's volatile years as one of Europe's less successful economies in the
1960s and 1970s: that all public borrowing is bad, and that
the state necessarily makes worse investments than the private
sector. When Thatcher conquered all in the 1980s – including
the mindset of the most successful election-winning leader in
Labour's history, Tony Blair – the idea that private-sector
investment was superior to public-sector investment had been
raised to the status of eternal truth.

That was mad. When the private sector finances or provides
important infrastructure or public assets, it tends to demand a
high return for its investment, so taxpayers end up paying
through the nose for NHS hospitals and schools built under the
Private Finance Initiative, or commuters pay a fortune in rail
fares. And just as bonkers is how rarely governments exploit
their ability to take long-term important risks to actually foster
wealth creation at comparatively low cost, by taking advantage
of their ability to borrow more cheaply than the private sector.

To repeat what is widely known but systematically ignored, if it were not for public-sector funding, we would not have the internet or many of our life-saving medicines.

Right now, one of the most urgent problems facing the country is the absence of affordable – or, it turns out, safe – housing. One of the more exemplary policies of the 1950s and 1960s was to build council housing on a massive scale, spurring the economy and improving the lives of poor people. After Grenfell, and with so many young people so far away from ever having the resources to own a decent home of their own, we need to regain that post-war ambition and confidence, to build as we haven't for decades; financed by a government borrowing without its habitual reluctance on global markets, for projects that will over time improve our economic prospects, as well as uniting our fragmented nation. Some of these homes would be for rent, some for purchase. What matters is that they should restore confidence that a proper home is within everyone's reach.

Healing Britain's wounds, coming together, that is the priority. Can any of the established politicians help with that, fixated as they are on the minutiae of Brexit, unable to see Brexit in the broader framework of what has gone wrong? I fear not. Dad, you and I always moaned about how a prevailing crop of leaders were pygmies compared with the giants of the past, but that was often arrogance born of finding ourselves older than those who somehow ended up in charge. This time, however, I fear we would be justified in weeping that the country we love deserves better than the leaders we have, or at least over their inability to see what matters.

Here is the funny thing, Dad. My most powerful memories of you are from the 1970s, when I was a teenager precociously passionate about politics, clothes and Bowie – banging on doors aged fourteen in the two 1974 general elections, urging those much older than me to vote Labour. Much of what is happening today feels redolent and resonant of that time: Labour and Tories offering seriously different programmes for Britain, but neck and neck again in a reawakened two-party system; consensus that the economy has been crocked, but no consensus on how to fix it; anxieties about immigration and race relations; the near constant threat of terrorism; instability in the Middle East; tension between the West and Russia. That turned out to be a period of transition – to the Thatcher–Reagan era of economic liberalism, the dismantling of the state in favour of the private sector.

There is no doubt that we are again in no-man's-land, purgatory, the waiting room. The new age, when it dawns, will see a rebirth of the role of the state, because when it comes to the vital ingredients of the good life, from health, to welfare, to education and the income we all require, focusing provision on the private sector would see the yawning gap between the lives and lifestyles of rich and poor widen even more, and will tear the country apart.

New Britain will not be a return to old-fashioned, mono-lithic socialist provision. It will not pretend that Thatcher's focus on individual choice was an error. There will be devolved, decentralised provision of public services – mainly by the institutions and agencies of central and local government, often by voluntary organisations, and by the private sector only when it is conspicuously clear that public and voluntary sectors are failing (the corollary of the dictum that the role of the state is to correct market failures).

I have not talked enough in this book about the growing importance of what is usually and opaquely called civil society, or the many charities, voluntary organisations and social organisations that fill the interstices between public and private sectors, and keep the whole show on the road. We need them more than ever, for both the vital work they do, and the opportunities they provide for volunteers to enrich their own lives at a time when well-remunerated and satisfying work may become scarcer. Crucially, public and voluntary services must be properly funded, through adequate direct taxation, especially of those on higher incomes – and not just from the kindness of sympathetic strangers.

There must also be a repudiation of the fetish of austerity, and a reassertion of the proper and benign role of government to borrow and spend to stimulate the economy, even when public-sector debt is relatively high, as it is for most rich nations. Dad, you were Keynesian and proud to the end, and will not be surprised that fashion in economics is at last returning to the idea that government should do more than the bare minimum to fill the breach when consumers and businesses are not shopping and investing enough; to protect the livelihoods of the poorest and most vulnerable, and through growth to stimulate tax revenues that can actually reduce the national debt.

Most important of all, Dad, you would agree that we would be certifiably insane to leave the EU only to recast ourselves as a fragile, living-from-hand-to-mouth nation. If Brexit is about accepting second best, there is no point to it. You and I have had to put up with too many years of being penny-pinching runners-up at Arsenal. If that is a shameful *modus operandi* for our beloved football team, it would be a disgrace for Britain. The time is now for government to do boldly and ambitiously what only governments can do, which is invest in the public services and public goods that enrich us all.

I love you and miss you,

Robert

ACKNOWLEDGEMENTS

I have loved writing this, in large measure because of the pleasure of working with Kishan Koria, who has been a brilliant researcher, adviser and friend. Huge thanks are due to him. I have also benefited from the brilliant insights of Laurence Knight, the BBC journalist who collaborated with me on my last book, *How Do We Fix This Mess?* Roland Rudd and Tom Baldwin have both nudged me away from silly mistakes. And I am deeply indebted to amazing friends – Suzy Taverne, Marc Vlessing, Kate Rothschild, Rebecca Nicolson and Sarah and Renshaw Hiscox – who generously let me camp in their beautiful homes and escape the noise.

To Michael Jermey and Geoff Hill of ITV, thanks for having me – and to Sam Haq, thanks for putting up with me. To Vicky Flind of *Peston on Sunday*, thank you for being such an imaginative and supportive partner in crime (and to Alex Gardiner, I will miss you). To my brilliant, adored Charlotte Edwardes, yes, I am listening. And to my wonderful boys or 'boyz', Max and Simon, please read this and let me know what you think. As with everything I do, it is for you (well most of the time).

INDEX

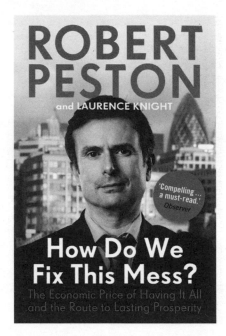

'Robert Peston's compelling account of global financial meltdown is a must-read . . .' – The Observer

The record-breaking unbroken growth between 1992 and 2008 wasn't the economic miracle that it seemed. It was based on a number of dangerous illusions – most notably that it didn't matter that the UK and US year after year consumed more than they earned.

But we couldn't go on increasing our indebtedness forever. The financial crash of 2007/8 and the subsequent economic slump in much of the West was the moment when we realised we had borrowed more than we could afford to repay.

So who got it wrong? Bankers, investors and regulators? And were they greedy, stupid or asleep? What was the role of government? And what part did we, as consumers, play in all this?

With the same probing lucidity he brought to WHO RUNS BRITAIN?, Robert Peston takes us step-by-step towards a common sense way to fix this mess.

9781444757125 | £9.99

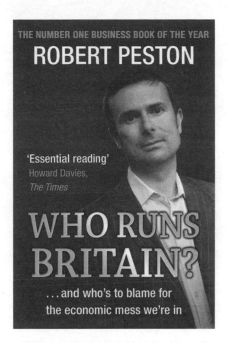

**'A compelling portrait of early 21st century casino capital-
ism . . . essential reading.' – The Times**

On 13 September 2007, Robert Peston broke the news that
Northern Rock had become a victim of the global credit crunch
and was seeking an emergency loan from the Bank of England

It was the latest in a long line of scoops by this award-winning journalist. Over the weeks that followed, the Government found itself
exposed to the Rock to the tune of 57 billion, or almost £2000 for
every taxpayer. As Robert Peston shows in his fascinating new book,
the seeds for the collapse of Northern Rock and the upheavals in the
financial markets were sown years before.

WHO RUNS BRITAIN? is the first time anyone has drawn all the
threads together to weave a story that's rich in extraordinary characters and outrageous feats of economic bravado. This book is about
the widening gap between the super-rich and the rest of us. It
explores and explodes the myth that the financial creativity of those
who are amassing these vast fortunes is good for the wider economy
and for all of us. Whether you're a financial expert or just have a
bank account, WHO RUNS BRITAIN? is a book you must read.

9780340839447 | £9.99